PETER GOODRICH

Reading the Law
A Critical Introduction to Legal Method and Techniques

Basil Blackwell

© Peter Goodrich 1986

First published 1986

Basil Blackwell Ltd
108 Cowley Road, Oxford OX4 1JF, UK

Basil Blackwell Inc.
432 Park Avenue South, Suite 1503,
New York, NY 10016, USA

British Library Cataloguing in Publication Data
Goodrich, Peter
   Reading the law: a critical introduction to
   legal method and techniques
   1. Law
   I. Title
   340   K230

   ISBN 0-631-14629-6
   ISBN 0-631-14631-8 Pbk

Library of Congress Cataloging-in-Publication Data
Goodrich, Peter, 1954–
   Reading the law.

   Includes index.
   1. Law——Great Britain.   2. Law——Methodology.   3. Law——
Philosophy.   I. Title.
KD640.G66   1986   340'.1'8   85–28692
ISBN 0-631-14629-6
ISBN 0-631-14631-8 (pbk.)

Typeset by Katerprint Co. Ltd, Oxford
Printed in Great Britain by Page Bros, Norwich

Contents

Preface

The title to this work has two conscious connotations. The first relates to the practices surrounding the Riot Act 1714 which stipulated that a particular form of wording contained in the Act was to be publicly proclaimed – the reading of the Riot Act – in front of riotous assemblies. If the assembled crowd refused to comply with the reading and failed to disperse, then, after one hour had elapsed, persons still so assembled were guilty of a capital felony and liable to summary execution. The notion of reading associated with the Riot Act is a highly active one. Far from being a question of a dry bibliophilic or literary exercise, reading the Riot Act was a direct speech-act, an exercise of power. It was a conscious performance upon the social and generally colonial stage, which removed reading from books to a context of life and death; the reading cajoled and threatened, and its meaning was quite as much a product of the circumstances of the occasion, of the status of the reader and of the magisterial and military authorization of the reading, as it was of the linguistic or internal structure of the text.

The second connotation derives from the first, although it has its more immediate origin in what has come, somewhat unhelpfully, to be termed post-structuralist theory. To the obvious truism that a simple reading of the Riot Act will tell us little of its effective social meaning and practice, its history and empirical readings, can be added the more general claim of recent literary and interpretative studies that the process of reading is an inherently social and political activity, that it constitutes a preferred text and actively selects and privileges meanings and accents. Nowhere, it has appeared to us, is such a process of constructive reading more obvious and more pernicious than in legal reading and it is the consequent objective of *Reading the Law* to outline and to question the prevalent and frequently unconscious methodology of such legal readings.

Moving from reading to writing, it is a pleasure to acknowledge the support, encouragement and help of those numerous friends and correspondents who read and commented on either part or all of this text.

Collectively I would like to thank the members of the Centre for Criminology and the Social and Philosophical Study of Law, of the University of Edinburgh, whose extensive hospitality and good humour sustained me during the inevitable crises of writing. Individually, I would like to thank Beverley Brown and Neil MacCormick who patiently read the larger part of the manuscript and saved me many infelicities and some outright inaccuracies. Patrick Durkin, Bernard Jackson, Andrew Miller, Judie Phillip, Kay Richardson, Denise Rokosz, Bill Sinclair, Pennie Taylor, David Walliker, Stephen Webster and Peter Young, all contributed by way of discussion, comment and encouragement and I would wish to thank them all for their time and patience. Finally, I am especially indebted to Tony Sweeney for his editorial help and encouragement and last and most significantly of all to Les Moran who selected examples for and helped research and prepare chapters 1, 2 and 3.

Table of Cases

Part I

Defining the Legal Text

1

Introduction: Ideational and Institutional Sources of Law

Sir, the law is as I say it is, and so it has been laid down ever since the law began; and we have several set forms which are held as law, and so held and used for good reason, though we cannot at present remember that reason.
(Fortescue J., 1458, YB 36 Hen. VI ff 25b–26)

One of the most longstanding and intractable of the debates surrounding the study of law concerns the nature and definition of the term law itself. At different times and in different cultures the term law may be taken to refer to institutions as radically different as magic, song-contests, vendetta (feuding), trial by ordeal and the rules of war. Even within the relative homogeneity of the western legal tradition, law has taken very diverse forms and has been derived from very distinct sources. At different stages in the development of western law it has been said variously that law 'comes from' God, from nature or the 'natural order of things', from the monarch, from the various forms of commonwealth or sovereignty, from the 'spirit of the people' or from custom and social usage, to name but a few of the more acceptable or prevalent views. Obviously the way in which we define law will, in terms of the examples given, make a considerable difference to the requisite manner of its study; if law comes from God then it would be best to be theologians or priests for the purposes of studying it professionally, whereas if it is really self-help or vendetta then skill with an axe or a gun is more likely to be useful than any knowledge of rules or texts or any ability to argue. The question posed by the difficulty of defining law is a serious practical problem for students and practitioners of the law, and it raises directly important issues of how law is to be differentiated from other social phenomena. Such issues go to the very heart of the professional status of law as a discipline and indeed of lawyers as its interpreters. In the present chapter we shall outline the traditional modes of defining law by reference to its ideational (conceptual) and institutional (legal) sources and shall then comment more broadly upon the practical meaning of the status law.

Commentary upon the wider social and political role of law and of the legal
discipline will form the introduction to the major theme of this work, that of
the need to develop a critical and interdisciplinary account of the way in
which law is read and interpreted. Such an account, a theory of reading the
law, will be the explicit subject of Part II of this work, while in Part I we
concentrate on establishing the object of legal reading, the texts and
discourses which attain the status of law: that is, by definition as law, by
being treated, recognized or assumed to be law by the institutions responsible for promulgating and sustaining the modern municipal legal system.
While we would note that the distinction between the two parts of the work,
between defining and reading the law, is not an absolute one, it is intrinsic
to our argument that it is precisely the historical and conceptual priority of
arguments as to the 'sources' of law, of definitions of the legal text, that
creates the method and techniques, the rigidity and orthodoxy, of legal
approaches to interpretation.

1.1   THE IDEATIONAL SOURCE OF LAW

To claim that law is a distinct enterprise, that it is independent of other
forms of social control and requires institutions and experts, indeed a
science, for its proper organization and functioning, is a fairly constant
claim within the western legal tradition. Despite the apparent diversity of
both the form and the content of law during the course of its lengthy history
and of the very different social, political and economic roles played by the
law, the legal institution itself has maintained a virtually uninterrupted
doctrinal belief in the distinctiveness of law, a belief in its unity and its
separation from other phenomena of social control. The two claims, those
of unity and of separation, have traditionally been closely linked in legal
doctrine; law is kept separate and distinct from other institutions and forms
of control precisely by virtue of being a unity, by virtue of having an
'essential' characteristic which distinguishes law from all else. That
'essence' or unifying feature of law has been variable in its content but
relatively constant in its form: the formal unity of law has traditionally been
based upon its derivation from an absolute source or origin; 'a unitary
necessity or cause' (Hirst, 1979, pp. 109–22) is singled out as the basis and
origin of all law. Although the content of the ideational source of law has
varied within legal doctrine, as we shall see, from being the divine commandments, to the dictates of nature or 'natural law', justice, the commands
of the sovereign or even the logical entailments of a basic rule or norm, the
conceptual characteristics of the absolute source of law do not greatly alter.
The divine origin of law becomes the secular sovereign, the State or even

the 'will of the people', but as a source of law it retains its quality as an external and absolute justification for legal regulation, discipline and law. This external, non-legal, legitimation of the legal order provides the law with its ideational unity and renders the wide spectrum of substantive legal rules into a 'system' of rules. It represents the foundation of law – in theology, politics or myth – yet paradoxically, this ideational source is always a deferred or absent source, it is always in its nature hidden rather than explicit, abstract rather than readily available, past rather than present. Truth, justice, nature or 'time immemorial' are, as we shall see later, neither easily definable nor easily refuted as the basis of law, yet they play a major if frequently indirect role in substantive legal regulation and will to some extent be challenged in the present work:

> Secularisation of the law has consisted not in doing away with the 'incompre-
> hensible nature of authority' but in censoring any mention of this. When
> formerly it was divine in its origins authority 'resounded', and its voice was
> heard like Biblical thunder, unassailable, irrefutable and unintelligible.
> Today, in its secularised form, authority still derives its effectiveness from
> being incomprehensible, with the centralised state installed on the Papal
> throne. (Glucksmann, 1980, p. 58)

The first and broadest sense of 'source of law' will be termed the ideational source of law and is metaphorical and conceptual rather than empirical in its reference. The ideational source of law refers to the 'idea' or 'belief' that lies at the basis of the system of law and provides, either directly or indirectly, an answer to the question of why law is authoritative, the question of why it should be obeyed. The commands and the judgments traditionally obeyed as 'the law' within a given community must 'come from' somewhere or be derived from some acceptable – even if mythical or notional – conceptual source of law. The question of the ideational source of law here invokes the profound and extremely contentious issue of the role of law as the form of communal order: what is it that binds the community, that gives rise to the sense of belonging and the habit of obeying which seem, historically, to be inseparable social functions? (Debray, 1981). We cannot here endeavour to answer directly such questions but we can point to the traditional doctrinal resolutions to the problem of the authority or ideational source and legitimacy of law, and we can also refer to the importance that this definition of law in terms of its source has for legal practice, for the interpretation and application of law.

The most obvious and one of the most long-lived examples of the ideational unifying 'essence', cause and source of law is to be found in Jewish law in the concept of God, the incarnation of justice who reveals the Torah (law) to Moses on Mount Sinai. The characteristic features of this exemplary act of biblical law-giving will be examined later in terms of written law, but it may nonetheless here be noted that God is explicitly represented as the unique source of law, as the conceptual basis of both the community and the order of law, as the authority that ties together the many different customs and texts which had hitherto formed the law.

> Now therefore hearken, O Israel, unto the statutes and unto the judgments, which I teach you, for to do them, that ye may live, and go in and possess the land which the Lord God of your fathers giveth you. Ye shall not add unto the word which I command you, neither shall ye diminish ought from it, that ye may keep the commandments of the Lord your God which I command you. (Deuteronomy 4:1–2)

The example of Jewish law and of the God of judgment and justice as the unique source of law is merely an extreme version of a much more general doctrinal concept of law as ideationally derived from the concepts of reason, justice, truth or nature rather than necessarily or always from God. This conceptual source of law, while it may change its guises, its personification and names, has generally played a fairly consistent role as a source of justification and argument, as an extreme and superior standard by which the law of the day may be, as occasion requires, either supported or (more rarely) challenged.

Within the classical Greek legal tradition, justice and the good of the community as revealed to humans through 'right reason' were seen to be ultimate sources of law, while within the later Roman legal tradition the Greek conception is adopted most forcefully at the time of the Republic by the legal orator Cicero. For Cicero 'there is in fact a true law – namely right reason – which is in accordance with nature, applies to all men and is unchangeable and eternal . . . there will be one common master and ruler of men, namely God, who is the author of this law, its interpreter and its sponsor' (*De Re Publica*). Elsewhere Cicero had argued in court that 'this therefore is a law, oh judges, not written, but born within us, which we have not learned, or received by tradition or read, but which we have taken, absorbed and imbibed from nature herself' (*Orations*). The concept of nature and of natural reason provides the conceptual and comprehensive source of law upon which Cicero can base his arguments as to both the rules and the interpretation of the law and it is this conception of a natural order which is carried into the *Corpus Iuris*, the compilation of that Roman law which survived the fall of the western Roman Empire and which, when rediscovered in AD 1090, became the foundational instrument of the medieval legal tradition in the west. Within that tradition the law of nature (*ius gentium*) is the explicit ideational source of the whole law. As the unifying element of the various branches and scattered texts of substantive law it is expressed, in comprehensive acknowledgement of the scope of natural law, in 1158, in the following way: 'what is common . . . to all men is called "natural" law from human nature, in which sense the law of nations (*ius gentium*) is called natural. Thus we say natural law teaches us to revere God and worship him and to keep faith in a promise. Another sense of "natural" law is the fairest law, by which meaning even civil law can be called natural law' (Kantorowicz, 1938, p. 271).

As the legal tradition develops from the twelfth century to the eighteenth- and nineteenth-century era of modern codifications and the rationalization of the system of common-law precedent, the role of the ideational source of law waxes and wanes in its substantive effects. However much the legal humanists and later lawyers claimed a secular basis for the legal order in the 'general will' of the people (Rousseau) or in 'custom' and memory of usage (Blackstone), to take but two examples, it would be wrong to end this discussion of the ideational source of law without stressing its continuing substantive relevance. The explicit link between a concept of God, nature, justice or even reason and the positive (human) legal order may have declined in respectability within legal doctrine but the ideational source of law remains as an important substantive mechanism for the unification of legal order, for the postulation of an 'order' or 'system' of law which is to be recognized and obeyed. While nature is replaced by references to logic and the idea of legal order, the fundamental influence of a conceptually unifying source of law remains within legal doctrine: the law represents the best available means of regulating human conduct; it forms a complete order of rules that are to be distinguished from mere coercion or brute force by their legal quality, namely the unity and rationality of the order (and mechanisms of application) to which they belong. In its most direct formulation:

> the norm that we ought to obey the provisions of the historically first constitution [i.e. ideational source of law] must be presupposed as a hypothesis if the coercive order established on its basis and actually obeyed and applied by those whose behaviour it regulates is to be considered as a valid order binding upon those individuals; if the regulations among these individuals are to be interpreted as *legal* duties, *legal* rights, and *legal* responsibilities, and not as power relations. (Kelsen, 1957, p. 262)

The courts are the simple mouthpiece, in short, of an order and of its rules which are imposed on them and declared by them, a proposition well expressed in Article 4 of the *Code Napoléon* which proclaims dogmatically that a judge cannot refuse to give judgment on the strength of the 'silence, the obscurity or the inadequacy of the law'. The judge is obliged to treat the system of law as complete and without gaps, as coherent and without contradictory prescriptions or even ambiguities. In French law, of course, the doctrinal reasoning behind the requirement that all judgements refer directly to the rules set out in the *Code Napoléon* is one which sees that Code as the culminating achievement of the French Revolution, as the expression of the will of the people and as a restraint upon the possible abuse of power on the part of the judiciary. The Code unifies the French legal order – it is the unitary source of law within a system purporting to consist purely of statutory legal rules. While it might be thought that this ascription of unitary authority might be peculiar to the civil-law systems of codified law, a comparable position can be briefly mentioned drawn from a system very different to French law, that of the United States, *c.*1928. In *Black and White Taxicab Co.* v *Brown and Yellow Taxicab Co.* (276, US Rep. [1928] 533–84) Holmes J. observes of the US legal tradition, 'law is a word used with different meanings, but law in the sense in which courts speak of it today does not exist without some definite authority behind it. The *common law* so far as it is enforced in a state, whether called *common law* or not, is not the common law generally but the law of that state existing by the authority of that state without regard to what it may have been in England or anywhere else.'

If we move now to look at the explicit practice, we may observe that historically, lawyers have been somewhat wary of attributing the status of law too directly to any single source. Rather than explicitly placing the entire status and function of law-creation in the hands of a sovereign, monarch, oligarchy (aristocratic class) or representative democracy, the tendency has more often been to place a greater weight upon the doctrinal 'idea' of law than upon its contingent manifestations and temporary human representatives. In this context of substantive rule-application, the ideational nature or conceptual source of law refers to the content of law, the standards or criteria to which the rule of law or legal utterance must in principle conform for it to be capable, other things being equal – ideational and institutional requirements being met – of being law (Fuller, 1975, p. 23 ff).

This mode of designation is concerned with the substance of the law. The failure of a statement to achieve a certain content will deny it the status of law. An example of this approach operating within the common-law tradition can be seen in the writings of Blackstone:

> This law of nature being coeval with mankind and dictated by God himself, is of course superior in obligation to any other. It is binding over all the globe, in all countries and at all times: no human laws are of any validity if contrary to this; and such of them as are valid derive all their force and all their authority, mediately or immediately from this original. (*Commentaries*, Vol. 1, p. 41)

This passage contains the essential elements of an ideational source of law: the universality of the legal content, the superior nature of that content, the validity of human law being contingent upon its concordance with an unwritten ideal of law. In the example drawn from the writings of Blackstone, the ideal or superior source has a divine origin. Other attempts to designate law by reference to a superior or ideal source locate the superior nature of the source by reference to reason, justice or moral law. In all accounts the abstract ideal purports to determine the possibility of law. In theory at least the validity of human (positive) law should be withdrawn in the event of its failure to comply with the ideal.

God, nature and reason are used in the practice of law and have on occasion operated significantly in disputes relating to issues of human rights. Charters of human rights, such as the European Convention on Human Rights, purport to state those rights that are natural or intrinsic to the human condition. Litigation before the Court of Justice of Human Rights at Strasbourg is centred on the failure of domestic law to comply with the European Convention, thereby threatening its status as law. A recent and interesting example of such a conflict between domestic law and a more abstract and ambitious conception of human rights is to be found in *Malone* v *United Kingdom* [1984] EHRR 14, a case concerning telephone tapping by government agencies in the United Kingdom. Under Article 8 of the European Convention on Human Rights:

> 1. Everyone has the right to respect for his private and family life, his home and his correspondence. 2. There shall be no interference by a public authority with the exercise of this right except such as is in accordance with the law and is necessary in a democratic society in the interests of national security, public safety or the economic well-being of the country, for the prevention of disorder or crime, for the protection of health or morals, or the protection of the rights or freedoms of others.

In the domestic hearing of a case brought by Malone against the Metropolitan Police Commissioner [1979] 1 Ch. 344, it was held that although there was no express legal authority for the interception of telephone communications by State agencies, such interception was well established in practice and was consequently to be regarded as lawful. The practice of interception did not infringe any legally recognized right and in the absence of any authority to the contrary it could not – however unfortunate or undesirable the conclusion might be – successfully be challenged in the English courts. On application to the European Court, the absence of direct legal authority for the practice of tapping weighed heavily against the domestic decision; the state of domestic law was thought to be 'somewhat obscure and open to differing interpretations', it was in essence 'uncertain' and 'to that extent the minimum degree of legal protection to which citizens are entitled under the law in a democratic society is lacking.' In a concurring opinion, Judge Pettiti observed that 'the danger threatening democratic societies in the years

1980–1990 stems from the temptation facing public authorities to "see into" the life of the citizen.'

The Court of Justice in the *Malone* case made use of a set of general propositions as to basic human rights to invalidate the otherwise lawful (not unlawful) activities of a signatory State. The practice of tapping telephones, because of the manner in which it was undertaken, because of the lack of adequate legal regulation and because of the inequality of power as between the citizen and the agencies of the State, was to be viewed as infringing fundamental freedoms or human rights, and was consequently to be ruled immoral and unlawful. What is interesting about the ruling is that the decision is based neither upon any explicit infraction of an established legal rule by the State agency, nor upon any substantively stated right to unimpeded or untapped telephonic communication. On the contrary, the case is decided upon the basis of a fundamental conception of natural rights and the morality of social life, upon notions which the Master of the Rolls had some years earlier remarked upon as being 'high-sounding' and 'drawn in such vague terms that [they] can be used for all sorts of unreasonable claims and provoke all sorts of litigation' (*Ahmad* v *Inner London Education Authority* [1977] 3 WLR 400). The European Convention, in other words, provides a very general body of fundamental or ideational restrictions upon the activities of signatory States and, however much national courts may occasionally abhor the fact, it enunciates moral rights and freedoms which can, as in *Malone*, occasionally render otherwise lawful activities and purposes, unlawful or void.[1]

Within the domestic sphere, constitutions often attempt to embody statements of essential or fundamental laws which are subsequently available to invalidate further expressions of a law-maker by reference to their failure to comply with certain substantive principles. For example, the Constitution of the Federal Republic of Germany, *The Basic Law*, contains the following statement:

Article 1. (Protection of Human Dignity)
1. The dignity of Man shall be inviolable. To respect and protect it shall be the duty of all State authorities.
2. The German people therefore acknowledge inviolable and inalienable human rights as the basis of every community, of peace and of justice in the world.
3. The following basic rights shall bind the legislature, executive and the judiciary as directly enforceable law . . .

The Constitution of the United States provides similar broad protection of individual rights, and to use an example relevant to the foregoing discussion of telephone tapping, the Fourth Amendment to the Constitution provides that: 'the right of the people to be secure in their persons, houses, papers, and effects against unreasonable searches and seizures, shall not be violated, and no warrants shall issue but upon probable cause, supported by oath or affirmation and particularly describing the place to be searched, and the persons or things to be seized.' As a consequence of this provision, the Supreme Court of the United States has held in *Katz* v *United States* (389, US 347) that telephone tapping is contrary to the Constitution and in *Lee* v *Florida* (392, US 378) introduced an exclusionary rule whereby all such illegally obtained evidence is inadmissible in court, taking the view that 'nothing short of mandatory exclusion of illegal evidence will compel respect for the federal law in the only effective available way – by removing the incentive to disregard it.'

Remaining with the example of telephone tapping, the English court in *Malone* was unwilling to develop the law solely upon the basis of a moral right to privacy or to freedom from State intrusion. While the judge was prepared to go so far as to declare 'I would have thought that in any civilised system of law the claims of liberty and justice would require that telephone users should have effective and independent safeguards against possible abuses' (381), it was nonetheless the case that 'however desirable it may be', the court could not provide a remedy on the strength of justice or liberty alone. While there are instances when the English courts will turn explicitly to liberty, justice or comparable natural-law categories as explicit sources of law, most famously in the criminal case of *Shaw* v *Director of Public Prosecutions* [1962] AC 220, where the court claimed the right to superintend the 'moral welfare of the State' and created a criminal offence on the strength of that power, it is generally the case that moral and political conceptions of the substantive role of the law influence the process of law-interpretation and law-application rather than being treated as an explicit source of law.

The explicit use of nature and natural reason as sources of law is not frequent within the common-law tradition. While examples can be drawn from doctrinal writings and most substantively from Blackstone, the major eighteenth-century literary exponent of the common law and herald of the renewed literary and academic tradition within the common law, this approach has rarely been explicitly used by the judiciary as a full substantive source of law. The classic example of its use is found in a decision of Lord Coke's in *Dr Bonham's Case* [1610] 8 Co. Rep 106 at 118, where Lord Coke speculated as to the relationship between the law enacted by Parliament and a higher order of law, concluding: 'And it appears in our books, and in many cases, the common law will control Acts of Parliament, and sometimes adjudge them to be utterly void; for when an Act of Parliament is against common right and reason, or repugnant or impossible to be performed, the common law will control it and adjudge such Act to be void.' Here Coke sees the common law as the historically established perfection of reason, as the higher order of law and ideational unity to which the legislative enactments of a Parliament must comply. The failure to do so will threaten their status as law, because, in the words of one historian, 'somewhere – in the breasts of judges, in Magna Carta, or in the liberties of Parliament – were laws so sacred and so essential to social stability, that no government could override them' (Hill, 1980). Whilst this approach to legislation has been criticized and in the main rejected (Lord Denning's support for it being somewhat exceptional), arguments based upon nature and reason as formal sources of law still occasionally find a place in the common-law system. For example in *Oppenheimer* v *Cattermole* [1976] AC 249, the house of Lords explicitly responded to an argument based upon nature as reason or natural law. The issue, which was ultimately found to be peripheral to the dispute, related to the status of a decree produced by the Nazi government in 1941 depriving German Jews resident abroad of their German nationality from the date of the decree. The house of Lords, while clearly of the opinion that the decree constituted 'unjust and discriminatory legislation', did not provide a consistent answer to the question of the legality of the decree. Lord Hailsham rejected arguments designed to deprive the decree of the status of law because of its content, taking the view that 'the only way known to English law of disregarding an unpleasant fact is to create the legal fiction that it does not exist. I do not think that such fictions always serve a useful purpose, and, where they do, among the criteria would certainly be included the effect of the proposed fiction on individuals, but not I venture to think the distasteful nature of the facts' (263). It was Lord Cross who provided the most extensive statement on the issue and argued in support of the conclusion that the court had the power to deny the decree the status of law because it contravened a superior (natural) order. After expressing the need for caution in so acting to deny the status of law to such a morally repugnant decree, irrespective of its institutional source, he concluded:

> what we are concerned with here is legislation which takes away without compensation from a section of the citizen body singled out on racial grounds all their property on which the state passing legislation can lay its hands and in addition deprives them of their citizenship. To my mind a law of this sort constitutes so grave an infringement of human rights that the courts of this country ought to refuse to recognise it as a law at all . . . it surely cannot be right for the question whether the decree should be recognised or not to depend upon the circumstances of the particular case. (278b)

In this rather exceptional instance its non-compliance with a superior order of 'human rights' was said to be capable of denying the 1941 decree the status 'law', a position interestingly summarized in a very different context by the American black civil-rights campaigner Martin Luther King in claiming that: 'there are just laws and there are unjust laws. What is the difference between the two? A just law is a man made code that squares with the moral law or the law of God. An unjust law is a code that is out of harmony with the moral law.'

1.2   INSTITUTIONAL SOURCES OF LAW

The assumptions that lawyers make as to the inevitability, the validity and the moral benefit of legal regulation are crucial to their practice and to the maintenance of legal rules, to the ideology of law within the industrialized western nations. Such assumptions as to the conceptual unity of law are, however, increasingly infrequently utilized as explicit sources of law, reference to moral, political and economic factors generally being seen as a function of interpretation and argumentation – of implicit or tacit sources of law – rather than of formally designated legal authority. At the same time as stressing the practical importance of the ideational source of law, we would also rapidly point out that the abstract and external, ideational source of law is neither the most obvious nor the most frequently stated meaning of source of law in contemporary legal cultures. The preferred view is currently one which stresses the institutional sources of law rather than directly or consciously elaborating the myth of an origin or essence of law or indeed the dogmatic status of legal science or legal reason as sources of law. The current legal wisdom views law as a tradition and as a process or practice of regulation. Rather than defining law, legal doctrine is now more content to see it as a series of traditionally established texts and similarly established techniques for the interpretation of those texts; 'laws have no necessary unity of content, form or function outside of that derived from the legislative processes and legal apparatuses' (Hirst, 1979, pp. 111–12). The institutional source of law is here seen to be the established practice of the legal institution and of its officials – law is taken to be what lawyers 'recognize' as law. In complex modern legal orders the material sources of law are various and far from simple; the manner of their recognition is correspondingly a complex 'professional' task, although legal doctrine does not attempt to formulate any explicit rule for verifying valid law. The rule of recognition is rather 'manifest in the general practice on the part of officials . . . of identifying rules . . . its existence is *shown* in the way in which particular rules are identified, either by courts or other officials . . . the rule of recognition of a legal system is like the scoring rule of a game' (Hart, 1961, pp. 98–9). While this definition of the sources of law suffers from numerous defects, not the least being that it is a circular or tautological definition which uncritically allows lawyers to define the law, it does carry a useful element of realism with it. Law is defined as the social fact of law, as a long-standing institutional practice subject to the internal discipline and rules of the institution itself. Within the legal institution the material sources of law are to be discovered in a hierarchically organized series of institutional functions or roles: provided that the given rule is not in conflict with some other, hierarchically superior, source of law, it will be deemed valid law.

The concept of recognition refers the student of law or other reader of legal texts to what are somewhat ambiguously termed the 'institutional' or legal sources of law within the specific legal tradition being studied. A classic formulation of this most basic doctrinal meaning of recognition can be taken from the writings of the Austrian jurist Hans Kelsen (1957): 'positive law is an order by which human conduct is regulated in a specific way. The regulation is accomplished by provisions which set forth how men ought to act. Such provisions are called norms and either come from custom, as do the norms of the common law, or are enacted by conscious acts of certain organs aiming to create law, as a legislature acting in its law-making capacity.' Clearly this view of law as defined by its source is too general to be of specific or substantive use: different institutions and different procedures will be found to designate the hierarchy of legal sources of law within different legal orders. The general point made by Kelsen, however, remains valid; it is by examining where the law or rule comes from – its institutional source – that law is recognized as valid within the official community of legal doctrine in a fashion broadly comparable to that whereby the institution of language determines the manner of recognition of utterances as being in a familiar or foreign tongue.

The most basic institutional meaning of source of law refers to the institutional behaviour and practice most generally accepted and adopted by the officials of the legal system examined. Institution is here most generally taken to refer to conventions or to doctrinally agreed roles, as for example in the (unwritten) British constitution and the sources of law within that constitution. The traditional view is one which is expressed by A. V. Dicey in his study of the law of the constitution (Dicey, 1885) in terms of institutionally arranged sources of law. The supreme source of law, then as now, is found in the duly expressed utterances of the institution 'Queen in Parliament', composed of the monarch, House of Lords and the House of Commons acting in agreement. This triumvirate was the supreme source of law within the United Kingdom at the time in which Dicey was writing, supremacy meaning that the enactments of this body could not be over-turned by any court of law nor by any other legislative institution within the United Kingdom. The power of the triumvirate is consequently the ultimate source of law emanating from any institution within the United Kingdom, there being traditionally no legal limit upon the subject-matter of its legislative expressions, save only that it cannot bind future legislative expressions. To this it should merely be added that since 1972 Britain has been a member of the European Economic Community and under Article 189 of the EEC Treaty, national law is subordinate to the legislative enactments, legal procedures and interpretative methods of the Community. In terms of the sources of law, however, the EEC merely superimposes a further institutional source of law to be recognized by the national legal institution and its officials by virtue of the European Communities Act 1972, s. 2.

The mode of recognition of a valid source of law within the United Kingdom varies according to the hierarchical status of that source: the higher the source in the hierarchy, the more literal and internal the recognition of it is likely to be. Thus in the classic case of *Edinburgh and Dalkeith Railway* v *Wauchope* [1842] 8 Cl & F 710, where it was pronounced by Lord Campbell – in an extremely legalistic vein – that 'all the Court of Justice can do is look to the Parliamentary roll: if from that it should appear that a bill has passed both Houses and received the Royal assent, no court of Justice can inquire into the mode in which it was introduced into Parliament, nor into what was done previous to its introduction, or what passed in Parliament during its progress in its various stages through both Houses.' Consequently the plaintiffs in the case in question, adversely affected by a duly enacted Private Bill, could not resist its adverse effects upon their interests on the grounds that they had received no notification of the Bill. The stated position of the courts in relation to legislation or written law is one of straightforward obedience and application save only in circumstances where there are formal irregularities in the enactment, as in *Stockdale* v *Hansard* [1839] 9 Ad & E 9, a case concerning Parliamentary privilege in which the court conclusively rejected the argument that one branch of the 'Queen in Parliament', the House of Commons alone, could by itself change the law: 'nothing is clearer than that the House does not have that power, and cannot by its own resolutions acquire it.'

As we shall have occasion to observe later, the courts of the common law have traditionally approached legislation and written instruments more generally with something approximating to mystical awe. While that attitude has changed somewhat over the past decades and certainly has not often extended to European legislation, it is still useful to distinguish, on formal grounds, the approach to the supreme source of law and that towards secondary or customary sources. The principal institutional distinction to be made is that between legislation (written) and common (unwritten) law.

Legislation, both primary and secondary, forms the institutional pinnacle of the hierarchy of sources and, in doctrinal accounts, these are followed by the courts themselves as institutional sources of law predicated upon the concept of a system of precedent. The decision of a higher court (*ratio decidendi*) binds a lower court and, as a general rule, the most recent decision or pronouncement of a court will be binding evidence of a common-law rule for all courts of equal or lower status.

Without at this stage entering too great a degree of detail with respect to the specific institutional sources and methods of legal recognition, we would wish to make certain brief critical observations as to the accuracy of the doctrinal definition of institutional legal source. This concept of an institutional source utilized in legal doctrinal writings is far more a justification for the procedures of law-application than it is an accurate description of legal methods of dispute-settlement or procedures of social control. The very notion of a hierarchy or indeed grammar of legal sources perpetuates, in a secular form, the essentially natural-law conception of the unity and the reason of legal order. It is, in short, an article of faith as much as it is a descriptive account of the workings of the courts. Certainly we may admit that systems of legal control in modern societies tend to adopt very strict criteria or rules governing the formal order of deference within the institution. It is a part of what Foucault (1977, p. 181) terms the 'order of discourse' within disciplinary social formations strictly to organize, enclose and delimit both the topics of speech and who may speak within each given institution of control. An 'analytical space' is organized within which roles and functions are partitioned and in more general terms highly technical rules operate to legitimate and authorize the speakers and discourses of the law.[2] There are, in brief, specifiable times and places and occasions of legal speech, there are ritual affirmations of what is spoken, there are procedures of social and communicational authorization and of sanction with respect to who may speak and what they may say. The legal institution and the rules governing sources of law are best understood not as a unique set of discursive procedures but as one institutional discourse – albeit of a formal, highly symbolic and political significance – within a society of diverse institutions and discourses of control. Analytically, it can be pointed out that law is simply one stage in a continuum of disciplinary and normalizing discourses which might very loosely be said to run from educational discourses, the rules of grammar, etiquette and the social, political and moral aspects of collective existence, through to the more explicitly coercive languages of psychiatry, therapy, law and religion. Finally, it should never be forgotten that beyond the discourses of normality and of law are the various arms of State coercion and terror; where law is ineffective or consent to legal order is lacking, then the discourse of order is simply and swiftly replaced by the politics of violence, of confinement, physical subjection and at its most extreme, death at the hands of the military and martial law.

What is peculiar to the legal institution is not that it has rules of office, of ritual procedures, of doctrine and heresy, as well as specific methods of interpretation and application of its rules but rather that such a tremendous degree of social affirmation is lavished upon those rules and procedures. The primary modes of recognition of valid legal rules have more to do with the symbols of administration and media power that surround the institutional sources of law than they have to do with either the formal procedures or substantive content relating to sources of law (Mathieson, 1981). Certainly there are strong arguments from very diverse theoretical positions which would forcefully claim that legal administrative power – in both its formal and its substantive aspects – is much less regulated and far more open to manipulation, negotiation and technique generally, interpretation and abuse, than is admitted by legal doctrine. The logic behind this claim can be subdivided along the lines of the distinction already outlined between ideational and institutional sources of law.

With regard to the ideational source of law – with regard, that is, to legal doctrine, the legal profession's belief in the logical and unified character of legal regulation – the argument is a simple one. There is no rational ground for supposing either that legal order is ultimately derivable from a concept of God or that the existent western legal orders in their actual practice come anywhere close to approximating a divine or natural order incarnate. While there are numerous possible arguments for ascribing divine, natural or rational status to legal regulation, these arguments have nothing whatsoever to do with the sources of law in their material functioning or official validity: beliefs as to the metaphysical import of human existence are characteristic ingredients of faith, philosophy and social and political ideologies; they should not be mistaken for substantive sources of law of either an ideational or institutional kind. The reason for this is not in the end so much to do with arguments as to divinity, metaphysics or the distinction between nature and culture as it is to do with the practical operation of legal orders and the methods necessary for accurately describing them.

In terms of institutional sources, we have already loosely indicated that the legal institution is to be seen as part of a continuum of disciplinary institutions within contemporary western social orders. It would be wrong in such circumstances to view the legal system as being a privileged or unique institution: to a large degree it shares its language, methods of self-regulation and techniques of discipline and decision-making with other branches of the State machinery of control. For that reason alone it would seem apposite to direct a number of relatively simple questions at the legal self-description of the rule of law and to take seriously the available evidence on the functioning of legal rules (Henry, 1984, pp. 1–31). Of the more important areas of discussion, areas we shall return to subsequently, the following are among the more interesting and illuminating. First, the pervasive yet little acknowledged role of discretion within decision-making processes throughout the legal order, and not simply within the process of explicit adjudication. The issue is one which we would term the politics of interpretation: the latitude technically available in virtually all areas of legal discourse allowing for judicial choice in the application of legal norms. There is, we shall suggest, an element of politics in virtually all decision-making procedures in both the legal and other arms of the administration, yet it is only in the realm of legal doctrine as to the sources of law that the existence of such discretion is routinely and vigorously denied. To acknowledge the element of discretion in rule-usage of any kind is to take up a position on the margins of legal doctrinal writing, the official view being a restrictive one, expressed, for example, by Viscount Simmonds in the case of *Scruttons Ltd* v *Midland Silicones* [1962] AC 446:

> to me heterodoxy, or as some might say, heresy, is not the more attractive because it is dignified by the name of reform. Nor will I easily be led by an undiscerning zeal for some abstract kind of justice to ignore our first duty, which is to administer justice according to law, the law which is established for us by Act of Parliament or the binding authority of precedent . . . If the principle of 'ius quaesitum tertio' [third party rights] is to be introduced into our law, it must be done by Parliament. (467–8)

Against such a view, a number of theoretical and substantive arguments can be put forward to emphasize the degrees of choice or to pose discretion as a source of law. In summary form, these would include the generality of legal language and the pervasive use of discretionary categories such as those of 'reasonableness', 'fairness', 'consideration of all the circumstances' and like phrases, both in legislative drafting and in the formulation of common-law rules. To issues of the ambiguity of rules, of competition and conflict between rules within a complex and vast system of substantive law, it should be added that in the end the court makes a decision on the specific case before it. Not only does this mean that the law has always to be interpreted and applied to the particular fact-situation before the court, but it allows the court to alter, vary or ignore the legal rule according to what it sees as the merits of the case. In the view of one important American school of potentially radical legal thought, rules are only ever as good as their application: the law is 'what officials do about disputes' (Llewellyn, 1950).

In looking at what officials do about disputes, it is necessary to take into account a vast array of political, economic, social, ethnic and psychological factors relevant to decision-making, and not simply the officially designated or 'recognized' sources of law. It would be extremely naïve or ill-intentioned to suppose that only legal factors determine legal outcomes, a point well refuted by sociological studies of courtroom practice (Carlen, 1976; McBarnet, 1981). The contemporary sociological view of legal sources pays greater attention to informal and discretionary factors than it does to officially designated written and unwritten sources of law. An adequate account of legal decision-making processes should thus take into consideration the entire process of social regulation, including also that preponderant number of disputes that never come to court. First, there is the process of selection of cases to be tried, the question of what happens before the trial. The vast majority of disputed social issues, including both private- and public-law conflicts, never come to court. Mechanisms of informal justice (Henry, 1984), of self-regulation and of social dominance – whether politically, economically or sexually based – more generally prevent the majority of conflicts becoming legal conflicts before the courts. Factors such as lack of knowledge and lack of money, as well as the availability of alternative remedies, will frequently resolve private disputes, while bureaucratic and official practices will frequently be directed towards preventing public and penal issues coming before the courts. When such issues do arise in court, the vast majority of defendants in criminal cases plead guilty and overall, where cases are disputed, informal rules concerning courtroom ritual, patterns of acceptable behaviour, modes of dress and modes of speech are likely to be as important to the outcome of the trial as are any formal legal sources. In the courts of first instance the predominant issue is that of establishing credibility with regard to facts, of substantiating a version of what happened, and is seldom a question of disputes as to the meaning or application of formal rules.

In briefly adverting to factors which can be taken to challenge the legal professional account of law and of legal sources, we are concerned to propose a wider definition of law, legal sources and legal texts. Such 'critical' issues will form a central theme in this study and will be analysed in depth in elaborating a theory of reading the law. For the present purpose of analysing the concept of source of law we would simply conclude that any remotely critical account of the legal institution should analyse it both in terms of its self-definition and also in terms of its more general social and political roles. The legal institution forms one branch of the political administration of the modern State. As one element within a complex bureaucracy it would be surprising if it did not have ambitions, goals, values and purposes closely allied to those of government itself. Its ideology is in that sense political and its functions and performances are political and social as well as being distinctively legal. Such a point is not of great originality but it is frequently forgotten or repressed: the law may be defined at its broadest as the characteristic discourse and practice of the legal institution. These discourses and practices should not be read simply in the formal terms of the specifically legal but also as social discourse, as part of a continuing political and administrative dialogue as to the terms and conditions of social life. Legal discourse is in this sense simply one of many competing normative disciplinary discourses, discourses of morality, religion and social custom to which it is closely related and from which it draws many if not all of its justificatory arguments. It is a discourse which should ideally be read in terms of control – of dominance and subordination – and of social power-relations portrayed and addressed to a far more general audience than that of law-breakers and wrong-doers alone (Goodrich, 1986, ch. 7). Finally, it is a discourse that combines both speech and action and consequently changes dramatically over time. It is a discourse which should be read as inherently historical and political in that it is a rhetoric aligned to historical and social change and it is in that context and at that level of social dialogue that we attempt in this work to read it.

NOTES

1 The Interception of Communications Act 1985, sections 7 and 8, implements certain of the recommendations of the European Court of Human Rights in the *Malone* case.
2 The contemporary hierarchy of common-law courts can be briefly outlined as follows: the judicial committee of the House of Lords is the supreme domestic court in both civil and criminal jurisdictions. Second to it is the Court of Appeal and, in civil jurisdiction, the County, Divisional and High Courts lie below the Court of Appeal. In criminal jurisdiction, the Crown Court and the Magistrates' Court lie below the Court of Appeal, while the Divisional Court acts as an alternative court of appeal. (See ch. 3, s. 3.1.2.)

REFERENCES AND FURTHER READING

Carlen, P. 1976: *Magistrates' Justice*. London.
Debray, R. 1981: *Critique of Political Reason*. London.
Dicey, A. V. 1885: *Introduction to the Study of the Law of the Constitution*. London.
Fine, B. 1984: *Democracy and the Rule of Law*. London.
Foucault, M. 1977: *Discipline and Punish*. London.
Fuller, L. 1975: *The Morality of Law*. Yale.
Glucksmann, A. 1980: *The Master Thinkers*. Brighton.
Goodrich, P. 1983: 'The rise of legal formalism'. 3 *Legal Studies* 248.
Goodrich, P. 1986: *Legal Discourse*. London.
Hart, H. L. A. 1961: *The Concept of Law*. Oxford.
Henry, S. 1984: *Private Justice*. London.
Hill, C. 1980: *The Century of Revolution*. London.
Hirst, P. 1979: *On Law and Ideology*. London.
Kelsen, H. 1957: *What is Justice?* California.
Llewellyn, K. 1950: *The Bramble Bush*. New York.
McBarnet, D. 1981: *Conviction*. London.
Mathieson, T. 1981: *Law, Society and Political Action*. London.

2

Law and Writing

The King, whose oracle is at Delphi, neither speaks nor keeps silent but expresses himself by signs.

(Heraclitus)

From the earliest times, law has been inscribed and codified, be it chiselled in stone, scratched on vellum or written in books. While the law codes and law books are not the only form of law, they are certainly in historical terms a frequently repeated one; the law is promulgated in books and found in books and it is, we will suggest, of the essence of legal power to take a written form. The nature of the relationship between law, writing and power is extremely complex; writing as a political and legal form of practice serves many functions, three of which we shall examine closely in the present chapter. The written law and particularly the codification or statutory law makes a series of assertions as to social relationships, it presents a broad model of society and acts as a resource for legal discourse and argument in court. Second, the writing of the law suggests the availability of the law; it may be known to its subjects and a restraint upon its interpreters and judges. Third, however, writing creates a need for interpreters and the historically constant feature of written law has been its protection by priestly and professional classes of interpreters and commentators, an issue which will form the principal focus of this chapter in so far as we argue that the democratic motive behind the written law is consistently belied or frustrated by a literary and interpretative practice which treats the written law as an encoding and a veiling of the legal rules.

The concept of writing as a source of law has a specific, confused and somewhat confusing legal meaning – that of *ius scriptum* – which will be discussed in detail later in this chapter. Prior, however, to any examination of the now rather narrow legal sense of written law it is useful to comment briefly upon the more general historical connection between law and writing or, more accurately, between writing and power. The history of systems of

writing clearly evidences a constant link between the invention of writing –
of pictograms (Mexico), hieroglyphs (Egypt), ideograms (China) as well as
alphabetic script[1] – and knowledge or control placed in the hands of elite
groups or classes within the societies in question. Writing was developed so
as to retain and control information relevant to the administration of
societies of an increasing size and it is in the listing and collating of
information, in the keeping of 'written accounts' and the recording of
information about persons, objects and events, that a form of power and
surveillance unavailable in oral cultures, the power of encoded (cryptic)
information, is generated. What Foucault terms the 'power of writing' in
modern societies is the indispensable and historically constant mechanism
of discipline and surveillance. Writing has always organized and separated
individuals for the purposes of administration, observation and judgment and
its history has in general been one of a growing sophistication in its role in
the retention and control of information or knowledge for the purposes of
ruling groups.

The written codes act as authoritative resources for administration,
control and the 'accounting' of social relationships generally. Writing
inscribes, enrols, documents, registers and examines in the whole multitude
of modern disciplinary institutions: the school, the factory, the prison, the
barracks, the hospital and the court are all centrally controlled institutions
of the modern State which depend upon codes of 'disciplinary individuality', upon systems of filing and writing. 'The turning of real lives into
writing . . . functions as a procedure of objectification and subjectification'
(Foucault, 1979, pp. 184–94), or, in less technical terms, it functions to
create a *system* of authority or control which the individual subject is to obey
without necessarily understanding. What is important is not so much the
content of the system or its rules but rather the simple recognition on the
part of those subject to them that the written texts do indeed form a system
or that there is a rule to be obeyed. 'In this way one enters a universe of
silence, the universe of the text, of the text which knows everything, asking
the questions and also answering them.' In more general terms, the anthropologist Levi-Strauss also observes and confirms that the State, bureaucracy, cumulative history and centralized administration, from the army to
teachers, all presuppose that 'leap forward' which was constituted by the
invention of writing, and is well illustrated in his discussion of the discovery
of writing amongst the Nambikwara tribe (Levi-Strauss, 1978). In imitating
the note-taking anthropologist, the leader of the Nambikwara borrowed
notepads and traced wavy lines on to the paper. Having collected a largish
number of such scribbled notepads, he began to use them as lists and would
pretend to read from them when deciding upon the correct measure of
exchanges amongst his people. Levi-Strauss observes that he 'immediately

understood [writing's] role as sign, and the social superiority that it confers
. . . The symbol had been borrowed but the reality remained quite foreign.'

The intimate relationship between techniques of writing and the growth
of administrative power, that of a centralized administration or State, is also
well evidenced in the available historical accounts of early systems of
writing, which appear almost universally to have been utilized to record and
to represent the interests of ruling groups. Writing seems to have been
everywhere destined to serve the dual functions of history and law. In the
Mexican Empire, for example, the pictogram (picture-writing) was utilized
first for the tax rolls of the royal treasury and for their civil code; the most
developed part of this law treats, interestingly enough, of patriarchal power
(*de iure patris*), the legal right of the father to the power of life and death over
his children (Pope, 1975). In ancient China and Egypt as well, a similar
correlation is apparent between priestly power, sacred law and the development respectively of the ideogram and the hieroglyph. Political power in
both Chinese and Egyptian societies rapidly became a question of knowledge of the written law: knowledge of the code and struggles for power
became a question of struggles over various writings, the struggle of priestly
groups to protect a favoured version of the scriptural past against competing
interpretations. 'Writing does not come to power. It is there beforehand, it
partakes of it and is made of it – struggles and contending forces permeate
writings and counter-writings: the political question of literati, of intellec-
tuals in the ideological apparatus, of the place and stockages of writing, of
caste phenomena, of "priests" and the hoarding of codes, of archival
matters – [these] should all concern us' (Derrida, 1979, pp. 117–18).

The point to be made is that written law is an early and exemplary form of
writing and it should not come as a surprise if legal writings, codes and
codifications, share many of the features of the early bonding of writing,
power and knowledge. As our discussion of the religious basis of legal
writing will endeavour to show, contemporary written sources of law still
need to be looked at in terms of their written context and of the general
history of such writings, the history of texts and of the single Table, Tablet
or Text as the source of tradition and territorial conquest. 'Love of texts is
what holds up tradition and not vice versa . . . texts do not simply serve the
exercise of power, they are that exercise, they subject people' (Glucksmann,
1980, pp. 34–65). It is to this issue that we shall now turn, after a brief
discussion of some of the terms to be used.

In discussing the history and traditions of written law, two terms of art
will be invoked, those of *code* and *codification*. The meanings of these terms
are not totally separate. *Code* will be used to designate the total body of
written law (*ius scriptum*) to be found in force at a given time within a
specific legal system. *Codification* will be used to designate a particular

process, a particular moment in legal history when a body of written law is produced which has particular characteristics and significance. Codification signifies the creation of a body of written law which is, for whatever purposes, intended to express a break in the history of the given legal and political tradition. Its most important political and ideological function would appear to be that it is seen to represent a process of reduction of law into a coherent, rational, discrete and complete form, setting down in a permanent and binding manner the agreed rules of law governing either a particular disputed area of social life or the entirety of the law. In either case, it purports to be a complete statement of law within its designated domain. Politically it dislocates law from its past and, typically, references to old sources of law are outlawed. The law in its codified written form is to be extensively privileged so as to render it the first and frequently the only institutionally designated source of law.

2.1 THE CIVIL-LAW TRADITION

The extreme importance and primary status of written law within contemporary legal traditions may best be understood by setting out the historical, political and ideological basis upon which it rests. The basis is complex and extensive; it must take account of the role of writing itself within western political culture and the extraordinary significance to be attached to the storage of information and the coding and keeping of knowledge, both legal and religious. In short, there can be no single, simple analysis, and the following account necessarily omits a great deal. For present purposes, the story may usefully begin with a brief excursion into the Old Testament, the original Scriptures and the first comprehensive written law within the western legal tradition.

2.1.1 *The historical foundation*

The foundational myth of western law, the ideal symbolic representation of legality, is fittingly a religious one and is to be found in the Book of Deuteronomy. God's chosen people, the tribes of Israel, had during the course of their journey (exodus) from Egypt to the promised land become somewhat disobedient and disrespectful towards God's unwritten law and its human representatives, the prophets and religious leaders of the tribes. For this reason, we are told by the Scriptures, God chose to appear to the people of Israel and did so on Mount Sinai, arriving as a voice in the midst of a fire: 'And ye came near and stood under the mountain; and the mountain burned with fire unto the midst of heaven, with darkness, clouds and thick darkness. And the Lord spake unto you out of the midst of the fire: ye heard the voice of the words but saw no similitude . . .' (4: 11–12). The people of Israel, frightened by this fiery manifestation, would not go up Mount Sinai and it was left to Moses to ascend the mountain to collect the two tablets of stone upon which were written down God's commandments. Moses tells us that he listened to the Lord – to the judge 'unbearable to behold' – and wrote down the Ten Commandments on the tablets of stone which he subsequently brought down, proclaiming to the people: 'I stood between the Lord and you at that time, to show you the word of the Lord: for ye were afraid by reason of the fire and went not up into the Mount' (5: 5).

The elements of this particular instance of law-giving are of extreme interest both in terms of the form and also of the source of the law. Of the elements of the story which may be singled out, the following in particular reappear fairly consistently as significant attributes to law-giving – to written sources of law – in the subsequent history of codification. First, both in terms of impact and of legal significance, the law comes from above, it is carried down from the Mount to the people below. The sacred status of the law, its derivation from God, is physically represented in the source or speaker of the law situated on the Mount, literally and legally, historically and physically, the hierarchical pinnacle of the Old Testament order of law. Interestingly enough, the term hierarchy, which takes on such enormous significance within later legal orders in terms of the hierarchy of sources of law, derives directly from the Greek 'hierarch', meaning priestly rule, and mediately from 'hieros', meaning sacred. It is the sacred that authorizes and establishes the hierarchical order of the law and the authoritative status of the legal word as written law:

> The authoritative word demands that we acknowledge it, that we make it our own; it binds us quite independent of any power it might have to persuade us internally; we encounter it with its authority already attached to it. The authoritative word is located in a distanced zone, organically connected with a past that is felt to be hierarchically higher. It is, so to speak, the word of the fathers. Its authority was already acknowledged in the past . . . It is given (it sounds) in lofty spheres, not those of familiar contact . . . (Bakhtin, 1981, p. 342)

Neither the sacred text nor the written law can be escaped or ignored or denied – they are there and already authoritative; one cannot, as is so well expressed in Kafka's *Trial*, claim to be innocent and yet not know the law, the simple reason for this being that the subject of the law is not in truth supposed to know or understand the law but rather is expected merely to acknowledge that it is law and leave it to the professionals to argue and explain its content and meaning.

If faith in the sanctity of the text of the law is a primary legal virtue, it finds further graphic expression in the constitutive form of the written law. The term code (*caudex*) itself refers to the physical, permanent, form of the law, that of tablets of stone, later of wood and subsequently of papyrus (parchment) and only later in scrolls and then in books or the book of the law. The permanent form of the law has several different implications. For the Israelites of the Old Testament the laws chiselled on stone represented a strongly symbolic response to prior disobedience: the law was now 'declared'; it was made public, visible and inescapably 'known'. The giving of the Ten Commandments to Moses represented a transition (fall) from an unwritten to a written law. The invisible and hidden was made visible and explicit in the form of ten concise commandments, the rules of behaviour to be observed and obeyed at all times and in all places; it was the written law and was to be returned to time and again in preference to the traditional ways recollected by the Pharisees. God is the only source of law – 'ye shall have no other' – and his laws are promulgated and known, a factor that underpins traditional religious and legal wisdom which has tended to regard the permanent written form of the code as an essential and democratic moment of legal development. The law is promulgated to the people, it is made known and unchangeable: what is permanent cannot be retracted, what is written and so promulgated cannot be denied or ignored. The law is now established and merely needs to be applied and obeyed.

A closer scrutiny of the story of the Ten Commandments does not lend support to this view of the written law as clarification and rationalization of prior (generally customary) law. First, and somewhat unfairly, the available historical evidence of the scriptural myth tends to confirm it precisely as myth or symbol: the Ten Commandments were in all probability written by priests in exile and were never fully accepted as law by the people of Israel. The history of the laws handed down from Mount Sinai is that of a power struggle between different competing ruling groups within the tribes, which did not settle or permanently promulgate the law but rather made it the object of political struggle. The Ten Commandments were simply one of several different versions of the divine law and were frequently rejected by the people while being fought over by their ruling groups who were also the interpreters of the law. The story itself can confirm this view if we examine in greater detail the terms of the myth. The giving of the law from Mount Sinai is a story concerned with establishing an 'absolute' source or foundation for a set of laws which had become contested. The myth endeavours to establish the legitimacy and the power of the law and it does so by ascribing the law to an absent, invisible, divine source. The purpose of the story – the fiery presence, the fear of God, the need for Moses to act as intermediary and interpreter – is not one of clarifying or secularizing the source of law, but rather of making it incontestable. Although the people of Israel have to rely upon Moses, it is God who we are told has spoken and it is God who must be obeyed through the written law, despite the fact that it is only Moses who has had contact with this 'source' of the law and even he has not seen, has not dared to look into, that source.

The last point raises the interesting and enduring question of the relationship of law as writing to legal interpretation. The code is not simply an expression of the law; it 'encodes' the law, it secludes it in a new form and guards it with a new class of interpreters. To codify the law, to reduce it to a written form, far from democratizing the law, takes it away from the people and renders it more rather than less hidden. Orally transmitted customs as sources of law at least have the benefit of being generally available within societies based upon traditions of story- and myth-telling. Writing in such cultures was always the monopoly of a restricted elite class and the reduction of oral to written law served to maintain the power and status of the literate classes within cultures where literacy was not widespread.[2] The written text of the law, far from being a clear and accessible statement of law, is rather to be understood as a coded representation of an absent source or speaker. The written text is to be read by specialized interpreters (hierophants/priests) who can, through skill, knowledge and inspiration, decipher the true meaning of the law by going behind it, by penetrating the written word to discover its absolute source in the word of God. The code, the written text, has to be deciphered and it is, in the terms of one recent study, in principle hieroglyphic and in constant need of interpretation or of priestly revelation; it is power which writing encodes, and knowledge of the code gives access to power: 'the dual figure of the priest and the hieroglyph occupies an exemplary position . . . bringing together the essence of social power qua power of writing or at least an essential moment of the two powers and of what is represented in them . . . No priests without a hieroglyphic writing, no hieroglyphs without a working priesthood' (Derrida, 1979, p. 125). In short, power is necessarily encoded, it being the historical role of government to separate the language of administration, of political and legal control, from the publicly available (oral) codes and rhetorical (democratic) traditions of law-giving. Ordinary language is annulled by a learned language although the learned language has no greater secret than that of annulling – of appearing superior to and so silencing – the ordinary language: 'one doesn't carry on a dialogue with the law, one makes it speak, using a scholastic method operated by the technicians of the written discourse . . .'

The written code of law functions to conceal the source of law quite as much as it purports to reveal the substantive laws themselves. The code establishes the social power of a priestly group of interpreters of the law and if we trace very briefly the history of legal codifications as sources of law, we find that the power of the code is time and again located in the hidden and ambiguous character of its source and the correlatively priestly status of its interpreters. The two categories, those of source and interpretation, are intimately and enduringly linked, it being the hidden and sacred character of the source of law that determines the rigidity and authoritarianism of its interpretation. Moving from the Old Testament to the Rome of 451 BC, a second powerful example can be drawn from the XII Tables, a codification which has traditionally been regarded as the foundation of Roman law, as, for example, in the first sentence of Maine's famous work *Ancient Law* (1880) where we are told that 'the most celebrated system of jurisprudence known to the world begins, as it ends, with a Code.' Conventional legal wisdom regards the XII Tables as a body of legislation or codification which was forced upon the Roman ruling class (patricians) by pressure from the lower orders (plebeians) and whose value, it is said, 'did not consist in any approach to symmetrical classification, or to terseness or clearness of expression, but in their publicity, and in the knowledge which they furnished to everybody, as to what he was to do, and what not to do (Maine, 1880, pp. 14–18). Among the chief advantages which the XII Tables and similar codes conferred on the societies which obtained them, was the protection which they afforded against 'the frauds of the privileged oligarchy and also against the spontaneous depravation and debasement of the national institutions'. The code was thus traditionally seen as law which came from below in the sense that it was enacted so as to render disputed customary rules of law clearer. Its general purpose was to declare what the law was in areas where it was unknown to the people or contested by them, so as to protect both the people and the laws themselves from potential abuse. Most importantly, the XII Tables were supposed to represent the defeat of the claim of the priestly class to a monopoly over knowledge of the law, and the replacement of their exclusive possession of this information by popular access to law. The rules set out in the XII Tables do not form a code in the sense of a complete body of written law, but they do perform a significant function in that they purport to settle the law in difficult areas and so, in the conventional view, they may be seen as binding the hands of the Roman lay magistrate (*praetor*) and his various interpreters and advisers on legal matters (Stein, 1966, p. 7 ff). While the XII Tables did achieve a status comparable to that of later codes – the rules set down were seen to supersede all earlier law and on the issues which they covered they could not be directly challenged or changed – they are best viewed not simply or only in terms of an intention to democratize the law but rather as re-establishing the priestly power of the early Roman legal classes, the College of Pontiffs and later the Roman jurists, and eventually as reaffirming the exclusion of plebeian participation in creating and determining the law. The commission that drew up the XII Tables based them in large measure upon the somewhat tyrannical law of Solon dating from the Athens of the sixth-century BC, and in writing down the laws merely extended the privileges of an ecclesiastical order of Pontiffs who alone could read and write. The early Romans were indeed 'remarkably illiterate', and since it was only the priestly classes who (from approximately the middle of the seventh century BC) could read, power in the form of a clear tradition of *interpretatio* (development of the law) remained very firmly in their hands (Diamond, 1971, pp. 114–23).

As a source of law the XII Tables conform quite closely to the religious tradition already outlined, a tradition in which the written laws were compiled by patrician 'priestly' experts in the customary 'undeclared' law. The XII Tables, however, codified only a limited number of substantive and procedural rules within a legal system which for the most part remained unwritten. In either case, the immediate source of law is the priestly legal interpreter, the Pontiff and later the predominantly patrician jurists (*hones-tiores*), and it is upon these interpreters that the subjects of the law must in general have depended. The permanent written form of a limited number of disputed legal rules served the function of legitimating the legal order as a whole. It temporarily outmanoeuvred claims to participate in the law-making process and it provided a potent symbol of the authority of law in the tables (wooden tablets) upon which were inscribed what were suppo-sedly the foundational rules of Roman law. The codification in question, however, was never comprehensive and in many of the areas which it covered it rapidly became overtaken by new interpretations, fictions and innovations and by the late Republic (131 BC) it was in large measure an archaic relic of ideological rather than practical legal value (Watson, 1984).

The XII Tables were not, however, the major codification of Roman law nor were they the longest lived. The codification of Roman law which was to have by far the greatest significance and which, both in its comprehensive written form and in its substantive content, in its classification and ordering of legal rules, was to have a foundational impact upon the development of the legal discipline, was the *Corpus Iuris Civilis*, compiled by the eastern Roman Emperor Justinian (AD 527–65) and published in AD 532–5. It was in the *Corpus Iuris Civilis* that the modern conception of code was fashioned and legal studies were from then on able to develop as an independent discipline or science. While the *Corpus Iuris* will be examined in much greater detail in terms of legal method and the techniques of legal reading that developed from it in a subsequent chapter (4.1), considerable attention should also be paid to this classic codification as an exemplary source of law.

The *Corpus Iuris* lies at the basis of the continental (civil-law) legal traditions, a civilian legal tradition meaning merely a legal tradition which, to a greater or lesser extent, takes Roman law and its representation in the *Corpus Iuris* as the basis, historical and conceptual, of legal order. It is to the *Corpus Iuris* indeed that modern western civil-law systems owe their principal categories and divisions and in the prevalent view, they owe to it also their 'formal rationality', their coherence, logical ordering and characteristic techniques of law-application (Watson, 1981). This issue of reason and technique will be returned to. For the present we would rather concentrate on the compilation as a source of law which conforms to the tradition of codification already discussed, although in many respects it surpasses that tradition in the quality and quantity, range and scope, of the written law. Amongst the more important features of the *Corpus Iuris* as codification and written law we would observe the following.

First, the *Corpus Iuris* itself. Divided into four parts – the *Code*, the *Digest*, the *Institutes* and the *Novels* – and published between AD 532 and 535 by the eastern Roman Emperor Justinian, it was a massive compilation of the law of Rome. Ordered by Justinian very early during his reign (527–8), it was to classify, cohere and codify the entirety of Roman law available at that date; custom, 'authorized' learned opinions (*ius respondendi*) and imperial legislation alike were to be annotated and inserted into the new, authoritative, compilation. Once complete, this new compilation was to be treated as final and definitive of the law; it became the statutory text of the law and reference to the original sources was expressly forbidden. Justinian even went so far as to order that copies of the original texts be burned and, for comparable motives, also prohibited subsequent commentaries on the compilation for fear that they would detract from the written law itself. The codification as a whole represented, for Justinian, the perfection of the earlier law and it bears with it both explicitly and implicitly all of the features of codification as it was later to develop within the civil-law tradition.

Of primary significance, of course, is the origin of the codification itself: it is a compilation self-consciously ordered by Justinian in the role of heir to the western Roman Empire and as overlord of the civilized world (*dominus mundi*). Justinian was the law-giver and his subjects were the recipients of his universal rule. Looked at more closely, however, the emperor as the conceptual source and authorization of the law is more symbolic than actual, more political than legal. The actual content of the codification was only in minor part the direct enactment of Justinian (*Novels*). The preponderant content of the compilation dated back several centuries to a foreign culture, that of Rome, and to the complex mass of Roman law. Overall, however, it is Justinian's status and sovereign power (*imperium*) that lend the compilation of materials the status of codified law and as will be observed later, also lend the compilation its character as a complete, coherent and discrete statement of the law. As is so frequently the case to the present day, the display of obedience to the personification of the law – to its source or agent – is of greater importance than obedience to the letter of the rule.

The source of the written law is again the status, the charisma, of its nominal or imputed author; it comes from above, is comprehensive and non-contradictory, and 'it arranges well both divine and human matters and drives out every iniquity.' It is, in short, the eminent qualities ascribed to the author of the text rather than the actual content of the text or of the rules themselves that are of the greatest significance in qualifying the written rules as law. The written law is to be treated as written reason (*ratio scripta*) – any imperfection in the law is to be seen in principle as an error on the part of the reader – while the law as a whole is of complete and final authority. The codification demands obedience and application and its rationality is unquestionable, although paradoxically the substantive content of the codification is far from being the law in force even at the time of its original promulgation. The law codified is archaic and alien and was never the law practically in force in the eastern Roman Empire, an observation which leads us to a further important feature of this exemplary written law – to these precious books.

In introducing the *Digest*, the largest of the four parts of the *Corpus Iuris*, Justinian comments that 'we find the whole course of our law which descends from the foundation of the city of Rome and the times of Romulus to be so confused that it stretches to infinity and is contained by no human capacity.' The vast compilation is consequently apparently intended to simplify and clarify the complexity of the Roman legal tradition and also to reduce its great bulk to manageable proportions, that of one set of books comprehending the entirety of the law. Again, in other words, the codification is presented as rationalizing and clarifying the law; if not at the direct request or demand of the people, it is at least apparently intended to benefit them, both the students of the law and also its subjects, the law of the *Code* being conceived explicitly as a concession from the emperor to his people. Again, however, the writing down of the law is more a symbolic than a practical simplification of prior law. While the *Institutes* were certainly a major intellectual achievement in the conceptualization of the law, they were an explicitly pedagogic text aimed at students of the law; the rest of the *Corpus Iuris* was of far greater complexity and made no pretence to clarity or lay accessibility. To those observations, of course, it should then be added that by the time of its compilation the Roman law set down in the *Corpus Iuris* was already several centuries old and relevant to an Empire that had been finally lost in AD 476 and that had even earlier been abandoned by Constantine the Great who had moved the administrative capital of the Empire from Rome to the east, to Constantinople (Byzantium), in AD 330.

It was not, in other words, either temporally, geographically or culturally at home in the Byzantine Empire of Justinian and it would be simply false to regard it as clarifying the local law of the east (Ullmann, 1975, pp. 59–64).

The greatest codification in the history of western law was a symbol of power and an object of reverence. It wrote down an archaic and alien law for political and ideological reasons, and that it subsequently became the object of an almost mystical awe had more to do with the political needs of the later western governments than it had to do with the substantive legal content of the codification as a whole. For the present, however, it is sufficient to note that the *Corpus Iuris* was compiled by teams of legal experts appointed by Justinian and led by Tribonian and, as its extraordinary later history amply evidenced, it was studied, learned, commented upon and utilized by experts in the 'divine and human' purposes of the law. It became the primary source of legal learning within the civil-law tradition and from the eleventh century onwards the books of the *Corpus Iuris* were the fount of all legal knowledge and the techniques and methods of the legal discipline were formed and developed in the course of the endlessly renewed interpretation of those texts. The texts became authoritative throughout much of Europe and they later represented the universality of legal science, of the written reason of the law, becoming, in the words of a nineteenth-century German legal historian, Rudolph von Ihering, 'the formal common possession of the law' whereby the 'formal unity of the science [law] . . . existed through the common possession of one and the same law book for the greater part of Europe' resulting in the 'working together of the jurisprudence of very different lands on the same material and the same problems'. In short, the *Corpus Iuris* became the model of written law for the later traditions of codification and it is, we shall argue later, only through an understanding of the status and techniques of interpretation relevant to the *Corpus* that it is possible fully to comprehend the contemporary authority of the written law. In one recent account, 'the formal rationality of western civil law systems is very much the result of treating the *Corpus Iuris* as authoritative' (Watson, 1981, p. 23).

2.1.2 *Political traditions and modern codifications*

The medieval history of Justinian's codification, the intricate development of the science of law from the founding of the first law school at Bologna in 1090 to the legal humanism of the seventeenth century which led to the modern vernacular codifications, will be dealt with later in terms of reading the law. Rather than attempting here to enter the details of scholastic legal studies, it is sufficient to observe that the *Corpus Iuris* defined the continental legal traditions, 'a working definition of a civil law system [being] a system in which parts or the whole of Justinian's *Corpus Iuris Civilis* have been in the past or are at present treated as the law of the land or, at the very least, are of direct and highly persuasive force' (Watson, 1981, p. 4). For five centuries after its rediscovery, the *Corpus Iuris* was either, as in Italy, southern France and latterly Germany, the substantive law of the land, or, as in northern France, pre-Reception Germany and Scotland, it was regarded as written legal reason (*ratio scripta*), as the universal form of law and the basis of legal method, of its concepts, classifications and argumentation. Even as if such a lengthy history were not enough, when the local languages and laws of continental Europe did begin to reassert themselves and gain a certain respectability along with the beginnings of the growth of the modern nation-state in the seventeenth century, the return to local law merely heralded a renewed influence of the Roman legal classifications and of the principle in particular of written law, of codes and codification.

The precise motives for the various codifications of the eighteenth century are much disputed. For F. H. Lawson, for example, the reasons are political and ideological:

> All the original codes have been in countries which have just undergone a revolution and wish to recast their law quickly from top to bottom, or in countries which had in the past suffered from a diversity of legal systems or had found themselves in that position because they have incorporated new territories or had come into existence by a union of territories governed by different laws. One or other of these factors must be at work if the lawyers of a country are willing to undergo the immense trouble and inconvenience of transforming their law and learning it afresh. (Lawson, 1953, p. 49)

Nationalism and imperialism would in this view appear to explain the movement towards codification which occurred in the eighteenth and nineteenth centuries, while more complex reasons have been suggested by Alan Watson and others in terms of the European legal tradition in civil-law countries and, specifically, the extreme ideational importance of the Roman law as set out in Justinian's *Institutes* to the seventeenth- and eighteenth-century systematizations of local law (Cairns, 1984). To these should be added the standard arguments as to the clarification, rationalization and indeed democratization of the law represented in the act of codification, the repetition, in short, of the foundational myth of law in its written mode, a myth which is by no means exclusive to the civil-law tradition.

Whatever the ostensible or academically imputed motives for the movement towards codification, it would appear indisputable that a major element in the explanation of this legal phenomenon must be political. If we refer, as does Watson, to the tradition of the civil law and the antiquity and importance of the written law within it, we should also recall the context and character of those written monuments as sources of law. The tradition is not, in sum, one of democratization or clarification; it is rather religious in its origins and its interpreters and is best explained, as we have argued, in terms of writing and power, in terms of the Roman concept of *imperium*, of imperial power or, more generally, 'the government free to do as it pleases; the personality of the magistrate in contradiction to the legislative power of the people' (Sherwin-White, 1968). In very crude terms we may observe that the eighteenth and nineteenth centuries saw major economic and political developments which inspired legal resort to codification. The most important general development was undoubtedly the rise of the nation-state in Europe (Poggi, 1978). One of the more significant of the techniques utilized to construct and consolidate the concept of the nation-state was precisely the process of codification and the production of codes of law. The process and the end product are capable of expressing a wide range of symbolic messages appropriate to the needs of the emergent nation-states. Codification is, for instance, symbolic of a fracture with the past, the new state being represented in the new code. The code symbolizes a national territorial identity, its application is coextensive with the geopolitical domain of the new state which may be the end product of revolutionary upheaval, of conquest or of an agreed political consolidation within an existing territory. The code may symbolize the naturalness of the new political configuration in that the code may be perceived as the end of a process of development which culminates in the expression of a perfected reason in the law, which law is taken to underpin the cultural tradition that has given rise to the new political order. The code may also, by reference to the superior (rational) quality of its content, be seen as symbolic of national qualities; the genius of the code is merely a reflection of the genius of that body of persons, of that historically or ethnically or politically defined group that makes up the nation-state. Finally, the code may be viewed as a symbolic technique, intended to foster obedience. The clear and cohesive statement of the new national order's rules of behaviour will foster obedience and support for the new order through the revelation of its basis in reason, be it seen to be economic, political or social in its most fundamental strata.

The history of Europe from the eighteenth century onwards abounds with examples of the above senses of codification. Revolution and international armed conflict were often followed by periods of consolidation to which the process of codification made a significant contribution. To take the most obvious example, the French Revolution of 1789 was followed by the codification of French law in the *Code Napoléon*, which came into force in 1804. The reconstruction of Germany after the Second World War produced a new constitution providing a written statement of the principles and institutions of power upon which the new Federal Republic of Germany would be constructed (*The Basic Law*). In both cases, that of the new

Code and that of the new Constitution, the written law was apparently designed to be symbolic of a political and social break with the past. In many senses, of course, the code does represent a dramatic development and is, as was the case both with the Napoleonic Code and with the German Constitution, originally motivated by a desire to restrain the exercise of power and to control its abuse both within the administration and within the legal arm of the State. Whether or not this symbolic function is matched by the content and application of the code is a very different question. The movement towards codification was European rather than peculiar to specific national legal systems. It gained influential representatives in the common-law tradition – notably through Bentham and Austin in England and slightly later the movement towards the Restatements of the common law in the United States – and in many senses a codified written law was the object of legal developments throughout Europe. That such codification was successfully achieved in the civil-law countries has to do with the Roman-law tradition which defines them and the model of the *Corpus Iuris* to which the modern codifications complied. In terms of their categories, classifications and content generally, the codes were not legally novel (Watson, 1981, pp. 99–130). The Napoleonic Code, for example, has its doctrinal origins in François Bourjon's *Droit Commun*, first published in 1743, a work which recent research has shown prefigured and largely determined both the arrangement and the content of the *Code Civil* upon a model which eventually returns to the *Institutes* of Justinian: 'this most influential of all civil codes is in the tradition of Justinian's *Institutes* and the institutes of local law. To some extent, the attractiveness of the *Code Civil* is to be attributed to the familiarity of its arrangement ... The French legal tradition was still very much that of civil law as distinct from natural law' (Watson, 1981, p. 114).

An earlier example of the same point can be taken from the Bavarian codifications of the 1750s, ordered by Frederick the Great of Prussia in 1746. The purpose of the project (which never came into force) was to rationalize and cohere the law of the Prussian territories; it was to express the unification of the Prussian Empire and to systematize and clarify the law that governed it. In introducing the project, however, Frederick clearly intends to base the new codification upon the ancient tradition of the *Corpus Iuris*, the purpose of the new codification being that of correcting and restoring the original certainty of that Roman law. The modern expression of national sovereignty and of a renewed political will actually finds itself couched in the humanistic terms of the recovery of the 'spirit' of Roman law: 'The incertitude of law which reigned in the collections of Roman law would still have been tolerable if one had observed Justinian's prohibition against making a commentary on this body of law, because the lawyers and judges would have been bound to rely solely on the laws, to search for their true meaning and to grasp better than they have done the spirit and principle which caused them to be published.'

The 'spirit' and 'principle' underlying the classical law as compiled in the *Corpus Iuris* is both historically and conceptually very far removed from the revolutionary rhetoric, the theories of natural law and human rights, which were the ostensible political motivation for the modern codifications. It is politically rather than legally, formally rather than substantively, that codification is to be seen as a technique whereby the excesses of the past can be controlled and thereby avoided by subsequent generations. A particular type of code, that of the constitution, is paradigmatically concerned with such a task. Constitutions attempt to define a body of basic principles and establish and delimit the operation of those institutions designated with the task of their realization. The many examples of constitutional code exemplify the great diversity of political interests and institutional forms rather than any more profound legal diversity of function:

> as soon as we begin to ask what has influenced . . . preferences we stumble on an additional reason for the wide variegation in the content of constitutions. It is a very simple and obvious reason . . . It is quite simply, that the constitution-makers in different countries, or for that matter at different historical stages in the history of one country, have quite different pre-occupations . . . Different historical contexts have generated different pre-occupations: different pre-occupations have generated different emphases. (Finer, 1979, pp. 21–2)

For example, the constitutions of both the USA and the USSR (1977) formally and symbolically enshrine democracy as central to the power structure of the State. In an attempt to avoid past abuses of civil and human rights, constitutions embody statements and rules purporting to protect those rights; a Bill of Rights figures prominently, for example, in the American Constitution (by early amendment) and in the opening articles to the Constitution of the Federal Republic of Germany (1949). Another frequent consideration is the need to limit the powers of interference available to a government and to limit the powers of the various arms of the State machine through the clear definition and separation of those powers. Such considerations are not confined to constitutional codes even though they tend to be concentrated within them. For example, the *Code Napoléon*, which is a code of private law, by Article 5 specifically forbids judges from giving judgments that purport to be statements of general rules with a view to establishing precedents for future cases. Such a provision not only reflects upon the principles relating to the nature of the code as the supreme source of law, but it is also a reflection of the legitimizing principle of the separation of powers which was particularly influential upon the reconstruction of the French State after the Revolution of 1789. The principles and presuppositions of codification were seen to provide a mechanism whereby political change could be effected and consolidated successfully. Such a view of the political role of codification as the restraint of power may find its most direct and symbolically complete form of expression in constitutions but, historically, there is no overriding reason for writing down and promulgating such expressions of legal right. In Britain, for example, there is no such constitutional document and legal doctrine has to perform the tasks elsewhere undertaken by the constitution and constitutional courts.

2.1.3 *Contemporary sources of written law*

The contemporary civilian legal traditions embody and express the principles and presuppositions outlined above in terms of the tradition of written law as the primary source of law. In form, codification dominates written law. It provides the fundamental law in both the public (law relating to the powers of the State and the State/individual relationship) and the private (law relating to relationships between individuals) domains. Codification is also supplemented by written laws of a secondary status (statutes, decrees) which may be used to add detail to the basic rules contained within the codes. The style of codified law throughout Europe has generally been influenced by one of the earliest modern examples of a code of private law, the *Code Napoléon*, which attempted to use simple, general statements of principle as the basis for legal regulation. The other end of the spectrum is reflected in the Code of Frederick the Great of Prussia who attempted to provide detailed rules to meet every eventuality; for example, the code contained clauses dealing with rules for deciding upon the sexuality of hermaphrodites and provisions relating to the practice of breast-feeding. Both approaches to the drafting of codes pose their respective sets of problems for the relationship between the primacy of the code and the task of interpretation. The demand that the code should at all times be *the* source of law and that this position should not be undermined, together with the political principle of the separation of powers, influential from the eighteenth century onwards in most European states, which demands that the law-making power be located in the legislature, are the main legal and political factors that influence the dilemma arising from the task of interpretation.

In practice the judiciary are involved in interpreting words and phrases whose meaning is unclear, dealing with lacunae within a text which purports to be a complete exposition of the law and applying the code to situations which could not have been foreseen by the legislature. Civilian systems have experimented with various mechanisms to resolve the problem of law-making through interpretation. As the legislature is the ultimate source of law, ideally it should resolve the problems of interpretation returning the definition to the judiciary for application. Such a mechanism was used after the French Revolution but was found to be impossible to operate in practice. A second technique is to provide a provision within the code which prescribes how the judges are to deal with the task of interpretation. For example in the Italian Civil Code (1942) the code provides that:

> In interpreting the statute, no other meaning can be attributed to it than that made clear by the actual significance of the words according to the connections between them, and by the intention of the legislature.
> If a controversy cannot be decided by a precise provision, consideration is given to provisions that regulate similar cases or analogous matters; if the case still remains in doubt it is to be decided according to general principles of the legal order of the State.

In practice neither the objective that the code be *the* source of law nor the complete separation of law-making from law-application is realized. In the French legal system, for example, judicial interpretations have, even in legal doctrine, over time become accepted as a source of law known as jurisprudence. This jurisprudence has been responsible for developing areas of law, as for example with Article 1384 of the *Code Napoléon* which states, in paragraph 1, that: 'A person is responsible not only for the damage caused by his own actions, but also for that which is caused by the actions of persons for whom he must answer *or that caused by things under his care.*' The jurisprudence of the French courts developed the words emphasized to fill a gap in the law (concerning the relevant standard of care owed) which had not been met by the legislature, and succeeded in providing for liability without fault for damage caused by things under one's care. The use of general statements of law creates the need for the judiciary to define the detailed application of the principles. The use of specific rules may raise the need for a creative style of interpretation to meet the demands of novel factual situations.

To meet the needs generated by the legal, political and practical contexts of law-application, the judiciary within civilian legal systems have developed a range of approaches to the task of interpretation. As most judges wish to be seen to be supporters of the prevailing legal and political ideology, preference is given to approaches to interpretation that follow the letter of the law, adopting and applying a grammatical construction of the text and a literal sense to the meaning of the words used. When the dispute before the courts cannot satisfactorily be resolved in this literal manner the courts depart from the technique. Numerous alternative styles have been developed and practised in the various civilian legal systems. An example from France is contained in a speech made on the occasion of the centenary celebrations of the French *Code Civil* by Ballot-Beaupré (1836–1917), president of the French Supreme Court (*Cour de Cassation*). He delivered a speech which confirmed his support for the literal approach to interpretation where the text is unambiguous, clear and precise in its application. However, when ambiguity or doubts arise, then the judge should have the widest powers of interpretation. The judge should not be confined by the historical context of the document to be interpreted. The judge must operate as if the clause were being drafted today. Having regard to contemporary ideas, social manners, institutions, economic and social conditions he must say 'justice and reason require that the text be liberally interpreted and humanely adapted to the realities and requirements of modern life' (David and Brierley, 1978, p. 110). Another technique found operating in the German courts involves the use of general clauses to neutralize or adapt specific provisions. For example the German Supreme Court (Reichsgerict) has used clause 826 ('Whoever intentionally causes injury to another in a manner violating good morals is bound to repair the injury') to alter the apparent meaning of other clauses. Clause 823, for example, was interpreted by reference to clause 826 to facilitate the award of damages as compensation which appeared to be excluded by the wording of clause 823, a more specific provision.

The status of jurisprudence as law is informally recognized in that reference to previous decisions containing interpretations of the law is made during the course of legal argument, and may be found in notes and commentaries made about the code. The politically and doctrinally important claim that the judiciary is not making law is maintained to varying degrees within the various civilian legal systems. For example, in the *Cour de Cassation* the French Supreme Court, judgments handed down do not contain references to interpretations provided in the court's previous decisions but refer only to clauses within the code, thereby supporting the fiction that the code is complete, providing all that is necessary to resolve the issues before the court. Similarly, the reports of the decisions of the Italian courts omit references to sources other than the code, it being the view of Italian jurists that 'the work of the legal [scientists] is like the work of other scientists, not concerned so much with the resolution of practical problems as with the search for scientific truth, for ultimates and fundamentals; not concerned so much with individual cases as with generic problems, the perfection of learning and understanding, not, in a word, with engineering, but with pure science' (M. Cappelletti *et al.*, 1967). The practices referred to are fictional in the very concrete sense that annual series of annotated case reports are published listing the decisions relevant to each section of the code and these are used both academically and in legal argument.

Whilst it is possible to observe from the behaviour of the courts that the codified law is not the sole source of law, codified law still plays a central role within the civilian legal culture as the ultimate source of legitimacy to which all other activities must relate. It is in this sense that it retains its primacy within the legal system. The secondary sources and techniques of law-interpretation more generally must all relate back to the codified law and claim their origin in it.

2.2 THE COMMON-LAW TRADITION

To understand the status of written law within the English legal system it is necessary to consider two preliminary matters: the relationship beween written law and unwritten law and secondly, the institutional history of the legal system.

2.2.1 *Written law and unwritten law*

In historical terms the primary source of law within the English legal system is unwritten law. Whilst in this respect it does not differ significantly from the early history of vernacular local legal systems in the rest of Europe, it does differ from those legal systems in that the unwritten law has retained its position as a significant source of law. Unwritten law (common law) is defined as custom derived from time immemorial. Written law is seen as a subsequent development. It has since medieval times been seen as a technique used to strengthen, interpret, regulate or amend the common law. This image of the relationship between written and unwritten law has persisted even through the economic transformations of the eighteenth and nineteenth centuries, and Blackstone in the mid-eighteenth century refers to legislation as fulfilling a variety of roles, 'either declaratory of the common law, or remedial of some defects therein' (Blackstone, *Commentaries*, 1825, vol. 1, p. 86). Remnants of this position can still be seen in operation contemporarily in that many of the presumptions brought to bear upon the interpretation of legislation have their basis in presuppositions as to the historical relationship between the common law and legislation. For example, there is the presumption against the alteration of the law, that Parliament knows the law and only consciously changes the law. More substantively, we would cite the presumption that, following the common-law principles of culpability, liability may not be imposed without fault. The presumptions, too numerous to be here detailed, collectively suggest that there already exists a seamless web of law, the common law, which may be changed but only as a result of a conscious act which will be interpreted accordingly as an interference with pre-existing law and principle and will be interpreted restrictively in its effects. A recent example of such controversy has centred on the relationship between legislation and unwritten law and is to be found specifically in a dispute based upon the interrelationship between the jurisdiction of local authorities to take children into care under the terms of a series of Acts culminating in the Child Care Act 1980, and the common-law or residual-wardship jurisdiction of the courts which is based upon their inherent power to care for the welfare of children. The existence of legislation has not been interpreted to deprive the courts of all their power and when questions of the welfare of children are concerned the basic common-law principles to a large degree retain their validity and effect, save where explicitly excluded. In *A* v *Liverpool City Council* [1982] AC 363, for example, a mother challenged a local-authority decision concerning the 'rehabilitation' of her child, in care under s. 1 (2) (*a*) and (3) of the Children and Young Persons Act 1969. Lord Wilberforce in the House of Lords observed first that the courts of equity have and retain an 'ancient jurisdiction' over minors. A number of Acts of Parliament had since come to place children in the care of local authorities, 'subject to the enacted limitations and safeguards, decisions for the child's welfare [being] removed from the parents and from the supervision of the courts' (371, 373). Immediately subsequent to that passage Lord Wilberforce remarks that 'this is not to say that the inherent jurisdiction of the High Court is taken away. The Court's general inherent power is always available to fill gaps or to supplement the powers of the local authority . . .' (373). For Lord Roskill, the ancient jurisdiction of the court to care for minors was guided by the paramount interest in the welfare of the child, a principle which survived the statutory jurisdictions 'the wardship jurisdiction of the court [can] properly be invoked in addition to the statutory jurisdiction of the local authority because it was only in this way that the result which [is] best in the paramount interest of the child [can] be achieved . . .' (378). This power to supplement the statutory rules and make them coherent, was examined again and applied in *Re J (a minor) (wardship jurisdiction)* [1984] 1 AER 29, Cumming-Bruce LJ taking the view that there was a lacuna in the relevant statutory scheme (s. 21 (2) of the 1969 Act) and in such circumstances the court would exercise its residual power to take jurisdiction and protect the child.

In effect, legislation is frequently ascribed a secondary role not only because it is seen to post-date the common law but also because it is not infrequently seen by the judiciary as a substantively inferior source of law. The common law is historically often represented as a statement of human reason that has been refined and perfected to such a degree that it is superior to other forms of law in its content, a view classically expressed by

Lord Coke in *Dr Bonham's \Case* (1610) 8 Co Rep 106. Blackstone, to take a later example, considered the common law to be the concentrated wisdom of the various peoples who had invaded and settled in Britain. They had brought with them their own legal system, imposing certain features upon the native system and refining parts of it. The resulting common law represented a body of law of superior quality. Legislation was therefore to be treated as a technique for the improvement of this body of law and confined to the extent that it improved the wisdom of ages rather than abrogating or ignoring that time-hallowed legal wisdom.

2.2.2 *Institutional history*

The second fundamental and historically distinctive influence within the common-law tradition is the development of the central institutions of the State. The history of the English State machine is important in so far as it represents one of the oldest and most stable institutional orders in the western world. Its embryonic base is found to be in operation at least as early as the Norman Conquest of 1066. The administrative skill of the later Norman and Angevin monarchs created an administrative and adjudicative structure which effectively pervaded all parts of the kingdom and was controlled by a small elite of centrally based royal administrators. The court system itself was composed of central courts located at Westminster together with travelling judges who regularly visited the rest of the kingdom which was for legal purposes divided into assize circuits. This system was fully operational by the end of the thirteenth century and remained largely intact until the middle of the nineteenth century. It provided an effective bureaucratic structure which was capable of producing a coherent body of law based upon the custom of the realm – common law. Secondly, it provided a system whereby that law could be brought to effect upon the kingdom as a whole. The small number of royal judges who presided over both the central courts and the assize courts could effectively control the development of the substantive law, generally claiming to foster the doctrinal values of consistency and coherence which contributed significantly to the status of common law. Common law was seen to represent a rational ordering of the rules governing human behaviour and it was the claim of the developing class of lawyers to provide a seamless web of regulation. All of these factors contributed to the ability of the common law to withstand the threat of codification and to provide an effective resistance to the incursion of piecemeal legislation.

A second important feature of the institutional history is the development of the dichotomy between the legislative and the judicial functions of the sovereign power. The separation of these two functions is a relatively modern and sophisticated development. Originally the king was the ultimate source of law, be it divine law, the custom of the realm or the creation of new law. The scale of the operation in practice demanded the delegation of tasks. In addition, changes in the structure of political power led to the transfer of power to a variety of administrative institutions. The capacity of the sovereign to declare what the law was represented the embryonic development of legislation. When the monarch was the sole source of knowledge as to both common law and new law (legislation), the likelihood of conflict between the two was minimal. Nor did the early delegation of the adjudicative function and the development of the role of the judiciary as the source of knowledge about the content of common law lead to problems, in so far as the judiciary were often intimately involved in the drafting of the new law and retained a close connection with the monarch which facilitated the relationship between legislation and the common law. A final factor in the early relationship was the infrequency of the use of legislation.

With the separation of the judicial and legislative roles of the sovereign the problem of the relative status of the two sources arises. From the time of the Tudor monarchs legislation begins to develop as a major source of new law. For example, in the reign of Henry VIII over 600 statutes were enacted, a number which probably exceeds the total number of statutes passed from the time of the Magna Carta of 1215. The importance of legislation and its incursion upon the field of interest of the common law and the activities of the judiciary at this time is also reflected in case law. For example, in *Dr Bonham's Case* (1610), Lord Coke provides one of the earliest reflections upon the nature of the distinction between the common law and legislation and it is also from this period that one of the earliest rules of statutory interpretation was formulated, the rule in *Heydon's Case* (1584), suggesting the growing importance of statutory law. The importance of legislation and the development of the power of the House of Commons continues throughout the Restoration until the crisis which culminated with the 'Glorious Revolution' of 1688 and led to the enactment of the Bill of Rights which provides a formal statement of the new balance of power within the State, establishing the supremacy of the two Houses of Parliament over the monarch.

The importance of Parliament and the primary status of its legislative statements was consolidated in the political and jurisprudential traditions arising from the seventeenth century through to the nineteenth century in the work of Hobbes, Bentham, Austin and Dicey, works which may generally be characterized as emphasizing the written law of the sovereign institution, Parliament, as the supreme source of law. The impact of the concept of the 'supremacy' of Parliament is to be found increasingly acknowledged in the contemporary decisions of the common-law courts, as

for example, in *Edinburgh and Dalkeith Railway* v *Wauchope* [1842] 8 Cl &
F 710, and in *Lee* v *Bude and Torrington Railway* [1871] LR CP 577, 582,
where it was acknowledged that although natural equity represented the
'law of laws' or the 'immutable law of nature', the substantive principles of
such law stand 'as a warning, rather than [as] authority to be followed. We
sit here as servants of the Queen and the legislature. Are we to act as
regents over what is done by Parliament with the consent of the Queen,
Lords and Commons? I deny that any such authority exists ... The
proceedings here are judicial not autocratic'; and the judiciary are correspondingly the servants and not the judges of the content of legislation. The
effect of this ideological tradition is that in the last instance legislation must
supersede all previous law, be it previous enactments or the established
common law.

The final institutional factor influencing the relationship between common law and legislation was the ability of both the legal and the political
institutions and forms of government to adapt to meet the needs generated
by the Civil War and the political revolutions which resulted from the
overthrow of the monarchy and the temporary instituion of the Cromwellian
Commonwealth, rapidly followed by the Restoration and the 'Glorious
Revolution' of 1688. Whilst the eruption of political change had not fractured
the institutional facade of the State, power had largely been appropriated
from the monarchy and aristocracy by the ascendant bourgeois classes and
by the middle of the eighteenth century the dominance of the middle classes
was indisputable. Paradoxically, the legislative and the judicial institutions
remained largely unchanged as a result of these shifts in the balance of
power. The judiciary illustrated their ability to transfer allegiance and
utilized their law-creating powers to adapt the common law to serve either
feudal or capitalist entrepreneurial interests. The absence of violent revolutions and the adaptability of the law, its capacity to satisfy the demands of
the newly powerful classes, reduced the need to symbolize the transfer of
power and the establishment of the new regime through the use of codification. In fact, the common law itself fulfilled many of the symbolic functions
undertaken by codification on the Continent. It already expressed the
geopolitical domain of the nation – the common law was already regarded as
national law and the common-law jurisdiction was expressly defined in
opposition to alien law and its languages, those of the civil-law tradition and
the competing jurisdictions of canon law and admiralty (Cairns, 1984). That
great value was attached to the common law as a symbol of nationalism is
nowhere better illustrated than in its use in the administration of the British
Empire during the centuries of imperialism: whatever the local practices or
law of the specific regions of the Empire, they were rapidly subordinated to

the principles and procedures of the common law, the law of the conquering nation. The British administrators brought with them their language and their national law and superimposed it on the culture of the colonized territories with surprisingly enduring effect. The linguistic and legal transplants dating from the eighteenth century onwards left a lasting mark on the cultures affected and it is only relatively recently that the indigenous cultures of former colonies (where they survived) have explicitly begun to challenge the hegemony of the common law.

The argument in favour of codification had at various times been voiced within the common-law system: by Francis Bacon, when Attorney-General, who had recommended 'the reducing of concurrent statutes, heaped one upon another, to one clear and uniform law'; or even earlier, by Reginald Pole (1500–58), who had argued in favour of codification on the grounds of the confusion, lack of order, uncertainty and instability of the common law. For Pole, as later for Bentham, it was the latitude available to the interpreters of the law that weighed most heavily against the system of unwritten law and he consequently proposed 'the same remedy that Justinian [brought to bear] in the law of the Romans', namely that of replacing the infinity of unwritten law by the institution of 'a few and better laws and ordinances'. The argument in favour of codification and against the common law gained its most dramatic and extensive exposition in the nineteenth century, its proponents including Jeremy Bentham and John Austin, both prominent representatives of a secular, positivistic theory of law.

The economic revolution of capitalism and the rapid industrialization of the second half of the nineteenth century brought major pressures to bear upon the legal system which had the effect of again raising the issue of codification. Economic development saw an expansion of the role of the State, which came to intervene increasingly in both public and private life. The rapid growth of statute law grafted on to the established and developing body of common law and equitable principles generated confusion and problems of knowledge of and access to the law. One response to the confusion generated was the demand for the codification of the law. Jeremy Bentham, a prolific philosopher and liberal reformer of the late eighteenth and early nineteenth centuries, played a leading role in initiating this debate on codification and can also be taken to represent one of the most extreme positions in that debate, advocating the complete codification of the law. Common lawyers first experimented with codification in subservient jurisdictions within the Empire. For example, in India large portions of the common law were reduced to codified form for use in India between 1830 and 1860. Attempts at home were not so grandiose. Consolidation, the reduction of several statutory provisions to one statute, was increasingly utilized, as for example in the Criminal Law Consolidation Act 1861. A Royal Commission established in 1866 suggested that digests be written of various branches of law as a preparation for codification. Two examples of digests produced as a result, the *Digest of the Law of Partnership* (1877) and the *Digest of the Law of Bills of Exchange* (1878) were subsequently enacted in 1890 and 1892 respectively. Their objective was to state in a clear way the main principles existing within the law. The process was seen primarily as a conservative operation, the justification being that a mere restatement of the law would not be controversial. Once the existing principles were clearly stated, controversy about the reform of the law would be less likely.

More recently, 1965 saw the institutionalization of an attempt to introduce codification to the English legal system with the establishment of a Law Commission empowered to examine the law of England and Wales (a second was established in the same legislation to deal with the law of Scotland). The Commission's powers are wide-ranging, with a duty to keep the whole of the law under review with a view to its systematic development and reform. One method singled out in the legislation to realize these objectives is codification of the law. In the annual report of the English Commission, the commissioners have expressed their support for wide-ranging codification including the law relating to landlord and tenant, the law of contract and family law. The scale of the task has led to the development of particular strategies for the realization of codification and a tempering of their original enthusiasm. The process of codification is initiated by the production of working papers which endeavour to state and analyse both the common law and the legislation upon a particular topic or area of substantive law, for example common-law public-order offences, the law relating to divorce, financial provision on the breakdown of marriage. The working papers are intended to initiate a process of debate amongst interested parties which it is hoped will help to contribute to the task of the Commission. As in the tradition of the Justinian compilation, the objective is to remove obsolete provisions, reorder and rearrange material and resolve conflicts within the law. The end result is not intended to be a complete codification of an entire substantive body of law, but rather the proposal is intended at this stage to be the first step in what has been described as 'creeping codification'. As more law is reduced to statutory form, the second stage of codification will be invoked, namely that of consolidation. Here several statutory provisions will be brought together into a single body of statute law. At this stage there will be no substantive change, merely a reordering of the existing provisions into a single coherent order. Examples of this second stage already exist. For example, the Matrimonial Causes Act 1972 is a consolidation of three earlier statutory provisions which embody the work of the English Commission: the Divorce Reform Act 1969, the

Matrimonial Property and Proceedings Act 1970 and the Nullity of Marriage Act 1971. This Act does not represent the end product of codification but merely a second stage in the process of creeping codification.

As codification has not yet been completed in any area of the Law Commission's work, it is difficult to evaluate its overall style and success. The enactments to date suggest that in style the common-law codifications are not going to follow in the continental tradition of the *Code Napoléon* for the simple reason that the drafting style follows the traditional common-law approach of providing detailed regulation as opposed to statements of general principle. A second and more fundamental feature to these compilations and reforms relates to the status of the codified law and its relationship with the old law and in particular the common law. The current state of affairs is one of transition.

In interpreting the enactments produced by the work of the Law Commission the courts have shown their willingness to continue to resort to the common law and to previous enactments as a means of interpreting certain provisions in the new codifications. Section 2 (1) (*b*) of the Divorce Reform Act 1969, for example, in defining irretrievable breakdown of a marriage as a ground for divorce, refers to the behaviour of the respondent being such that 'the petitioner cannot reasonably be expected to live with the respondent.' In *Katz* v *Katz* [1972] 3 AER 219, the question before the court was whether the behaviour of the respondent, who was mentally ill, would fall within the terms of behaviour covered by s. 2 (1) (*b*). For Sir George Baker P 'the true test to apply now that we are no longer dealing with cruelty but with behaviour is that propounded by Lord Reid in *Williams* v *Williams* [1963] 2 AER 994, with the appropriate amendment to fit it to the new law.' The test, in short, is to be derived not from the Act but from the pre-existing law, the character and gravity of the behaviour having to be such that the petitioner could not reasonably be expected to live with him, a test which precluded the need to establish any intention on the part of a mentally ill respondent. Elsewhere, in *Pheasant* v *Pheasant* [1972] 1 AER 587, a slightly different issue arose with respect to the same section, 2 (1) (*b*). The respondent had starved the petitioner of affection 'which his nature demanded and for which he craved'. For Ormrod J. the test to be applied under sub-paragraph (*b*) 'is closely similar to, but not necessarily identical with, that which was formerly used in relation to constructive desertion. I would not wish to see carried over into the new law all the technicalities which accumulated round the idea of constructive desertion . . . It would be consistent with the spirit of the new legislation if this problem were now to be approached more from the point of view of obligation than in terms of the now outmoded idea of the matrimonial offence' (591). In short, the legislation has to be fitted into the pre-existing

law, both written and unwritten, and the concepts, methods and classifications of interpretation are to be derived by and large from prior law and the
general methodology of the legal discipline, a factor tacitly recognized by
the consistent use of vague terms in legislative drafting: where the legislation is ambiguous, vague or in some fashion incoherent, then it is for the
courts to re-establish the unity of jurisprudence and their reference will be
the traditional methods and meanings of the common law (Atiyah, 1985).
Many other examples can be provided which suggest that at least in the
transitional period it will not be possible to effect a break between the
restatement of the law in the new statute and the preceding law. It is only
possible to speculate as to the future willingness or ability of the courts to
realize this goal of treating the law as a single and complete body of codified
law. The Law Commission has given some time to this problem in its
consideration of the role of the judge in interpretation (Law Commission
Report No. 21) but little progress has been made in this respect. It is likely
that this issue will create major problems in the path of any successful
realization of complete codification of the English legal system.

   This introduction to written law as a source of law within the common-law
tradition outlines, we hope, certain of the issues that are specific to that
tradition, or at least are less apparent within legal cultures dominated by a
tradition of written law. The common-law tradition is one of unwritten law
on to which a body of written law has been superimposed. The interrelation
of these two bodies of law has had a significant impact upon the contemporary legal culture, and especially upon the methods and techniques used to
discover and interpret the law. It is to these methods and techniques as they
affect the contemporary common-law tradition that we shall now turn.

2.3   WRITTEN LAW AND CONTEMPORARY COMMON LAW

In this section our concern will be with the following issues: the realization
of the supremacy of the statute within the tradition of unwritten law, and the
interrelationship, within the written law, of the various different categories
of written law, namely primary and secondary legislation. The style of
legislation within the common-law tradition and finally the formal rules
governing methods of interpretation will be outlined and analysed.

   Domestic legislation may be reduced to two main categories: primary and
secondary legislation. Primary legislation is the supreme source of law,
being the expression of the will of the supreme legislative institution known
as the 'Queen in Parliament' (Dicey, 1959). This institution is a combination of the monarch, House of Lords and the House of Commons acting in
agreement. Under the traditional characterization of supremacy, Parliament

can make or unmake any law. This has several effects. First, it renders legislation superior in the last instance to the common law. Legislation can be introduced to amend or abolish common-law rules, as in *Attorney General* v *De Keyser's Royal Hotel* [1920] AC 508, where an action was brought by the petitioners, De Keyser's Hotel, for compensation in use and possession after the Crown had taken compulsory possession of their hotel under Defence of the Realm Regulations then in force. The House of Lords took the view that the Crown could successfully be made to pay compensation: the statutory power under which the possession was authorized gave very wide powers to the Crown but required payment of compensation. The existence of alternative common-law prerogative powers allowing the Crown compulsorily to possess the land of a subject could not invalidate, circumscribe or avert the statutory provision. A more recent example can be taken from *A* v *Liverpool City Council* [1982] AC 363, a case concerning the competing wardship jurisdictions of the High Court and local authorities. To Lord Roskill it was clear that:

> while the prerogative jurisdiction of the court in wardship cases remains, the exercise of that jurisdiction has been and must continue to be treated as circumscribed by the existence of the far reaching statutory code which entrusts the care and control of deprived children to local authorities. It follows that the undoubted wardship jurisdiction must not be exercised so as to interfere with the day-to-day administration by local authorities of that statutory control.

Second, it is the most recent expression of Parliament upon a matter governed by legislation that is the law on that issue; earlier enactments are either expressly or impliedly repealed by later enactments, as for example was stated in *Ellen Street Estates* v *Minister of Health* [1934] 1 KB 590 at 595, 597, where Lord Maugham observes, 'the legislature cannot, according to our constitution, bind itself as to the form of subsequent legislation, and it is impossible for Parliament to enact that in a subsequent statute dealing with the same subject-matter there can be no implied repeal. If in a subsequent Act Parliament chooses to make it plain that the earlier statute is being to some extent repealed, effect must be given to that intention just because it is the will of the Legislature.' Thirdly, the statute is superior to legislation produced by subordinate legislative authorities (secondary legislation). An area of some controversy which has recently arisen in this field concerns the relationship between the legislation of the UK and that of the European Economic Community (EEC). The dispute centres upon the question of which sovereign body is the ultimate or supreme law-maker in the event of an overlap of jurisdiction. In practice it would now seem settled that the UK legislative institutions are willing to accept an inferior role in the final instance, as for example with regard to the recent amendments to the Equal Pay Act 1970, the Equal Pay (Amendment) Regulations 1983, which were introduced as the result of the inability of UK law to satisfy obligations imposed under EEC primary and secondary legislation. In legal theory however, it is possible and is still argued both that the UK Parliament must take an inferior or subservient role to the EEC and/or that it is still, in the last instance, the supreme legislature. Until the legislature openly provokes dissent it is likely that the legislative, executive and judicial branches of the State will foster concord and thereby reduce the likelihood of conflict.

Whilst the legal rule central to the resolution of a dispute may be in written form, the rule may be dispersed amongst both primary and secondary sources of written law. It may require consideration of the relationship between the written law and the unwritten law which it purports to supersede or to which it relates. Finally, it may require consideration in the context of its relationship with written sources of Community law. To take an example of the first issue, in *R* v *Secretary of State for the Home Department, ex parte Benwell* [1984] 3 AER 481, the court was concerned with the law relating to the employment and dismissal of prison officers. To ascertain the law relating to this problem the court referred to three sets of provisions: the Prison Act 1952 s. 47 (1) (primary legislation) giving power to the minister to produce rules (secondary legislation) which would include provisions dealing with the terms of employment of prison officers, the Prison Rules 1964 r. 84. Finally, under these powers the Secretary of State produced a code of discipline which prescribed acceptable patterns of work practice and listed disciplinary offences. The applicant, who admitted an offence under the code, was held to have been duly dismissed.

The problem of rules spread through primary and secondary legislation may develop a further dimension when questions are raised about the legality of the secondary rules; secondary rules may be made beyond the scope of the powers delegated to the secondary law-maker, they may be ultra vires. For example *R* v *Secretary of State for the Home Department, ex parte Anderson* [1984] 1 AER 920, considered the law relating to prisoners' access to legal advice. The relevant legal provisions were made under powers contained within the Prison Act 1952 s. 47 (1), pursuant to which the Secretary of State made the Prison Rules 1964. A dispute arose as to the legality of r. 33 (1) allowing the Secretary of State to impose restrictions either generally or in a particular case upon the communications to be permitted between a prisoner and other persons 'with a view to securing discipline and good order or the prevention of crime'. Pursuant to r. 33 the Secretary of State made standing orders for prisons under which order, 5 A (34), a prisoner could not be visited by a legal adviser where the purpose of the visit was to discuss complaints about prison treatment. At this point a further level of complexity was added in that the court now resorted to common-law principles to determine the scope of the powers delegated by Parliament and in particular invoked the right of inmates of prisons, like other citizens, to have access to the courts. It was decided on this basis that order 5 A (34) was an impediment to the right of access to a solicitor and consequently, on the strength of the common-law right of access, order 5 A (34) was to be deemed ultra vires the powers contained in s. 47 (1) of the 1952 empowering Act.

Finally, *R* v *Secretary of State for the Home Department, ex parte Dannenberg* [1984] 2 AER 481, provides an illustration of a dispute where the domestic legislation had to be considered in the context of EEC law. The dispute related to the deportation of a person after conviction for a criminal offence. As Dannenberg was a national of a Member State, the powers of deportation contained within s. 6 of the Immigration Act 1971 had to be read in conjunction with Articles 6 and 9 (1) of the EEC directive 64/221 dealing with the powers of deportation and the notification of the reasons for deportation: 'the difficulty is to reconcile the procedure for the co-ordination of special measures concerning the movement of foreign nationals on grounds of public policy provided by EEC Council Directive 64/221, which, by reason of s. 2 of the European Communities Act 1972, is part of the law of this country with the procedure for the deportation of aliens under the Immigration Act 1971.' The conclusion arrived at by the court was that compliance with Article 9 and with the general purpose of the directive necessitated the quashing of the deportation order under the 1971 Act for failure to comply with the EEC directive.

The superiority of the legislature logically implies the 'inferior' constitutional position of the judiciary, who fulfil the role of the readers and the interpreters of the legislation. This should not, however, lead to the conclusion that the judiciary may only resort to sources of law emanating directly from the legislature, but it does mean that in the last instance Parliament determines the source and substance of the law. The most frequently cited example occurs in *Burmah Oil Co. Ltd* v *Lord Advocate* [1965] AC 75, where the House of Lords decided that under the common law compensation was payable by the government to Burmah Oil Co. Ltd for damage to one of their planes incurred as a result of armed conflict. The government of the day disapproved of their Lordships' conclusion and passed retrospective legislation effectively nullifying the effects of the judgments (War Damage Act 1965). To take a somewhat more complicated example, in *Madzimbamuto* v *Lardner-Burke* [1969] 1 AC 645, the court refused to recognize the new political regime of Ian Smith even though the domestic courts of Southern Rhodesia (Zimbabwe) had accepted the new regime as the legitimate law-maker and thereby a legitimate source of law within that territory.

The courts could not accept a change in the status quo until this was accepted by Parliament, subject only to a test of efficacy expressed in the view that 'it is an historical fact that in many countries . . . there are new regimes which are universally recognised as lawful but which derive their origins from revolutions or *coups d'état*. The law must take account of that fact' (724).

2.4 LEGISLATIVE STYLES

Drafting styles are said to fall into two broad categories: the common-law style and the civilian style. To appreciate the common-law approach it is important to recall what has already been said about the relationship between the common law and legislation, particularly that legislation is seen as a restatement or correction of common law and, more generally, that legislation is always seen in the context of an established body of law. The common-law style of legislative drafting suggests a preoccupation with the need to state clearly this interrelationship and thereby avoid attempts to overconfine or overextend the legislation within the established domain of the common law. The common-law drafting techniques emphasize detail and precision and tend to result in complexity. The legislative drafter attempts to predict and to provide for every eventuality: 'the draftsman is instructed to deal with every small point, block every loophole, tie up every loose end. The result is legislation of great complexity and length' (North, 1985, p. 123). To take a recent example, in the Police and Criminal Evidence Act 1984, stronger police powers were created to deal with 'serious arrestable offences'. This phrase is defined in s. 116 which includes eight subsections and incorporates a schedule (schedule 5) which specifies sixteen named offences. To take a further topical example, s. 1 of the Equal Pay Act 1970, as amended, contains a lengthy and complex expression of the general ideal of equal pay. By way of contrast, the EEC Treaty Article 119, containing the main provision on equal pay, succeeds in realizing the task in a few lines:

> Art. 119   Each Member State shall during the first stage ensure and subsequently maintain the application of the principle that men and women should receive equal pay for equal work.
>
> For the purpose of this article, 'pay' means the ordinary basic or minimum wage or salary and any other consideration, whether in cash or in kind, which the worker receives, directly or indirectly, in respect of his employment from his employer.
>
> Equal pay without discrimination based on sex means:
> (a) that pay for the same work at piece rates shall be calculated on the basis of the same unit of measurement;
> (b) that pay for work at time rates shall be the same for the same job.

The doctrinal position is well summarized in one recent comparative study: 'the continental lawmakers, influenced by their heritage of codes, think out their laws in terms of principle, or at least of broad intention, and express the principle or intention in the legislation. This is the primary duty of the legislator – to make his general will clear' (Dale, 1977).

In many respects the treaties of the communities follow the civilian approach which has its immediate origins in the style reformulated by Napoleon in the drafting of the *Code Civil*. This model emphasizes simplicity and the statement of the law by reference to general principle using a fairly high degree of abstraction. The general tendency, as noted, is to avoid complexity in the drafting of the law, and correspondingly to interpret the legislative provisions in the broad context of their economic and social purposes. Thus in *Defrenne* v *Sabena* (case 43/74 [1976] 1 CR 547, 565, ECJ) the European Court of Justice remarked on the construction of Article 119 in terms of two broad aims, economic and social, to the equal-pay legislation as a whole:

> First, in the light of the different stages of the development of social legislation in the various member states, the aim of article 119 is to avoid a situation in which undertakings established in states which have actually implemented the principle of equal pay suffer a competitive disadvantage in intra-Community competition . . . Secondly, this provision forms part of the social objectives of the Community, which is not merely an economic union, but is at the same time intended, by common action, to ensure social progress and seek the constant improvement of the living and working conditions of their peoples, as emphasised in the Preamble to the Treaty.

It was on the strength of these very broad social and economic purposes of the Article that, to take but one example, the European Court rejected an interpretation of that legislation which insisted upon a strictly literal interpretation of the contemporaneity requirement whereby, under the domestic legislation (Equal Pay Act 1970) equal pay for equal work is to be assessed on like work done at the *same time* and nothing else (*Macarthys* v *Smith* [1980] 3 WLR 929).

Legislation in the English legal system is presented in a particular format. Primary legislation follows the pattern illustrated by the Police and Criminal Evidence Act 1984. The format may on occasion have significance as it may contribute to the means available to assist in the interpretation of the law. The 'body of the Act' is the primary source of the expression of Parliament. This part of the document is split into sections and subsections and ordered under subject headings to facilitate use. Marginal notes are also designed to facilitate the easy use of the statute. The sections of the Act may fulfil a variety of purposes. They may deal with the substance of a right or duty (substantive), as for example in s. 1 of the Police and Criminal Evidence Act 1984; they may define procedures, as for example in s. 40 of the same Act, or they may provide definitions, as for example in s. 116. Schedules frequently follow the 'body' of the Act. Strictly speaking, they are not classed as part of the legislation though reference to them in the 'body of the Act' can incorporate them into the Act (*Buchanan* v *Babco Ltd* [1977] QB 208). Schedules fulfil a range of functions. They may be used to set out detailed provisions which are excluded from the main section of the Act in an attempt to avoid an excess of detail likely to generate confusion. For example, in the Bail Act 1976 the considerations to be taken into account when a court is considering the exercise of its power to refuse bail are contained in the schedule (No. 2) of the Act. Schedules are often used to detail the amendments to other statutes affected by the new statute and to document the statutory provisions repealed as a result of the new law. Finally, schedules are used to provide examples of standard forms referred to in the body of the Act, as, for instance, with schedule 8 to the Unfair Contract Terms Act 1977 which bravely attempts to define reasonableness for the purposes of the Act.

The formal layout described for primary legislation provides the pattern adopted by most categories of secondary legislation.

2.5   FORMAL METHODS OF INTERPRETATION

On numerous occasions judges, during the course of giving judgment in a dispute, have taken the opportunity to make statements as to how they approach the task of interpretation, not only to justify their own conclusions as to the meaning of statutory provisions under consideration, but also to provide models of behaviour for others to follow. The content and the taxonomy of the techniques is a reflection of many of the matters relating to the relationship between the legislature and the judiciary and the distinction between the written law and unwritten law discussed earlier. The methods of interpretation embody a vast collection of frequently overlapping and on occasion conflicting rules, principles and presumptions which have accumulated over several centuries.

The general approach which is said to be the primary method of common-law statutory interpretation is usually referred to as the *literal approach*. The classic statement of this technique is found in the *The Queen* v *Judge of the City of London Court* [1892] 1 QB 273: 'If the words of an Act are clear, you must follow them, even though they lead to a manifest absurdity. The Court has nothing to do with the question whether the legislature has committed an absurdity.' The literal approach demands that the court apply the ordinary, natural meaning of the words used, a mythical task which we will subsequently examine in depth.

An adaptation of this first approach is often referred to as the Golden Rule. Its concern is to provide an alternative approach in the face of an absurdity resulting from the literal interpretation. The rule, however, is inadequate in that it provides little guidance as to how interpretation is to proceed beyond the conclusion of absurdity. The classic exposition of the rule is to be found in *River Wear Commissioners* v *Adamson* [1877] 2 AC 743, where Lord Blackburn stated:

> But it is to be borne in mind that the office of the Judge is not to legislate, but to declare the expressed intention of the legislature even if that expressed intention appeared to the court to be injudicious; and I believe that it is not disputed that what Lord Wensleydale used to call the Golden rule is right viz. that we are to take the whole statute together and construe it all together, giving the words their ordinary significance unless when so applied they produce an inconsistency or an absurdity or inconvenience so great as to convince the court that the intention could not have been to use them in their ordinary signification and to justify the court in putting on them some other significance which though less proper is one which the court thinks the words will bear. (763)

The third and oldest statement relating to techniques of interpretation is found in the rule known as the Mischief Rule or the Rule in *Heydon's Case* [1584] 3 Co Rep 7. This rule emphasizes the interrelationship between the status quo prior to the legislation and the objectives of the new law: 'four things are to be discussed and considered: 1. what was the common law before the making of the Act; 2. what was the mischief and defect for which the common law did not provide; 3. what remedy the Parliament hath resolved and appointed to cure the disease of the commonwealth; and 4. the true reason for the remedy.' In following this line of approach the ultimate objective is to interpret the law in such a fashion that the objectives of the enactment are realized.

Finally, a technique which is reminiscent of the rule in *Heydon's Case* is referred to as the *purposive approach*. It embodies the general ethos of the previous method in that it stresses the need to interpret the enactment in such a way that the objectives (purposes) of the statute are realized. It differs from Heydon's formulation in that it does not locate the approach purely in the context of the common law, nor does it confine objectives to their historical origin though this may be one source of information about the objectives. In *Royal College of Nursing* v *DHSS* [1981] AC 800, Lord Diplock discusses the interrelationship of approaches with respect to the interpretation of the Abortion Act 1967: 'whatever may be the technical imperfections of its draftsmanship, however, its purpose in my view becomes clear if one starts by considering what was the state of the law relating to abortion before the passing of the Act, what was the mischief that required amendment, and in what respect was the existing law unclear.' The historical, social and economic aspects to abortion were then examined as well as the more obvious features of its moral and legal history to the conclusion that 'the wording and the structure of the section are far from elegant, but the policy of the Act, it seems to me, is clear. There are two aspects to it: the first is to broaden the grounds upon which abortions may be lawfully obtained; the second is to ensure that the abortion is carried out with all proper skill and in hygienic conditions.'

The relative importance of these styles of interpretation is itself a source of considerable controversy which raises theoretical and substantive issues about the role of the judge, the law-making dimension of interpretation and the threat this poses to the abstract supremacy of written law. The controversy can be reduced, for present purposes, to two positions which have both a descriptive and a prescriptive quality. The first represents the judge as a passive actor in the process of interpretation, merely giving the words of the Act their natural meaning and applying that meaning to the situation in the dispute. It stresses a mechanical representation of interpretation, emphasizing the impartiality involved in adjudication. The model is most sympathetic to the adoption of the literalist style of interpretation. The second model rejects the notion that this can be the only role-model for a judge. This model represents the judge as a party who necessarily undertakes an active role in the task of interpretation. Whilst the judge is not a completely free agent, this model stresses the role of the judge as an active participant in the process of creating legal meaning and the need for the judge to resort to the whole range of resources within the legal culture which may lead variously to references to social policy, economics, and other broad-ranging administrative and political considerations of the 'consequences' of the rules to be applied. This model suggests a dynamic role for the judiciary. It is most sympathetic to those techniques of interpretation which seek to realize the purpose and objectives of legislation, the Mischief Rule and the purposive style of interpretation in particular. The first model, on the other hand, provides no threat to the law-making role of the legislature, as the judge is the passive servant merely reading the written law and applying it. The second model potentially threatens the superiority of the written law in that the judge may be seen as a law-maker with the capacity to change or even to undermine the supremacy of the written law by resorting to sources and materials outside the statutory provision, and thereby threatening its status.

Judicial observations on the merits and demerits of the various styles of role-model are numerous. One of the most quoted examples is found in a confrontation between Lord Denning when in the Court of Appeal and Viscount Simonds in the House of Lords in the case of *Magor and St Mellons Rural District Council* v *Newport District Council* [1952] AC 189. A more recent example of the controversy, and one which provides a clearer expression of the political considerations which underpin the debate is to be found in the judgment of Lord Diplock in *Duport Steels Ltd* v *Sirs and Others* [1980] 1 WLR 142:

> When Parliament legislates to remedy what the majority of its members at the time perceive to be a defect or a lacuna in the law (whether it be written law enacted by existing statutes or the unwritten common law as it has been expounded by the judges in decided cases), the role of the judiciary is confined to ascertaining from the words that Parliament has approved as expressing its intention, what that intention was, and to giving effect to it. Where the meaning of the statutory words is plain and unambiguous it is not for the judge to invent fancied ambiguities as an excuse for failing to give effect to its plain meaning because they themselves consider that the consequences of doing so would be inexpedient or even unjust or immoral.
>
> A statute passed to remedy what is perceived by Parliament to be a defect in the existing law may in actual operation turn out to have injurious consequences that Parliament did not anticipate at the time the statute was passed . . . it is for Parliament, not for the judiciary, to decide whether any changes should be made to the law as stated in the Acts . . .
>
> It endangers continued public confidence in the political impartiality of the judiciary, which is essential to the continuance of the rule of law, if judges, under the guise of interpretation, provide their own preferred amendments to statutes which experience of their operation has shown to have had consequences that members of the court before whom the matter comes consider to be injurious to the public interest.

In addition to the collection of primary techniques of interpretation, the judiciary has developed a collection of second-order rules, principles, presumptions and policies to facilitate interpretation. In general these are resorted to as part of wider strategies of interpretation usually characterized in the terms already outlined. For example, a collection of rules has been developed to regulate the use that can be made of various components of the documentary format in which statutes appear. The long and short title, preamble and section headings are only available as aids to construction to facilitate the interpretation of the words in the sections where there is a controversy over the meaning of those words. They cannot be used to introduce questions of ambiguity where the words of the section are clear in themselves (*R* v *Bates and another* [1952] 2 AER 844). Rules have also been laid down by the courts as to the status and use that can be made of material contained in schedules (*Buchanan (James) & Co Ltd* v *Babco Forwarding and Shipping (UK) Ltd* [1977] QB 208). Special rules prescribing how certain commonly used combinations of words are to be interpreted have arisen.

For example, the *ejusdem generis* rule deals with the combination of specific and general terms. It requires that where three or more specific examples are followed by a general word, then the parameters of the general category are to be determined by the common characteristics of the specific words (*Palmer* v *Snow* [1900] 1 QB 725, at 727). The *noscitur a sociis* rule prescribes that words are to take their meaning from their context (*Muir* v *Keay* [1875] LR 10 QB 594). A further category of aids to interpretation are general principles by which the task of interpretation is to be assisted. Many of the principles are general guides describing the attributes of the activity of legislation. For example in *Morris* v *Beardmore* [1980] 2 AER 753, the court had to consider the legislative provisions relating to the taking of specimens of breath by the police. The dispute related to the power of the police to enter private premises to effect a breathalyser test. In interpreting the statutory provision, Lord Scarman made the following reference to a general principle:

> When for the detection, prevention or prosecution of crime Parliament confers on a constable a power or right which curtails the rights of others it is to be expected that Parliament intended the curtailment to extend no further than its express authorisation. A constable, who in purported execution of his duty has infringed rights which Parliament has not expressly curtailed, will not, therefore, be able to show that he has acted in execution of his duty, unless (and this will be rare) it can be shown by necessary implication that Parliament must have intended to authorise such infringement. (763 b–c)

The narrow construction of penal provisions is another example of a similar principle, as seen in *R* v *Cuthbertson* [1980] 2 AER 401 where Lord Diplock applied a restrictive principle to the interpretation of the Misuse of Drugs Act 1971 s. 23 in the following fashion: 'the fact that the section is a penal provision is in itself a reason for hesitating before ascribing to phrases used in it a meaning broader than they would normally bear' (404). The above selection of secondary techniques is not exhaustive; it is merely a selection to draw attention to various general categories of method and technique.

A final matter which demands consideration again focuses upon the relationship between the judiciary and the legislature. As has already been noted, the act of interpretation through the ascription of meaning to the text may be viewed as a law-making function. Whilst reference has been made to strategies available to the courts which purport to deny the law-making nature of interpretation, such strategies are not completely successful; even in explicit practice, successive readings purporting to follow a literal interpretation, for example, may not be in total agreement as to the meaning of the text. In the event of such an outcome a question arises as to the status of the respective interpretations. Suggestions that one judicial interpretation may or must be privileged can be read to imply that the interpretation is a source of law superior to the actual words of the statutory text, which directly challenges the position of the text as the supreme source of law. In *Ogden Industries* v *Lucas* [1970] AC 113, Lord Upjohn considered the matter and concluded:

> It is quite clear that judicial statements as to the construction and intention of an Act must never be allowed to supplant or supersede its proper construction and *courts must beware of falling into the error of treating the law to be laid down by the judge in construing the Act rather than found in the Act itself.* No doubt a decision on particular words binds inferior courts on the construction of those words on similar facts but beyond that the observations of the judges on the construction of statutes may be of the greatest help and guidance but are entitled to no more than respect and cannot absolve the court from its duty in exercising an independent judgment. (Emphasis added)

His observations provide a striking illustration of the narrow political line formally espoused by the judiciary, one which in the last instance predictably asserts the superiority of the legal text over its interpreters and wittingly or unwittingly denies that the ritual claim to 'literal obedience' to the statutory text may mask any number of strategies of interpretation.

NOTES

1 General histories of writing which can usefully be consulted on issues of the anthropological and political features to the development of the various forms of script, include: M. Pope, *The Story of Decipherment* (London, 1975); also, I. J. Gelb, *A Study of Writing* (Chicago, 1963); D. Diringer, *Writing* (London, 1962); J. Goody, *The Domestication of the Savage Mind* (Cambridge, 1971). For a general sociological introduction, see: A. Giddens, *A Contemporary Critique of Historical Materialism* (London, 1981); also W. Ong, *Orality and Literacy* (London, 1982).
2 The question to be asked is always that of who has control over the written information or archive. The argument may be taken further if we consider the historical tendency for ruling groups to invent new forms of codification once literacy, or knowledge of a particular script, becomes widespread. In many senses it can be argued that the contemporary professionalization of legal language functions precisely to encode legal knowledge in a culture where literacy is reasonably widespread, 'wherever a code is unveiled, disencrypted, made public, the mechanism of power produces another one, secret and sacred, "profound"' (Derrida, 1979, p. 138). Despite its apparent function of clarifying and communicating laws and the order of the city, writing was always opaque, the history of economy and government being the history of the various forms of cryptography.

REFERENCES AND FURTHER READING

Atiyah, P. S. 1985: 'Common law and statute law'. 48 *Modern Law Review* 1.
Bakhtin, M. 1981: *The Dialogic Imagination.* Texas.

Cairns, J. 1984: 'Blackstone, an English institutist'. 4 *Oxford J. of Legal Studies* 318.
Cappelletti, M., et al. 1967: *Introduction to the Italian Legal System*. Stanford.
Dale, Sir W. 1977: *Legislative Drafting: A New Approach*. London.
David, R. and Brierley, J. E. C. 1978: *Major Legal Systems in the World Today*.
      London.
Derrida, J. 1979: 'Scribble (writing-power)'. 58 *Yale French Studies* 116.
Diamond, A.S. 1971: *Primitive Law, Past and Present*. London.
Dicey, A. V. 1885, 1959: *An Introduction to the Study of the Law of the Constitution*.
      London.
Finer, S. E. 1979: *Five Constitutions*. London.
Foucault, M. 1979: *Discipline and Punish*. London.
Glucksmann, A. 1980: *The Master Thinkers*. Brighton.
Lawson, F. H. 1955: *A Common Lawyer Looks at the Civil Law*. Oxford.
Levi-Strauss, C. 1978: *Tristes Tropiques*. London.
Maine, A. 1861: *Ancient Law*. London.
North, P. 1985: 'Is law reform too important to be left to lawyers?' 5 *Legal Studies*
      119.
Poggi, G. 1978: *The Development of the Modern State*. London.
Pope, M. 1975: *The Story of Decipherment*. London.
Robinson, O. *et al.* 1985: *European Legal History*. Abingdon.
Sherwin-White, A. N. 1963: *Roman Society and Roman Law in the New Testament*.
      Oxford.
Stein, P. 1966: *Regulae Iuris*. Edinburgh.
Ullman, W. 1975: *Law and Politics in the Middle Ages*. London.
Watson, A. 1981: *The Civil Law Tradition*. Harvard.

3

Law, Custom and Adjudication

On the question of what the law is, so long as the rule of action is kept in the state of common, alias unwritten, alias imaginary law, authority is everything. The question is what on a given occasion A [a judge] is likely to think: wait till your fortune has been spent in the inquiry, and you will know.

(Bentham)

In historical terms, the status of written law or of codifications has varied over time and between different cultures. While it is certainly the case that codifications have played a pre-eminent role in the development of western legal culture and that written law has always been treated – by lawyers at least – as the supreme source of law in civil- and common-law systems alike, the codified law has had to perform varying functions. The importance of the code as a symbol of the foundational source of law or as a politically unifying element of new national regimes should not blind attention to the practical limitations of the code as a substantive source of law. The written law may be deliberately vague, it may be archaic, it may not deal with relevant local issues. Its role, in short, may be one of enunciating principles and of stipulating the general scheme of desirable social relationships either without governing or without directly stipulating the conditions for the resolution of particular disputes. In such circumstances the code of written law is either substantively irrelevant (a relic) or one of several factors loosely limiting the choice of decision in the particular case. In the latter instance the legal tradition has most generally resorted to the courts, the judiciary and customary law to fill the gaps or to interpret the written law.

The traditional view of written law has tended, as has been seen, to view the code as the function of a law-giver whose subjects were the recipients of that law. Law was conceived as a concession or donation whereby the will of the emperor or pontiff was made known to the people. The codification of law was viewed as benefiting the people in so far as it would from then on be possible to know directly and accurately the content of the law as laid down (*lex posita*). Thus, on occasion, the people were thought to have petitioned for the writing down of the law, their purpose being that of limiting and restraining the power of those who sat in judgment over them and who were entitled to state the content of the unwritten law. Unwritten or customary law was seen as the precise opposite of written law or law from above. The customary law consisted of rules that became binding by practice or usage within a particular group or community over a more or less well-defined stretch of time. Rather than being part of an essentially political discourse as to the 'right' forms of social interaction and exchange, the customary rule supposedly states the traditional manner of social contact and communication. In this sense the customary rule purports directly to express the will of the people (*voluntas populi*) and the authorities, by recognizing usage, accept popular action as having the force of law. As early as the Roman Republic, Cicero observed a source of law wherein 'law is thought to be created by custom which, by the wish of all, a long period of time has approved without a statute.' Justinian's *Digest* also recognizes 'inveterate custom' as a source of law of equal standing to reason and statute 'for since statutes themselves bind us for no other reason than because they were accepted by the judgments of the people, deservedly these also that the people approved without writing will bind everyone. For what does it matter whether the people declare its intention by vote or by acts and deeds?' (*D*. 1.3.32.1.) The historically dominant tendency, however, has been to place the customary rules in a position subordinate to that of written law (or *voluntas principis*), either by means of practice or on occasion by explicit command, as in AD 319 when Constantine declared that 'the authority of long custom and use is not small but it is not strong to such an extent that it conquers reason or statute.'

In analysing the functioning and interpretation of written law, we argued that despite the traditional view of codification as clarification and democratization of the law, as a concession forced from the sovereign, the better view of law and writing was one which recognized the code as a political *encoding*. Writing was the preserve of a literate elite and even where the written meanings of the code became publicly known the power of the interpreters of the code was maintained either by supplementing the code or by creating new codes. Related to this concept of encoding and decoding through writing and interpretation was the notion that the written text represented a religious or imperial source of law which pre-existed the code and had to be discovered through it. The formal (ideational) source of the law was never present; it was either long past, invisible, or wholly immanent in the law itself. The origin of the written law is always, in one form or another, a protected origin – it is necessarily hidden and obscure – and a similar argument can be seen to prevail in relation to unwritten law as well. The will of the people embodied in practice, custom and usage is neither an immediate expression of popular desire nor is it, in its origin as law, especially democratic.

Just as the priesthood has always been careful to push the origin of divinity or deification beyond familiar time or has encouraged the belief that immemorial time has passed since the time of origin, so too custom is only admitted as customary law once it has become 'ancient custom', 'immemorial usage' or of origins forgotten to the common classes. This view of custom is perhaps best expressed in English common law where 'the judges provided a remedy by holding that if the proof was carried back as far as living memory would go, it should be presumed that the right claimed had existed from time of legal memory, that is to say, from the time of Richard I' (*Dalton* v *Angus* [1881] 6 App. Cases, 740). To attain the stature of law, the customary rule had to pre-exist living memory and bear the character of established tradition or 'immemorial usage'. Precisely as such, as a practice of forgotten or hidden origins, it was esoteric in its nature, feudal in its content and in large measure obscure in its applications. It was for the courts to decide the nature of any given custom and it would be naïve in the extreme to suppose that the early local courts were immune to the political and economic pressures of the feudal nobility they served. There is no reason to suppose, in short, either that the unwritten law was the democratic expression of the will of the people as a whole or that its interpreters were free of sectarian interests: the common law was neither commonly available nor readily accessible to the people it supposedly represented. However, before expanding this theme, certain distinctions and preliminary clarifications of the terms, history and content of unwritten law are necessary.

3.1   CUSTOM AS A SOURCE OF LAW

In the very broadest of terms, custom refers to established patterns of order-maintenance and dispute-settlement within a given social group. In this wide anthropological sense, custom includes the entire array of mechanisms of social cohesion or group solidarity: a shared language, common expectations of barter and exchange, socialization and initiation rituals as well as traditions of story-telling and of oral history would all be included within the general designation of custom as the means of sociality. Clearly there is nothing specifically legal about custom in this sense; it pre-exists law and it coexists with law in cultures organized according to the doctrine and principles of legal order (Unger, 1978; Roberts, 1980). There is, in short, no necessary relationship between custom and law and, contrary to the prevalent view of law as the perfection and inheritor of custom (Hart, 1961, p. 99 ff), it is probably a more accurate generalization to see law or 'legal order' as a destructive force, as the assassin rather than the pinnacle of non-legal or customary orders. Such an observation is certainly true in terms of the relationship between European and non-European cultures during the centuries of expansion and empire. Colonization of territories invariably brought with it a greater or lesser degree of western legal order: centralized courts and enforcement agencies, rules and formal methods of adjudication were imposed upon non-legal cultures in the interests of domination, exploitation and administrative expediency. It is salutary, in short, to recall that the western tradition of law is the product of a very specific, localized yet imperialistic culture and that it has never been the indigenous tradition of more than one small but highly expansionary group of European cultures.

To the cultural relativity of legal order should be added its historical and social limitations. Even within western cultures the history of legal order is relatively recent and short-lived (in its contemporary meaning it dates back barely beyond the sixteenth century) and of restricted social and political effect. Law is an essential aspect of the modern western political tradition and of the ideology of government; it justifies authority and makes it appear natural, but as it is studied and reported it is of limited practical significance. Custom surrounds the law and exists within it; corporate self-regulation, shared expectations and specific local and ethnic practices are as likely if not more likely to prevent or resolve disputes or disorder than the centralized, bureaucratic and highly expensive legal administration. In such a context it is essential to recall that custom and law exist side by side and frequently in a relation of conflict: when lawyers past and present speak of custom they do not mean custom in general but rather the various legal forms of custom, that is, customs selected, interpreted and applied by the privileged class of experts in the law. Custom here is of limited accessibility and of restricted availability; it is legally recognized custom or practice, custom either formally or tacitly ascribed the authority of law. The procedures available for selecting and instituting customary rules as legal rules vary both between the civil and common law traditions and between different historical moments within those traditions.

Within the civil-law tradition, custom has played a changing and uncertain role as a source of law (*ius non scriptum*). In classical Roman law, as has been noted, custom played an important but diminishing role and was eventually replaced by imperially compiled or formulated legal rules. By the time of the *Corpus Iuris Civilis*, law, within the civilian tradition, meant written law or *lex scripta* and it was the written law as a whole which formed what was termed *ius commune* (common law) within the later civil-law tradition. That tradition of written law was, however, something of an anachronism within the various political traditions of western Europe and while it would be wrong to underestimate the conceptual, political and practical significance of the *Corpus Iuris*, its reception as substantive law was piecemeal over much of Europe. The *Corpus Iuris* was, in a formal sense, authoritative throughout most of Europe and it was of extreme persuasive value even where it was not substantively the law. The *Corpus*, however, represented a model of law and of social and political relationships, of empire and of sovereign order; both the rulers and the lawyers of the west were often keener to emulate and follow this model than they were to be concerned with the technicalities of Roman law. Side by side with that model of legal order existed important bodies of local, customary law. Such 'particular customs' (Blackstone, vol. 1, p. 67) existed throughout Europe and consisted of secular, non-professional, bodies of traditional practice associated with the specific locality, be it village, town, city or district, and it was from such 'particular customs' that the civilian model of law could be fleshed out, adapted and applied to contemporary and local problems.

The earliest literary evidence of customary rules emerges in the thirteenth century and the most widely known took the form of law books called *spiegel* (mirrors) providing unofficial accounts of local customs. The *Sachsenspiegel* (Saxon mirror) in Germany, for example, was compiled by one Eike of Repgow in the early thirteenth century. It was written originally in Latin but was subsequently translated into the vernacular and constituted one of the first non-Latin legal treatises. Equivalent compilations were provided in France (*coutumiers*) and in England during the same period. The local and vernacular character and unofficial status of the 'mirrors' and *coutumiers* should be carefully distinguished from the meaning and status of custom within the English legal system of the period, where custom officially designated the 'common law' of the king and the baronage (his tenants-in-chief) and was recorded, as by Bracton, in Latin and subsequently in law French. The national status of English common-law custom ('general customs') was, as will be seen, an important distinguishing feature of the common-law tradition, although its historical significance should not be exaggerated. By the mid-fifteenth century, and in many areas of Europe considerably earlier, extensive official systematizations (redactions) of local law were compiled and published and routinely referred to by the judiciary. Systematized fairly universally according to the principles of Roman law and of the *Institutes* in particular, the customary rules became the equivalent of one branch of the national law and it was these institutional writings and compilations, primarily the work of the universities, which became the basis for the later codifications of national law, and somewhat later, in England, of the 'system' of binding precedent.

3.1.1 *The common-law tradition*

In very broad terms it would seem permissible to generalize that the continental legal tradition has been overwhelmingly a tradition of written law. The status of law has been attributed sparingly to specific texts and specific performative acts or institutional discourses. In terms of the conceptual or formal source of law, it is consequently by and large accurate to observe that customary law, while it played an important role in the early history of the continental legal systems, was never a full source of national law within the civilian tradition. Certainly customary rules, as found and guarded by the doctors of law, were an important substantive element in legal decision-making in the period prior to that of the modern codifications. Further, it was vernacular law and local rules that to a large extent provided the content of the codifications themselves, although the act of codification was intended to sever for good the power of the judge to discover unwritten law. Within the contemporary civil-law tradition, custom officially refers to local customs which will occasionally be referred to in interpreting elements of the code, while in a less official and technical sense, custom and the vernacular legal traditions provide elements of the general legal doctrine and jurisprudence by which and in relation to which the civilian codes are interpreted and applied (Perelman, 1976).

By way of contrast to the civil-law tradition, the common-law or Anglo-Saxon legal tradition is generally treated as being predominantly a system of customary, unwritten law. Based in custom and in the 'natural reason' or will of the people, the common-law tradition is supposedly the unique product of the English people and their legal class and is supposedly vernacular in its form and democratic in its functioning. While there is some measure of historical truth in such a perception of the common law as a distinctive tradition, it both exaggerates the national quality of the common law and actively misleads the student of the contemporary legal order, which is effectively the product of much wider political and economic developments dating from the late seventeenth century to the present day. However politically pleasing or doctrinally desirable it might be to view the national legal system as a unique national product, we will argue here and subsequently (chapter 5, s. 5.1) that such a view is very far from being an accurate account of either the historical or contemporary workings of the common law. To the limited extent that the early common law was systematized into any coherent form of jurisprudence, the important intellectual influences upon it during its formative periods were those of Christianity and of Roman law, while as a body of disparate customary norms, the common law was distinctive primarily for its inaccessibility, obscurity and formality. Neither of such features supports the popular image of a native system of law emanating from the people or from below. They suggest rather the necessary complexity and, more specifically, the political and economic dependency of law upon other strata of the social whole. We shall look briefly at each of the two features mentioned, first at the formal or intellectual basis of the common law and secondly at the content and accessibility of the purportedly national customary law.

The conceptual source of the common law can be traced with considerable precision to the Anglo-Saxon monarchies of the period before the Norman conquest of 1066. In keeping with the general historical tradition which displays so close a relationship between law, power and writing, it is interesting to note that the earliest known law within the common-law tradition was both sacred and written. The tradition in question is one of a theocratic kind, rule being the rule of God as represented through the king, and the law of God was collected and promulgated in a codified, written form from a very early date, with major collections being associated with Aethelbert (602–3), Wihtred and most famously with King Cnut (1016–38). The single distinctive feature of these codes was that they were written in the vernacular, rather than in Latin, while their content was principally and fairly directly drawn from the Creed and other biblical passages. The model of law upon which these early codes were based was that of Rome: the codes were theocratic in their form and expressed fairly directly the political authority of government both in the elaboration of a relatively sophisticated body of penal norms but also in the growing use of charters as a means of conferring, 'by the grace of god', rights, duties and concessions upon individuals, groups, institutions and so on. The most famous example of such a charter is the very much later Great Charter (Magna Carta) of 1215, a concessionary charter extracted from King John, which commences, significantly and typically enough: 'First, we have granted to God, and by this our present charter have confirmed for us and our heirs for ever, that the English church shall be free and shall have all her rights and liberties, whole and inviolable. We have also given and granted to freemen of our realm, for us and our heirs for ever, these liberties underwritten, to have and to hold to them and their heirs, of us and our heirs for ever.' The early charters provided a formal expression of the king's will and were of greater practical importance, in all probability, than the general law promulgated by the king.

The influence of Christian law and the sacred status of the royal source of law tends to undermine more democratic conceptions of the origins of the common law. The other influence, of course, was Roman law and Roman ideas of government which played an increasing role throughout Europe. The early English legal tradition did not escape the latinization of European culture and by the time of the conquest Latin was the major legal language.

More importantly, the centralization of the legal system which occurred soon after the Norman conquest was very much an exercise in developing and systematizing native law according to the precepts and principles of Roman law. The first centralized courts were royal courts and the first judges were royally appointed from amongst the clergy and legally trained in canon law and Roman law (Dawson, 1960, 1968). It was precisely the king's courts, located at Westminster, and the king's judges, who first fashioned the 'general custom' of the land into a system of legal rules and provided, in a highly complex set of royal 'writs' governing the situations in which remedies were available from the courts, the rudiments of the centralized administration of justice or common law.

Remaining with 'general custom' and the early centralization of authority, the crucial period would appear to run from the late twelfth century through to the end of the thirteenth century. It was during this period that Henry II consolidated the central control of the king's courts and royal judges, both based in Westminster though increasingly peripatetic, and the early emergence of the legal profession based around the Inns of Court followed soon after. The theocratic tradition of law-making was supplemented by the influence of Roman law and the first literary expositions of the common law, most notably those of Glanvill (*De Legibus*) which appeared around 1187 and that of Bracton (*De Legibus et consuetudinibus Angliae*) which is dated 1256 and was praised by the historian Maitland as the 'crown and flower of English medieval jurisprudence'. Bracton was himself both a prominent cleric, eventually becoming chancellor of Exeter Cathedral, and also a royally appointed judge; his work on the law and customs of England draws extensively upon his experience as a judge and his knowledge of and access to earlier transcripts of pleadings before the royal courts. The form of systematization which Bracton brought to the common law was, however, that of the Roman law in which, as a cleric, he had originally been trained; 'it is clear that he (Bracton) has used Roman terms, Roman maxims, and Roman doctrines to construct upon native foundations a reasonable system out of comparatively meagre authorities' (Holdsworth, 1909, vol. II, p. 286).

The rapid development and stabilization of a system of common law during the thirteenth century was accompanied by the emergence of an early professional legal class, based at Westminster and skilled in oral pleading. Paradoxically the notions of oral pleading (narrators) and of an unwritten law were short-lived and the history of the common law is by and large a history of the recording and documentation of custom in a professional and extremely obscure language, that of law French, and hidden in technical and often verbose reports, initially of pleadings (plea rolls) and later of arguments and judgments (*Year Books*). In many senses it would be inaccurate to regard the common law as ever having been wholly unwritten in its character; it is simply unwritten in the technical sense of not being 'written law' (*ius scriptum*) or legislation. From a very early date, and certainly from the ninth century, the basic rules of general custom – of royally approved practices – were collected and recorded, most famously by King Alfred who compiled a dome-book or *liber judicialis* for use throughout the kingdom of Wessex. The book was lost but is known to have been a resource for information and knowledge of common law until the mid-fifteenth century and is said by Blackstone to have 'contained, we may probably suppose, the principle maxims of the common law, the penalties for the misdemeanours and the forms of judicial proceedings'. The substantive significance of the dome-book as a record of law and procedures is limited, however, by the subsequent Danish and Norman invasions and the separation of local and general customs.

At the level of particular custom, the Norman monarchy brought with it feudal law based upon the grant of land and the rights and duties which went with the land. It was feudal law which, in general, the common lawyers sought originally to systematize and record as common law. Originally the recording of the unwritten law was in the exclusive hands of the royal judges and emanated fairly directly from the monarch in the form of writs (the writ – originally referring to sacred writ or writings – means both command and writing) devised and issued by the king's secretariat, the Chancery. The system of writs was extremely formalistic from its earliest days and by 1258, by edict (the *Provisions of Oxford*), had congealed into a largely static and closed system of extremely complex pleadings. More general evidence of the common law was no less specialized. The plea rolls were written records of pleadings made at Westminster which frequently did not include the judgment in the case while the *Year Books*, which start reporting cases from 1292, report the oral arguments before the court in law French and are, in terms of the legal knowledge they presuppose, extremely demanding upon the reader. The law administered as the common law from Westminster was already inaccessible, esoteric and extremely technical, an 'occult science' which needed to be extracted with great difficulty and skill from the lengthy and arcane books of the law. These reports of arguments and judgments were neither official nor necessarily accurate. As Plucknett describes them:

> The whole business of pleading orally . . . was an immensely skilful and recondite game, conducted with great virtuosity by the leaders of the bar, and keenly relished by all others who were sufficiently learned to understand what it was all about. After such a display, it was an anti-climax to think of a decision. Time after time the Year Books will give pages of subtle fencing until we get the words: 'and so to judgment'. What the judgment was, nobody knew and nobody cared; what interested the reader was not the substantive law involved in a case, but the technique of conducting the pleadings . . .

The *Year Books* were eventually superseded by the *ad hoc* development of law-reporting from the early sixteenth century, when named private reporters would recall and publish more or less detailed and more or less accurate accounts of cases; Plowden, Dyer and Coke were among the most significant of the early reporters. The quality and content of the reports produced by the named reporters between 1550 and 1790 varied greatly and while frequent reference was made to earlier decisions, the reporting was frequently 'casual and careless' and on occasions 'grossly inadequate' (Dawson, 1968, p. 77). Again we would observe that such a haphazard written record of the common law hardly indicates any great certainty, predictability or widespread knowledge of law and procedure. Nor could one view the system of common-law judgment as a coherent and complete system of legal rules or as, in its modern sense, a legal order. It is only in the late eighteenth and early nineteenth centuries, with the renewed influence of Roman-law doctrines and classifications, with the shift from law French to the vernacular and with the emergence of professional and later official law reports that it becomes possible even to contemplate referring to the common law as a coherent system of rules or as an order of precedent.

3.1.2 *Precedent*

The emergence of reliable law reports in the early 1800s, together with the somewhat earlier revival of the academic and literary expositions and systematizations of the common law, provided the basic preconditions of the modern conception of common law as precedent. While the broad nature of precedent as a system of reading and interpreting authorities will be examined in detail in a later chapter (chapter 5, s. 5.2), we do need here to outline and comment upon the doctrinal conception of precedent and its specific institutional workings.

The modern and purportedly highly distinctive conception of a common-law system of binding precedent, of *stare rationibus decidendi*, meaning to follow the reasoning of previous decisions (*stare decisis*), dates back to the early years of the nineteenth century, if not before. In broad terms, the conception of binding precedent refers to the following of the rules (*rationes decidendi*) laid down in previous decisions and its logical form and entailment are classically set out by Justice Parke in *Mirehouse* v *Rennell* [1833] 1 Cl and F 527, 546, in the following terms:

> Our common law system consists in the applying to new combinations of circumstances those rules which we derive from legal principles and judicial precedents; and for the sake of attaining uniformity, consistency and certainty, we must apply those rules, where they are not plainly unreasonable and

inconvenient, to all cases which arise; and we are not at liberty to reject them, and to abandon all analogy to them, in those to which they have not yet been judicially applied . . . It appears to me to be of great importance to keep this principle of decision steadily in view, not merely for the determination of the particular case, but for the interests of law as a science.

In short, legal decisions are to be arrived at, where the dispute is governed by the unwritten or common law, by reference, either directly or by analogy, to the rules set down in previously decided cases. Such pre-existent rules or principles (reasonings) are to be followed, according to Justice Parke, even where the deciding judge does not view them to be necessarily the best means of deciding the disputed issue: predictability and consistency of legal decision-making are accorded greater value than particular justice.

This early view of precedent was developed during the nineteenth century into what is traditionally regarded as one of the strictest and most extreme systems of precedent known in the history of western legal systems. While the rest of Europe entered the age of codifications and the emergent nation-states placed their faith in publicly available written codes of national law, the English developed and refined an antiquated system of highly technical and highly particular legal decisions into the modern common law. The motives behind the development belong firmly in the European political and economic context of the nineteenth century. For the common-law system, the nineteenth century was also an age of statute law, of partial codifications and of consolidating Acts, the great upsurge coming in the 1830s and continuing unabated to the present day. Parallel to this development of what were seen as systematizing, simplifying and democratizing statute laws was the development of the common law as national law, it being the peculiar view of English lawyers that common law represented a unique and jealously guarded national legal achievement. It was, however, only with the aid of principles drawn from the academies and the civil law, that the common law could be developed into a coherent and largely self-sufficient system of legal decision-making. In 1861, in *Beamish* v *Beamish* [1861] 9 HL Cases 274, the House of Lords decided that precedent decisions of the House were to be binding in future cases, even upon the House itself. Only Parliament could alter the decisions of the House of Lords, a view reiterated in *London Street Tramways Co. Ltd* v *London County Council* [1898] AC 375, 380, by Lord Halsbury in a succinct statement that 'a decision of the House on a question of law is conclusive', a view which remained the law until in 1966 the House of Lords issued a Practice Statement declaring that, in a limited number of circumstances, the House would no longer be bound to follow its earlier decisions. The lower courts, the Court of Appeal in particular (see *Davis* v *Johnson* [1979] AC 264), however, remain bound by their own earlier decisions and the system of precedent in general is still doctrinally stated to be one of binding or strict precedent. The strongest legal argument is one which cites the *ratio decidendi* of a relevant precedent case; the issue of the forms which a precedent may take and the manner of its discovery and application are still the central methodological issues within the common law, although, paradoxically, 'theorists have not been able to agree upon an answer to the question, what is a *ratio*? Nor is there agreement as to the test to be used to identify a *ratio*, once the basic meaning of the term has been defined' (Andrews, 1985, p. 209). We shall examine this issue of the formal definition of precedent texts first in terms of their internal structure, second in terms of their role within substantive jurisprudence, and third in terms of the external constraints of the hierarchical organization of precedent texts.

(i) *Internal readings*. The traditional, somewhat mechanistic, view of precedent sees the common law as developing over time in an ordered and logical manner according to the application of rules established in prior cases. Each case, in this view, contains either one or more than one rule of law. It is the task of the subsequent court to discover and extract such rules of law from earlier cases, and, having done so, it simply has to apply them. The task of legal reading is in this view one of rigorously distinguishing, by purely internal, textual means, the relevant and the irrelevant portions of the authority studied: the rule or rules contained in the case, the *rationes decidendi*, are to be isolated and extracted from their surrounding context of general justificatory argument, termed *obiter dicta*. While *obiter dicta* have considerable persuasive force and, depending upon the authority of the enunciating court, can on occasion dramatically alter the law, as in the famous if short-lived example of *Hedley Byrne* v *Heller* [1964] AC 465, they have neither the status nor the binding effect of a precedent.

In traditional terms the somewhat mythical entity, the *ratio* of a case, has received numerous definitions, each of which attempts to limit in some slight variation of verbal form the inevitable discretion or choice facing the court or other professional lawyer reading the precedent authority. For A. L. Goodhart, to take an early and celebrated example, the procedure for determining the *ratio* of a case was a lengthy one and involved a number of salutary negative propositions as well as a positive principle of determination. Negatively, it was to be observed, the principle of a case was not to be discovered from the reasons given in the opinion, nor in the rule of law set forth in the opinion, nor necessarily by a consideration of all the ascertainable facts of the case and the judge's decision. The *ratio* was rather to be found by combining '(a) the facts treated by the judge as material, and (b) his [the judge's] decision as based on them' (Goodhart, 1931). While the definition is helpful in providing a broad outline guide for distinguishing separable features of the precedent text, it raises as many problems as it resolves. Some of these problems relate to the nature of the material facts, their degree of generality and their combination, and others relate to the language, scope and reasoning underlying the rule or decision enunciated.

To pursue the problem via the work of another eminent authority on precedent, the late Professor Cross, his most clearly expressed view was 'that it is impossible to devise formulae for determining the *ratio decidendi* of a case.' While he does at the same time propose a definition of *ratio* as being 'any rule of law expressly or impliedly treated by a judge as a necessary step in reaching his conclusion, having regard to the line of reasoning adopted by him' (Cross, 1977), the difficulties – factual, theoretical and contextual – that face its practical application are formidable and unresolved. At the level of the internal structure of the case reports we shall conclude by simply listing some of the problems to be accommodated in distinguishing and defining the *ratio*. First, the *ratio* is the rule established by the case and as such it entails a level of generality which necessarily involves a selective approach to the facts of the case. The problem is well posed by the American jurist Karl Llewellyn in terms of degrees of abstraction:

> Each concrete fact of the case arranges itself, I say, as a representative of a much wider abstract category of facts and it is not in itself but as a member of the category that you attribute significance to it. But what is to tell you whether to make your category 'Buicks' or 'motor cars' or 'vehicles'? What is there to make your category 'road' or 'public highway'? The court may tell you. But the precise point that you have up for study is how far it is safe to trust what the court says. The precise issue which you are attempting to solve is whether the court's language can be taken as it stands, or must be amplified, or whittled down. (Llewellyn, 1950, p. 48)

To the generality, the materiality and the precise concatenation of facts in a given case must be added further problems of the relationship of the facts to the rule and the language of the rule enunciated in relation to them.

The initial problem in accurately or definitively etablishing the *ratio* or *rationes decidendi* of a precedent decision is only in part an isolable question of the generality and combination of the facts of the earlier decision. The legal notion that, at the end of the reading of the earlier case, a conclusion must be arrived at as to the materiality or pertinence of the given facts raises a broader problem, that of the relationship of the rule stated in the case to the facts of the case. The decision or outcome of a case is not necessarily coincident with the rule in the case: the precedent rule is defined not as the outcome (stated at whatever level of generality) but rather the 'reasoning' of the prior decision. In terms of the internal structure of the text it is the reasoning of the decision, the relevant justificatory argument contained in the judgement, which will ideally determine both the materiality of the facts and the level of abstraction at which the rule is to be stated. It is precisely at this point, at that of determining the logic underpinning the precedent authority with a view to applying it to novel situations, that the internal distinction between *ratio* and *dictum* must give way to an analysis of the legal context or jurisprudence of the decision analysed: 'there is a distinction between the *ratio decidendi*, the court's own version of the rule of the case, and the true rule of the case, to wit what it will be made to stand for by another later court' (Llewellyn, 1950, p. 52).

(ii) *Substantive jurisprudence.* For any of a large variety of reasons, because of the varying possible combinations of fact and rule, because of alternative reasonings contained in the precedent judgment or because of ambiguity or vagueness in the language of the enunciated rule, a choice has to be made as to the legal import of a prior case. The problem of interpretation facing the subsequent court is not, in essence, what the *ratio* of the previous decision is but rather what can be made of or done with the prior arguments in the novel circumstances now before the court. The question is one of considerable complexity and it has been usefully – if grudgingly – recognized by recent writers as being a question which combines issues of law with questions of the politics and values underlying and determining interpretation. The full significance of reading as interpretation will be examined in a later chapter (chapter 5, s. 5.3) but we here pause to state and evaluate the technical problems raised by the issue of interpretation at the level of establishing precedents.

If there is no single reliable internal textual mechanism for establishing the *ratio decidendi* of a case it would seem both plausible and persuasive to look beyond the instant decision to the body of law or decisions to which it belongs; to look, in brief, for meanings and principles, substantive structures, which will cohere the instant case with wider areas of law. For Ronald Dworkin, for example, 'propositions of law are not simply descriptive of legal history, in a straightforward way, nor are they simply evaluative in some way divorced from legal history. They are interpretative of legal history, which combines elements of both description and evaluation but is different from both' (Dworkin, 1982, p. 181). Interpretation as the means of access to established legal rules necessarily relies, according to Dworkin, upon broader principles and rights than those established in any single case. The case will rather exemplify a principle or right which, in its turn, belongs to a higher order of legal abstraction and ultimately to that political or moral theory which best justifies the given legal order.

Without entering the often tortured details of Dworkin's many theories of rights and principles, it can be observed that even in the brief description of the theory given, the pursuit of the *ratio decidendi* of a case involves both description and evaluation, a jurisprudence of interpretation which endeavours to cohere substantial bodies of case law and statute according to their underlying reasoning, the legal principles and rights which they establish and exemplify. In this view the decided cases within any particular body of substantive law represent the equivalent of a literary canon or, in the view of Professor MacCormick, a specific speech-community within which the possible choices of the court are strictly defined and delimited by reference to legal criteria, by reference to rules, principles and values established in the prior case law. In this view, 'the whole idea of treating "like cases alike" can in fact be rendered intelligible only if we envisage decisions in individual cases as decisions of principle, indeed as decisions the principles of which have to be articulated and expounded' (MacCormick, 1978, p. 154 ff).

The law developed by means of individual decisions can only be properly understood in terms of the slow, incremental and fluctuating tradition of common-law textual practice. It is the general categories of law which the individual cases examine and expound, and by restricting or expanding the general categories the common law both develops and adapts itself while deciding and judging specific instances of dispute. The study of theories of precedent and of case-law reasoning can to some extent elucidate the nature of the common-law tradition and the manner in which it endeavours to decide cases in consistency with past practices and decisions. The nature of the tradition is not, however, one which can be properly comprehended or assessed in terms of an individual rule or *ratio decidendi*. It is the general framework of surrounding rules, principles and practices that delimit and to some degree determine the choices before the court in the individual case. While it would be quite wrong to say that the process of choice was necessarily a logical one, it would also be incorrect to view the exercise of legal discretion in selecting a rule or *ratio* as being necessarily arbitrary or irrational. The better description of both the tradition and the immediate practice would be one which recognized variant levels of reason, value and policy within the overall rhetoric of legal logic, a view liberally expressed by MacCormick whose opinion is that

> Legal rules (let me for this purpose call them 'mandatory legal rules') singly, or more commonly, in related groups may be conceived of as tending to secure, or being aimed at securing, some end conceived as valuable, or some general mode of conduct conceived to be desirable: to express the policy of achieving the end, or the desirability of that general mode of conduct, in a general normative statement, is, then, to state the 'principle' of law underlying the rule or rules in question. (MacCormick, 1978, p. 156)

The problem of the *ratio decidendi* at the level of what we have termed substantive jurisprudence in effect concerns the entire process of decision-making. It concerns not simply the meaning to be attributed to a specified authority but also the significance and purpose of that authority within the legal tradition and in the light of the likely or desirable future development of the law in that particular substantive area. The issue of the *ratio decidendi* relates to the question of ascertaining and interpreting first the rule, then its justification, and finally the consequences of sustaining, restricting or expanding the rule in the factual circumstances before the court. Precedent, in this view, is an art and not a science, a proposition which we would qualify only by remarking that as an art its practice conforms fairly closely and reasonably predictably to the interests, both political and economic, of the class to which the legal profession and institution belong. As an arm of government it has been persuasively, if somewhat broadly, argued that legal decision-making discretion is consistently exercised in protection of the status quo and to the benefit of the economically dominant groupings within contemporary social and political formations (Mathieson, 1980; Griffith, 1985). A final issue to be assessed thus concerns not how the *ratio* is found and interpreted but what, in social, political and economic terms, are the *effects* of the broad development of bodies of law. That issue, which some would term that of consequentialist arguments, is best defined in terms of the politics of law and the rhetoric of malleable legal rules, both of which are issues to which we shall return. Here, however, we shall conclude our consideration of substantive jurisprudence by referring briefly to the terminology within which the courts discover, interpret and apply precedent rules.

In formal terms we would observe that once the subsequent court has, to its own satisfaction, isolated a precedent rule, it is faced with the prospect of either directly applying it, or in certain cases of revising or rejecting it. A number of techniques have been developed to deal with these possibilities and while their terminology is too broad to be of any great practical utility or instrumentality it is worthwhile briefly to list them. First, there is the possibility of *distinguishing* the precedent authority. Material differences between the precedent case and the instant case allow the judge in the latter case to decline to follow the precedent case. Thus, for example, in *Rondel* v *Worsley* [1969] AC 191, it was authoritatively laid down by the House of Lords that barristers are not liable in tort to their clients for any negligence in the presentation of their case in court. The exemption from liability established in *Rondel* v *Worsley* was distinguished in the later case *Saif Ali* v *Sydney Mitchell and Co.* [1980] AC 198, the principal distinguishing feature of the later case being that the negligence complained of occurred prior to the presentation of the case in court and indeed was responsible for preventing the case from coming to court at all. Thus, for Lord Wilberforce, '*Rondel* v *Worsley* was concerned and only concerned with matters taking place in court which resulted in an outcome unfavourable to the client.'

Whether or not a court has good reason or motive for distinguishing an earlier decision, is, of course, a matter of much greater complexity than the simple definition of the technique would suggest. Granted that no two disputed sets of facts are ever identical, it is always open to the court to distinguish material particulars and similarly it is always open to the court to discover material likenesses or *analogies*. Analogy, which may be simply defined as the predication of a relevant similarity between the precedent and instant cases, plays a pervasive if ill-defined role in legal reasoning and legal justificatory argument. Analogy is not a logical operation, nor can analogies be proved; they are rather questions of degree, ultimately determined by reference to policies and consequences rather than to logic or necessity. In each instance the question is one of evaluation, of the ends furthered or served by either restricting or extending the given rule. In *Dillon* v *O'Brien and Davis* [1877] 16 Cox CC 245, for example, it was accepted by the court that there was a well-established common-law rule that upon arresting someone on suspicion of having committed a felony (a serious criminal offence), property in his or her possession believed to have been used in the offence could be seized and detained without the need for a specific warrant to search for the property in question. The plaintiff was arrested for a misdemeanour (a minor criminal offence) and the police at the same time seized papers, bank notes and coins belonging to the plaintiff. The seizure of evidence was held to be lawful despite the absence of a warrant on the basis of an analogy between felonies and misdemeanours. Underpinning the analogy was the view that the State's interest in detecting, apprehending and convicting persons guilty of crime should be expedited in relation both to felonies and misdemeanours.

Finally, two less extensive possibilities are to be found in the categories of *per incuriam* and of *overruling*. A decision can only properly be labelled *per incuriam* where a binding rule of law which, if taken into account, would have materially affected the outcome of the instant case, has been ignored by the court in the precedent decision. The previous decision is in such circumstances 'demonstrably wrong' and cannot be followed (*Morelle* v *Wakeling* [1955] 2 QB 379, 406). It is not open to the court, on such a definition of *per incuriam*, to avoid decisions it finds simply inconvenient or undesirable; there must be a 'manifest slip or error', a view forcefully re-emphasized in *Cassell* v *Broome* [1972] AC 1027, in terms of fidelity to law and the overriding value of legal certainty. Lord Hailsham concludes that 'the fact is, and I hope it will never be necessary to say so again, that, in the

Defining the Legal Text

hierarchical system of courts which exists in this country, it is necessary for each lower tier, including the Court of Appeal, to accept loyally the decisions of the higher tiers.'

(iii) *Hierarchy.* The above justification for restricting the category of *per incuriam* called in aid the doctrinal significance of the hierarchy of the courts and it is in the context of the hierarchy of the courts that we shall briefly deal with the issues of overruling: the power of courts higher up in the legal hierarchy to overrule or not to follow the decisions of courts lower down in that hierarchy, and in certain instances, precedents of their own or co-ordinate courts.

The doctrine of binding precedent is dependent upon a hierarchy of superior and inferior courts and rules that indicate the relationship between such courts. The rules of hierarchy relate principally to what are traditionally referred to as 'ordinary courts', the House of Lords, the Court of Appeal and the High Court. Although the details of the rules may vary, they are generally relevant to all institutional hierarchies which operate a system of binding precedent and it is worth observing that the ordinary courts are by no means the only example of adjudicative hierarchy within the contemporary Welfare State. The contemporary State has fostered numerous parallel and usually subordinate adjudicative hierarchies, some of which operate systems of precedent, as, for example, the decisions of the Social Security Commissioners. Furthermore, the differing institutional hierarchies are often themselves interrelated, usually through the inherent supervisory jurisdiction of the High Court to review the decisions of inferior tribunals, a power of judicial review which generally concentrates upon the fairness or legality of the procedures by which the decision was arrived at. Subject to this acknowledgement of a much broader and more complex system of adjudicative hierarchy, we shall here briefly examine the hierarchy of the ordinary courts.

As a result of the United Kingdom's accession to the European Economic Community through the European Communities Act 1972, the Court of Justice of the European Communities is the supreme court dealing with issues of European law. By section 2 (1) of the Act it is provided that in disputes relating to the meaning and effect of European primary and secondary law, the United Kingdom courts must act in accordance with the decisions and principles of the Court of Justice. Article 177 of the EEC Treaty lays down the details of the relationship between national courts and the Court of Justice on matters of the interpretation and validity of European law. In paragraph 2 it provides that the courts and tribunals of a Member State may, at their own behest, refer questions of law to the Court of Justice, while by paragraph 3 it creates an obligation to do so in situations where the adjudicating institution is one against whose decision there is no appeal. While there has been some dispute as to when a court is, in practice, the last court of appeal within the domestic legal system, the Court of Justice has understandably tended to encourage reference both in terms of the empowerment provision and in terms of the obligatory provision.

Within the purely domestic sphere the House of Lords is the supreme court and, at least from 1861, it claimed to be bound by its own previous decisions. Such remained the position until the Practice Statement of 1966 when, on behalf of the Lords of Appeal, Lord Gardiner LC announced that, in certain circumstances, the House of Lords would no longer be bound by its own previous decisions. While affirming that precedent was an 'indispensable foundation' for legal decision-making it was now also to be recognized that 'too rigid adherence to precedent may lead to injustice in a particular case and also unduly restrict the development of the law' (1966, 1 WLR 1234). While clearly not itself a precedent the statement has been accepted – for obvious reasons of the standing of its authors – as law. The proviso that the power to overrule earlier decisions be used sparingly has effectively limited its practical application and a recent review of the House of Lord's use of the power of overruling has evidenced a number of restrictive criteria (Paterson, 1982, p. 154 ff). The tacit jurisprudence of overruling would appear, amongst other things, to take into account:

(i) that the freedom ought to be exercised sparingly;
(ii) that a decision ought not to be overruled where to do so would upset the legitimate expectations of people who have entered into contracts or settlements or otherwise regulated their affairs in accordance with existing decisions;
(iii) decisions on questions of statutory construction ought not to be overruled except in the most exceptional circumstances;
(iv) that the mere fact that a decision is considered to be wrong is insufficient;
(v) a decision ought only to be overruled either if it creates too great a degree of uncertainty in the law, or if in reaction to some broad issue or principle it is no longer considered just or in keeping with contemporary social conditions or public policy.

The classic example of the last situation is the case of *Herrington* v *British Railways Board* [1972] AC 877, where the House of Lords decided to use its new power to overrule *Addie* v *Dumbreck* [1929] AC 358, a case which set out a particularly harsh and stringent test for liability on the part of an occupier of land to trespassers. While it should be pointed out that the courts for a long time managed to evade the harshness of the rule in *Addie* by means of interpretation and specifically by the implying of a licence to be on the land, it was only in 1972 that the issue could be directly faced. For Lord Pearson then, '*Addie's* case has been rendered obsolete by changes in physical and social conditions and has become an incumbrance impeding the proper development of the law . . . It has become an anomaly and should be discarded' (929–30).

During the 1970s the Court of Appeal on occasion attempted to acquire a power similar to that of the House of Lords in relation to its own previous decisions, Lord Denning most notably arguing plausibly that it would be both desirable and also a common-sense recognition of actual practice so to empower the Court of Appeal (*Davis* v *Johnson* [1979] AC 264, 278). The Court of Appeal in both its Civil and Criminal Divisions has traditionally been bound by its own previous decisions subject to the guidelines laid down in *Young* v *Bristol Aeroplane* [1944] AER 293; Lord Greene MR in that case, after acknowledging that the court was in general bound both by decisions of the House of Lords and its own past decisions, noted that there were three exceptions to the latter principle. First, that where there are deemed to be two conflicting decisions of the Court of Appeal, the subsequent court may choose which of them to follow. Second, the court is bound to refuse to follow a decision of its own which, though not expressly overruled, cannot, in its opinion, stand with a decision of the House of Lords. Third, the court is not bound to follow a decision of its own if it is satisfied that the decision was given *per incuriam*. In *Davis* v *Johnson*, despite plausible arguments to the effect that the list of exceptions to the general rule both was and should be much broader than those enunciated by Lord Greene MR, the House of Lords took the opportunity, in Lord Diplock's words, 'to re-affirm expressly, unequivocally and unanimously that the rule laid down in the *Bristol Aeroplane* case as to *stare decisis* is still binding on the Court of Appeal.' Finally, it may be noted that in *Police Authority for Huddersfield* v *Watson* [1947] 1 KB 842, the High Court ruled that it was in its turn bound by its own previous decisions in the same way and subject to the same exceptions as the Court of Appeal.

3.2 EQUITY

It would be wrong to conclude a discussion of unwritten law without some reference to *aequitas* or equity as both a general principle of legal interpretation and as a specific form of jurisdiction. It has, after all, frequently been under the label of equity that the law-making power of the courts and the moral and political affiliations underlying that law-making power have been most explicitly exercised.

In its most general meaning equity connotes equality and fairness and in its earliest Greek usage is closely connected to the concept of justice. Equity in this sense is an aspect of the law of nature, an aspect of the overriding and eternal law to which human law (positive law) must endeavour to conform and comply. Such, at least, is the most general meaning of the term as used by the Greeks and Romans. It represented a mode of approaching and interpreting the law so as to do justice to the principles underpinning the law and, where the occasion required it, correcting or reforming or abrogating the established law so as to ensure justice. Thus, in the *Rhetoric* Aristotle defines equity: 'it is equity to pardon human failings, and to look to the law-giver and not to the law; to the spirit and not to the letter; to the intention and not to the action; to the whole and not to the part . . .' (I. XIII.1374a). Equity in this sense represented an unchanging yet unwritten law, the principles of justice as proportionality to which legal orators could appeal in attempting to soften or to avoid the strict application of settled legal rules; 'what creates the problem is that the equitable is just, but not the legally just but a correction of legal justice. The reason is that all law is universal but about some things it is not possible to make a universal statement which shall be correct' (*Ethics*, v.x).

In Roman law equity played a somewhat similar role. Again derived fairly explicitly from the law of nature (*ius gentium*) it increasingly grew in importance as a source of civil law and formed a major part of the praetorian law of the Republic and early Empire. Decisions were given and edicts issued according to general considerations of equity and utility (*ex bono et aequo*). General equitable principles of good faith in contractual relationships, of interpretation according to intention rather than form in the construction of documents, and of the prevention of unjust enrichment were all developed so as to mitigate the rigour of the law. The purpose of practical or particular equity (*ius honorarium*) was 'to aid, supplement or correct the civil law', and such, in a limited form, remains the role of equity within the modern civil-law tradition. While codification purports as a general rule to settle the law and to limit if not totally to exclude the law-making power of the judiciary, it would be wrong to see codification as wholly antithetical to equity. In substantive terms the compilers of the code may often incorporate principles of general equity which leave the judiciary areas of discretion empowering them to mould and develop the law according to the humanistic sentiments of justice and fairness in the individual case. Thus, for example, Article 1226 of the Italian Civil Code directs the judge that if the precise amount of the damage to a plaintiff resulting from a breach of duty on the part of the defendant cannot be proved, the judge shall fix the amount according to the principles of equity. Article 1337 of the same code provides that parties to a contract shall act in good faith in the negotiation and formation of contracts. Further, it may often be the case that equity plays a more general role as a style and principle of interpretation of the code explicitly designed to justify decisions in the abstract language of justice and humanity. Where codification adopts a general style and, as is quite frequently the case, resorts to broad discretionary categories and broad statements of principle, then the judiciary are likely to resort to equity in its general sense in actively defining and applying these principles.

Although it developed by means of distinctive institutions and was for a long period of its history a separate jurisdiction, the role of equity in the common law is in principle comparable to that of *aequitas* in the civil law. If anything, the explicitly political character of legal decision-making and of law-interpretation are even clearer in the early development of equity in relation to common law than was ever the case in relation to the *imperium* of the Roman praetor and the correlative growth of the *ius honorarium*. Within the English tradition it was the King's Council and later the Chancellor who took the place of the praetor yet carried with them to the woolsack 'precisely the same training and . . . the same qualifications' as their Roman counterparts (Maine, 1880, p. 44 ff).

Equity acted primarily as a supplement and gloss to the common law. Its most general source was the unwritten or divine law and it is significant that during the early period of equity, up until the end of the seventeenth century, Archbishop Williams (1621–5) being the last, the Chancellors were ecclesiastics rather than mere lawyers. The Chancellors were from the beginning political appointees and to this day they have played an important political role. In terms of the early development of equity the religious training of the Chancellors meant that equity was aligned fairly directly with the development of the common law and with the theological conceptions of conscience and of moral or natural law which were seen in principle to underpin the positive law. For Cardinal Morton in the mid-fifteenth century, for example, 'every law should be in accordance with the law of God; and I know well that an executor who fraudulently misapplies the goods and does not make restitution will be damned in Hell, and to remedy this is in accordance with conscience, as I understand it' (Plucknett, 1956, p. 687 ff). To take a slightly later example, St Germain in his work *Doctor and Student*, which appeared in the early sixteenth century, remarks that 'if thou take all that the words of the law give thee, thou shalt sometimes do against the law . . . for such causes might come, that he that would observe the law should break both the law of God and the law of reason.'

The general and essentially religious conception of the source and function of equity gains a more specific and political expression in the development of the jurisdiction of 'particular equity'. In its substantive sense, equity developed as a way of mitigating the severity of the exegetical reading of the law. The medieval sciences in general were founded on books of authority in which the medieval scholars believed all possible knowledge could be found. The various disciplines were all essentially concerned to initiate the student in the books of an earlier and superior civilization, that of Christian antiquity, and legal method also developed in a scholastic and backward-looking atmosphere. Equity existed to gloss – to comment upon and supplement – the apparent literal meaning of the strict law (*rigor iuris*). Initially, equity developed in a piecemeal way internal to the common law, equity simply meaning the correction of undue formality, a process described by Maitland in its thirteenth-century form as meaning that:

> The royal tribunal is not so strictly bound by rules that it cannot defeat the devices of those who would use legal forms for the purposes of chicane; it means also that the justices are in some degree free to consider all the circumstances of those cases that come before them and adapt the means to the end. In the days of Henry II and Henry III the King's court wields discretionary powers such as are not at the command of the lower courts, and the use of those powers is an exhibition of 'equity'. (Pollock and Maitland, 1968, p. 189)

Specific and specialized remedies and rights were developed by means of a general equitable power of the court. This was derived relatively directly from the divine right of the king, the 'immemorial belief that inherent in the King are the right and power to remedy all wrongs independently of common law or statute law and even in the teeth of these; the right and power, in fact, to do as he likes whatever hard law and still harder practice may dictate' (Boland, 28). The source of equity was Scripture, and later Reason and Principle as perceived by the judiciary (Simmonds, 1984, p. 19 ff). Equity, in short, became a major source of legal development, of remedies *in personam* (against the person) as opposed to *in rem* (mere damages) and of exceptions and supplements to general rules of common law. The Lord Chancellors and the Court of Chancery from the fifteenth century onwards *de facto* exercised a jurisdiction separate from that of the common law although it was only in 1616 that the two jurisdictions were formally separated, a separation that lasted until the Judicature Acts of 1873 and 1875.

Equity as a distinctive source of unwritten law has been largely inoperative for over a century. It simply forms one historically distinctive source of particular rules which are distinguishable from common law by virtue primarily of their direct political provenance. Sir G. Jessel MR, for example, comments in 1880 that: 'the rules of Equity are not, like the rules of the common law, supposed to be established from time immemorial. It is perfectly well known that they have been established from time to time –

altered, improved and refined from time to time. In many cases we know the names of the Chancellors who invented them. No doubt they were invented for the purpose of securing the better administration of justice, but still, they were invented' (*Re Hallett's Estate* [1880] 13 Ch. D. 696). In contemporary terms it merely remains to observe that equity and trusts, equitable procedures, maxims and remedies form a substantive part of the common law and if it makes sense to speak of any distinct category of equity it will be as a specific mode of approach to interpretation of the law which attends specifically to the particularities or peculiarities of the instant case.

3.3 AUTHORITATIVE WRITINGS AND DOCTRINE

Literary expositions of the law, learned texts, commentaries, critical dissertations and textbooks all play a significant if variable role in the development and interpretation of the law. Extra-judicial, professional and academic writings on the law have, historically, contributed extensively to the reform, explanation and definiteness of the law, yet official recognition of these doctrinal sources of legal argument and legal judgment has often been slow and less than explicit. The most persuasive reason for such reticence, within common-law tradition at least, is expressed by a contemporary judge and scholar, Justice Megarry, who argues judicially that:

> The process of authorship is entirely different from that of judicial decision. The author, no doubt, has the benefit of a broad and comprehensive study of his chosen subject as a whole, together with a lengthy period of gestation, and intermittent opportunities for reconsideration. But he is exposed to the perils of yielding to preconceptions, and he lacks the advantage of that impact and sharpening of focus which the detailed facts of a particular case bring to a judge. Above all, he has to form his ideas without the aid of the purifying ordeal of skilled argument . . . Argued law is tough law . . . Today, as of old, by good disputing shall the law be well known. (*Cordell* v *Second Claufield Properties Ltd* [1968] 3 WLR 864, 872)

Whatever may be meant by the expression 'tough law' and the curiously medieval and agonistic image of law by 'ordeal', we would briefly suggest that the argument underrates the historical influence of literary expositions of the law and underestimates the potential value of academically informed, reasoned, researched and empirically substantiated studies of the logic and effects of legal regulation.

Informed and open dialogue as to the content and development of the law was a feature of both the Greek and Roman legal systems during their classical eras. In classical Greece, handbooks of legal argument were compiled by the early forensic rhetoricians who were teachers of both law and argument as well as being, on occasion, advocates in particular law suits (see chapter 6, s. 6.2). Technical accounts of the forms of argument and increasingly systematic commentaries were as important to the determination of the law as any judicial decision, established precedent or legislative rule: 'an Athenian could not even imagine relying on official registration procedures, written documents and the interpretation by legal experts of an unambiguous body of written rules to define his status and secure him his rights' (Humphreys, 1985, p. 313). In classical Rome priestly and broadly academic interpretation (*interpretatio*) was essential to knowledge and growth of the law and the first systematizers of the law were upper-class jurists whose writings on the law and, in particular, opinions (*responsa*) on specific disputed issues gradually acquired increasing authority from the middle of the second century BC, the time of Publicus Mucius Scaevola, right up to the compilation of the *Digest* in the sixth century. The writings of the jurists were gradually recognized to be legally authoritative, forming a recognized source of law (*ius respondendi*) in Gaius' *Institutes* and in Justinian's *Digest*. The authority of the work of any given jurist appears originally to have depended upon the status of his public office while later the emperors appear to have specifically authorized certain jurists to make law by way of *responsa* and in AD 426 the Emperor Valentinian promulgated the Law of Citations which ranked named jurists past and present according to their degree of authority.

The example of the Roman jurists indicates one important theme in the development of the civil law, that of the importance of academic and literary glosses, of legal doctrine or science, to the definition and development of the law itself. The interpreters and systematizers of the law had very real law-making power and the subsequent history of the civil law amply evidences such a proposition in the form of the reception of Roman law in medieval Europe. The doctors of the law, the glossators and commentators, forged a law from the venerable text of the *Corpus Iuris* and at several stages in the development of the civil law the maxim '*quidquid non agnoscit glossa, non agnoscit curia*' (what the gloss does not recognize, the court does not recognize) explicitly stated the direct authority of the critics of the law and later of the institutional writers.

Within the common-law tradition, willingness to accept explicitly critical debate and open dialogue on the content and development of the law have been more limited. Traditionally only a small group of extremely ancient literary authorities, Glanvill, Bracton, Littleton, Coke, Hale and Blackstone in particular, have been recognized as acceptable sources of knowledge of the common law. In the late eighteenth and early nineteenth century textbook literature began to emerge in a significant bulk, associated especially with names such as Bayley, Park and Sir William Jones, the forerunners of the modern textbook expositions of the law. Such works may be cited, preferably once their author is silent and dead, although Lord Diplock did observe in 1975, in the context a panegyric note, that 'in contrast to the judicial attitude adopted in my early days at the Bar, judges no longer think that the sources of judicial wisdom are confined to judgments in decided cases and, exceptionally, some pronouncement of the illustrious dead. In appellate courts, at any rate, when confronted with a doubtful point of law we want to know what living academic jurists have said about it' (Diplock, 1975).

While frequent and extensive citation of academic writings is the norm in legal argument and judgment in the United States, it would be misleading to view Lord Diplock's above-cited remark as indicating a similar position in England. It is still the case that it is primarily the classic and antiquated common-law literary sources which are cited, as, for example, in *Button* v *Director of Public Prosecutions* [1969] AC 591, to provide evidence of common-law rules relevant to obscure and little litigated issues, in that case the law of affray. Lord Gardiner LC reviewed common-law literary authorities going back as far as Lombard's *Eirenarcha* (1581), Fitzherbert's *L'Office et aucthortie de Justices de Peace* (1548), Dalton's *County Justice* (1618), Hawkin's *Pleas of the Crown* (1716) amongst other works, to correct an erroneous statement of the common law of affray which derived from Blackstone's *Commentaries* (1769) and was repeated in Archbold's *Criminal Law* (1882), from whence it made its way into legal practice. A comparable, more recent, example, can be taken from *L* v *K* [1985] 1 AER 961, where Hale's *Pleas of the Crown* (1678) was the principal source of evidence as to the common-law rules governing the sexual capacity of fourteen-year-old boys in criminal law: 'An infant under the age of fourteen years is presumed by law unable to commit a rape, and therefore cannot be guilty of it . . .'. While contemporary textbooks are referred to as persuasive sources (in *L* v *K* Smith and Hogan's *Criminal Law* (1983) textbook was briefly mentioned), their status is more argumentative and supportive than in any sense authoritative and even where cited the issues tend to be local and technical rather than substantive questions of general principle.

The judiciary, and to a greater extent the writers of contemporary textbook expositions of the law as well (Twining, 1973) do not appear to welcome independent academic enquiry into the modes in which the legal institution in general and the courts in particular exercise their law-creating discretions. The predominant tendency is one which treats the law – according to the evidence of the reports and the majority of textbooks at least – as a monistic discipline whose intrinsic logic allows lawyers to eschew the methodologies of other disciplines and to a large extent to ignore as well the empirical research that would substantiate the policy factors which so frequently determine legal outcomes. There are, however, strong arguments for increasing the status of research, scholarly writing and contemporary commentary and criticism as explicit sources for the systematization and development of law (Watson, 1984; Simmonds, 1984). The reasoning behind such an increased status is threefold.

First, and most generally, it would open the law to normative debate of greater consequence and greater depth than is often currently the case where purportedly technical issues and 'professional' problems of interpretation are at issue. In short, commentary and criticism as active sources of law could render the law more responsive to social need and social change.

Second, whether or not it is viewed as desirable to accord treatises, commentaries and textbooks the status of law, they to a large degree take on that status in the reality of legal practice. It is not only that textbook sources of law are the student's first and frequently only source of knowledge of the law, but more significantly they are, as Bentham observed, the only available systematic account of the principles and purposes of the law. The substantive jurisprudence of the textbook reading of the law is the only available sustained abstract reflection upon the law, concerned not simply with the facts of the dispute at hand but with the broader issues of interpretation, criticism and development of the law. While the treatise may be in Bentham's terms 'the shadow of the shadow of a shade' from the traditional point of view with respect to the origins of common law in custom, it would at least seem arguable that the treatise should be brought into the sphere of official legal discourse and legal judgement as being too important a factor in legal development to pass either unnoticed or unchallenged.

Third, we would stress that the law is open to numerous different readings and that the entire tradition of western law can plausibly be seen as a complex amalgamation of religious, political, economic and ethical discourses concerned precisely to provide models for contemporary social relations. If such is accepted to be the case, then time and again legal judgment and the rhetoric of legal reasoning hides the complex economic, political and ethical choices that the judiciary are inevitably making in their decisions as to how best to apply the law. Nowhere are the law reports more inarticulate and secretive than in their attempts to elaborate and substantiate policy arguments, yet, as will be the theme of Part II of this work, an interdisciplinary reading of the law provides ample evidence of a tradition and textual practice based neither in logic nor in a uniquely legal reason so much as in the politics of reading and interpreting the law.

REFERENCES AND FURTHER READING

Andrews, N. H. 1985: 'Reporting case law'. 5 *Legal Studies* 205.
Cross, R. 1977: *Precedent in English Law*. Oxford.

Dawson, J. P. 1960: *A History of Lay Judges*. Cambridge, Mass.
Dawson, J. P. 1968: *The Oracles of the Law*. Ann Arbor, Michigan.
Diplock, Lord. 1975: 'A.L.G.: a judge's view'. 91 *Law Quarterly Review* 457.
Dworkin, R.M. 1982: 'Law as interpretation'. *Critical Inquiry* 9.
Goodhart, A. L. 1931: *Essays in Jurisprudence and the Common Law*. Cambridge.
Griffith, J. A. G. 1985: *The Politics of the Judiciary*. London.
Hart, H. L. A. 1961: *The Concept of Law*. Oxford.
Holdsworth, W. S. 1909: *A History of English Law*. London.
Humphreys, S. 1985: 'Social relations on stage'. 1 *History and Anthropology* 313.
Llewellyn, K. 1950: *The Bramble Bush*. New York.
MacCormick, D. N. 1978: *Legal Reasoning and Legal Theory*. Oxford.
Maine, H. 1880: *Ancient Law*. London.
Maitland, F. and Pollock, F. 1968: *The History of English Law*. Cambridge.
Mathieson, T. 1980: *Law, Society and Political Action*. London.
Paterson, A. 1982: *The Law Lords*. London.
Perelman, Ch. 1976: *Logique Juridique*. Paris.
Plucknett, T. F. T. 1956: *A Concise History of the Common Law*. London.
Roberts, S. 1980: *Order and Dispute*. London.
Simmonds, N. 1984: *The Decline of Juridical Reason*. Manchester.
Simpson, A. W. B. 1973: 'The common law and legal theory', in *Oxford Essays in Jurisprudence*. Oxford.
Strathern, M. 1985: 'Discovering social control'. 12 *J. of Law and Society* 111.
Twining, W. 1973: 'Treatises and textbooks'. 12 *J.S.P.T.L.* 267.
Unger, R. M. 1978: *Law in Modern Society*. New York.
Watson, A. 1984: *Sources of Law, Legal Change and Ambiguity*. Philadelphia.

Part II

Reading the Law

4

Exegesis: The Attribution of Authority and Statutory Texts

> That the prime virtue of the Christian sage was humility, submission to the divine thought and will, this was an idea on which Francis Bacon the Lord Chancellor insisted no less firmly than Saint Augustine.
>
> (Perelman, 1976)

The study of law is a very specialized form of literary pursuit. It is the acquisition of a knowledge of legal texts, of written law or of the discourse of the legal institution, rather than an empirical or factual study of how law affects and controls actual behaviour. The first and most important stage of legal education is concerned with the techniques relevant to finding and interpreting written authorities or sources of law. The student is taught a method for the correct discovery and reading of the texts of the legal tradition. He or she is taught a series of discursive techniques which allow for the reading of legal writing in terms of its authority – its place within the hierarchy of legal texts – and in terms of its specifically legal meanings – its role within the system of legal rules. These discursive techniques, the way in which the legal profession reads the law, are the primary distinguishing feature of legal regulation or of the discipline of law. They are the means whereby legal texts are recognized, taught and applied as law, they are the substantive mechanisms of legal regulation: the control of behaviour and of social relations, generally by reference to binding texts authoritatively interpreted and ultimately by the imposition of those textual meanings, if necessary, by physical force.

In its most typical forms the legal text is a coercive text; it is writing which compels or, in a direct or indirect way, commands. What is commanded must be communicated and it is the role or purpose of the study of legal techniques to set out the rules that govern the communication, the system of transmission, of legal meanings as compulsory meanings. Just as there is a hierarchy of legal texts, based upon the proximity of the text to the supreme source of law, so there is also a corresponding hierarchy of techniques. The more authoritative or sacred a text is, the greater the doctrinal importance of its literal application and observance. Within the common-law tradition the supreme sources of law are statutory texts or legislative rules and in the present chapter we shall examine those primary techniques which relate to the authority and interpretation of such primary legal texts. Our subject-matter is statutory texts and the interpretation of statutes, a topic which will be approached in three stages. First, we shall examine the coercive status of statutes within the legal tradition and more specifically within legal doctrine, the issue here being classified as that of *exegesis* or of commentary upon a binding text. Second, we shall analyse the general features of statutory exegesis in terms of the language of the authoritative text and the linguistic rules that determine its meaning. Third, we shall group and detail the specific techniques relevant to the citation and application of statutory rules. The grouping of techniques provided is not intended to be exhaustive, nor is it intended to suggest that such techniques are relevant only to statutes.

4.1   THE EXEGETICAL TRADITION: COERCIVE TEXTS

It has already been stressed at a number of points that the legal tradition is primarily a written tradition and that legal studies is correspondingly a scriptural discipline or method for the decipherment and reading of specific texts. Both historically and hierarchically, the first task of the lawyers of the western legal tradition has been that of defining and of attributing authority to a text or set of texts. Their task has been that of establishing the parameters or scope of the law as a specialized discipline or science and the technique that has been used to achieve this purpose has been that of the delineation and exegesis of a code or of a *system* of written law. We shall examine first the general characteristics or rules of exegesis and second its practical and political nature and history.

4.1.1   *Biblical and legal codifications*

In its earliest form, exegesis was the primary technique of religious study or theology. It was the technique used for reading the Bible and the writings of the Church Fathers as the word of God, as the source of Christian teaching and as the foundation of the authority of the established Church. Although the tradition of biblical study goes back to rabbinical writings on the Old Testament, the Christian tradition of patristic exegesis dates from the first century AD and two features of its exegetical treatment of the Bible are of especial importance in the present context. First, the authoritative status of the text. The Bible was a sacred text and from the point of view of the Church, each word and each letter was authoritative – every syllable of the

Bible could potentially show or 'reveal' the will of God: 'this is an exegesis, which listens, through the prohibitions, the symbols, the concrete imagery, through the whole apparatus of revelation to the word of God' (Foucault, 1976, p. xvii). In St Augustine's words, we walk by faith and not by sight through the Scriptures. For him the authority of the biblical text was therefore a feature of its source, of where or who it came from, the text in question being the word of the Father, the written law which was to govern both the Church and indeed, for many centuries, the lawyers of the west. The second point of significance is that the authoritative status of the Bible was not only or not so much a feature of the text itself, of what it said, but rather of the way in which it was read, the system of techniques and authorities or churches by which it was transmitted to the followers of the Church. In one recent description, 'the whole history of medieval exegesis is the story of the establishing of exegetical authorities' (Eco, 1984, p. 151) – the establishment, that is, of institutionally authorized interpretations of biblical law and the clear definition and distinction of heresy from orthodoxy. Sacred writing has to be protected, the way in which it is read has to be controlled or authorized and its meaning must be agreed and uniform. Together these requirements define the early religious meaning and function of exegesis: it was the technique of commentary upon and control of sacred meaning. The Church and priesthood who interpreted and promulgated the sacred work over the vast territories of the western world and later of the New World, the Americas, were concerned to preach a single teaching and to form a single Church, the order of God on earth. Their approach to the primary religious text was literal, narrow and restrictive. They were not concerned to evaluate this truth which came from above; they were rather to systematize it, to reduce it to a single meaning by studying all its parts as the signs of one truth or as the will of one God.

The purpose and method of the early religious exegesis developed within the Judaeo-Christian tradition and most often associated with the work of St Augustine, is reducible to a set of general rules or techniques of textual analysis which will be briefly outlined here. There is first the requirement of a *code* or of a codification; the object of exegesis is to comment upon a primary text, to provide a secondary literature that explains and systematizes an authoritative body of writing. The code is defined by its divine source and is primary in the sense of being the highest point within the hierarchy of religious writings. Later commentaries and doctrinal writings, later churches and the priesthood generally as interpreters of the Bible, are secondary in the hierarchy in the sense of being defined by and limited to the exposition or teaching and application of the text itself. The first and earliest sense of exegesis was thus one which established both an authoritative code and also a secondary hierarchy of authorities, that of the order of writings which commented upon and explained the original text. Each of these secondary sources was assigned its own special status, its place within the order of authorities that constituted, as a whole, the doctrine of the Christian Church.

The second requirement of exegesis parallels the first; it is that of *unity* or uniformity of meaning. It is precisely because the code is authoritative that it is not to be criticized or appraised or questioned. The code is definitive: it contains, if properly understood, a complete and consistent set of meanings and the proper (exegetical) method of reading it is to search for that consistent meaning. Thus for St Augustine, the Bible is in principle reducible to a single meaning: 'in those places where things are used openly we may learn how to interpret them when they appear in obscure places', and for St Thomas Aquinas too, the exegetical reading must produce agreed, uniform meanings (concordances) and should eventually result in a single, literal, meaning for each passage of the Bible (Goodrich, 1985). The biblical teaching is to be applied and obeyed because God, and by association the priesthood which represents God as the interpreter of his word, is to be obeyed. The uniform meaning of the code is thus the combination of its authority with the requirement of obedience to the meaning established by its interpreters. There is a correct meaning and an incorrect or heretical meaning. In practical terms there is the authorized meaning, a singular and agreed meaning within the teaching of the Church, and there are numerous unauthorized meanings which the Church and Christian doctrine generally will seek to suppress or correct, by its teachings, by its preaching and ultimately, where argument and persuasion fail, by brute authority and, most famously in the work of the Spanish Inquisition, by torturing and by burning the adherents and proponents of false doctrine.

This religious origin or derivation of the method of exegesis is obviously not directly applicable to the description of the legal tradition which has its own special requirements and needs. These will be examined in greater detail in the present and subsequent chapters. It remains the case, however, that a broad analogy can be drawn between religious and legal exegesis. As a method, exegesis or commentary was originally a crucial part of Christian doctrine and indeed was the direct source of the method of the canon lawyers in their study of the *Corpus Iuris Canonici*. It would be surprising if the later secular legal usages of exegesis were not affected by the history of the method itself. The strongest support for such a proposition lies in the fact that the early western systems of law were systems of religious law and that no differentiation was made between law and religion as institutions and practices. A legal profession distinct from the priesthood only really emerged in the eleventh century AD and even then the sources of application of the law were based very closely upon religious models and existed in uneasy conjunction with canon law, the law and jurisdiction of the Church. Prior to the emergence of the various legal professions of medieval Europe, the source of law was universally religious in all its jurisdictions; the law came from God in the theory of natural law or it came through the 'divine right' (*imperium*) of the emperor or monarch, and in both cases law was sacred law. Further, it was generally found and applied by a priesthood, in Greece by the king and later the councils of elders (*arkhon*) up until about 440 BC, in Rome by the College of Pontiffs (*pontifices*) and later by elite groups of the 'legally privileged' (*honestiores*).

The law which was applied within the Greek and Roman legal systems was not always written law, but it was frequently so. Within the Greek legal tradition the earliest known codifications of law date from the sixth century BC, from the codes of Drakon and Solon which were principally concerned with rules relating to homicide (murder) and theft although the earlier code, that of Drakon, was also famous for its severity: all offences, including idleness, were punishable by death because there was no better sentence for lesser offences and no greater punishment for greater offences. Within the Roman tradition the first code, the XII Tables, dates from the fifth century BC. It is a partial code which deals with disputed and politically contentious areas of law by writing down on wooden tablets general rules governing the issues in question, issues primarily concerned with ownership and possession, succession and marriage. The early codes took the form of inscriptions upon stone or wood, while later codes were placed on scrolls, parchment (papyrus) and later in books of law. The written form of the code was by the sixth century AD, the date of the Justinian codification (*Corpus Iuris Civilis*), well established. The code was the written law (*ius scriptum*); it set down rules which were previously known only in the unwritten form of elite or priestly knowledge or in the form of divine inspiration and *imperium*. The code was the written representation of a divine source. It was to be read and studied reverently, obediently and literally as was appropriate to the sacred nature of its origin, and the study of law, in the classical definition of the *Corpus Iuris*, is given precisely as 'knowledge of things divine and human'.

The above are certainly the characteristics of the first major code, that of Justinian, which lies at the basis of the western legal tradition or of western legal science as it is contemporarily known. The Justinian codification has a peculiar importance within the western study of law and the development of legal vocabulary and method, and a brief analysis of it will provide the basis for a series of general introductory observations as to the character of legal codes and legal codifications, as the object of the exegetical techniques of reading the law. Justinian was Emperor of the eastern, Byzantine, Roman Empire from AD 527. His time as Emperor was marked, more than anything else, by a nostalgia for the western Roman Empire and the Latin culture

which had been overrun by Germanic tribes over a century earlier. He was
even responsible for an ultimately unsuccessful attempt to conquer the
western Empire. His memory of or longing for a return to the days of
imperial Rome did, however, have one peculiarly far-reaching product, the
codification of Roman law, predominantly the law of the third and fourth
centuries AD, which was completed and published in AD 532–5. The *Corpus
Iuris* was a vast compilation of the laws and legal opinions (juristic writings)
of an earlier culture. While the commission which prepared the collection
was empowered to exclude outdated law, the entire codification was by now
largely foreign or engrafted rather than local or indigenous. For practical
purposes we know of it in three parts. First, the *Code* (*Codex*), a collection of
all kinds of imperial enactments, arranged according to their subject-
matter, with contradictions and repetitions purportedly removed. Justinian's
constitution on the construction of the *Digest* explains the promulgation of
the *Code* in terms of its being: 'our first objective to make a beginning with
the most sacred emperors of old time, to amend their constitutions and put
them in a clear order so that, collected in the book with every repetition and
evil discord removed, they may present the ready protection of their ideal
character to all men.' The original *Code*, however, has not survived, but a
revised *Code* published in AD 534 has, in the form of twelve books,
predominantly consisting of the enactments of the Christian emperors and
set down in chronological order. Second was the *Digest*, an immense
compilation of the legal writings, opinions and doctrinal discussions of the
Roman jurists. It takes the form of fifty books, a vast patchwork of legal texts
ranging from statements of principles, discussions of rules and commentary
upon statutes to problems of interpretation and real or hypothetical cases.
Again the compilers were instructed to exclude anything that was superfluous, imperfect, contradictory or repetitious. The third part of the compilation is the *Institutes*, a systematic textbook of the law as a whole, prepared
primarily for students of the law, so that, in Justinian's introductory words,
'you might acquire your first rudiments of law not from ancient stories but
through the splendour of the emperor and that both your ears and eyes
might receive the truth in these matters without that which is unnecessary
and erroneous.' It is in four books subdivided according to topics – sources
of law, persons, property, succession, obligations and the law of actions –
and, excluding Justinian's own later enactments (*Novels*), it completes the
Corpus Iuris Civilis.

The entire compilation takes the form of statute law in the original
meaning of the term, *statutum* – that which is set up or authoritatively laid
down. It is statute law in the sense of being an authoritative statement of
binding legal rules coming from the supreme source of law, in this instance
the Emperor Justinian, and promulgated in general written form. At the

time that it was published, the *Corpus Iuris* was already outdated and alien to the society and legal system to which it applied. It is in many ways a defining paradox of the most significant codification within the history of western law that large portions of it never represented the law actually in force, that its purposes were from the very beginning as much political and symbolic as they were in any sense distinctively practical or strictly legal. The most interesting feature, however, of the *Corpus* lies not in the intention and effects of its original publication but rather in its adoption as law over 400 years later in western Europe. The manuscripts of Justinian's codification were lost to the west until 1090, when they were rediscovered in a library in Pisa in Italy. Their subject-matter, the law of imperial Rome, was now nearly 800 years old and yet the first law school in the west was established by a scholar named Irnerius at Bologna in Italy at the end of the eleventh century, specifically and almost exclusively for the purposes of studying the *Corpus Iuris*:

> To say that law was taught and studied in the West as a distinct science at a time when the prevailing legal orders were only beginning to be clearly differentiated from politics and religion, raises a number of questions. What did the first law teachers teach? The answer surely sounds curious to modern ears. The law first taught and studied systematically in the West was not the prevailing law; it was the law contained in an ancient manuscript which had come to light in an Italian library towards the end of the 11th century. The manuscript reproduced the enormous collection of legal materials which had been compiled under the Roman Emperor Justinian in about 534 AD – over five centuries earlier. (Berman, 1977, p. 898)

The first lawyers within the western legal tradition treated the Justinian codification as a comprehensive, authoritative and self-consistent body of statute law, 'the general objective of their program being to make the Roman law available for legal practice, as though the codification of Justinian had never ceased to be in force' (Franklin, 1966, p. 23). The *Corpus Iuris* was, for the early lawyers, to be treated as a 'monumental design for a whole society' (Dawson, 1968), as a complete statement of a way of life. It was written reason (*ratio scripta*) and so could not be questioned or evaluated as to its social utility or moral value. It was rather the 'source of all authority from which all deductions were to be made' (Vinogradoff, 1929), a binding statement of the law to be applied despite its antiquity and despite its originally unsystematic character: 'as in the case of theology, the written text as a whole, the *Corpus Iuris Civilis*, like the Bible and the writings of the Church Fathers, was accepted as sacred, the embodiment of reason' (Berman, 1977, p. 909). In brief, the *Corpus Iuris* represented something of a golden age of legal rationality belonging to a past imperial culture which the medieval western emperors were extremely anxious, for political reasons, to emulate. The reception and assimilation of the *Corpus Iuris* suggests not simply a legal continuity with the earlier Roman Empire (*imperium Romanum*) but a direct line of descent from Justinian to the medieval Europe not only of the fragmented Italian city-states, but also of the Gallic and Germanic empires of Charlemagne, Frederick and Barbarossa: 'the ideological opulence of this Roman *Corpus* proved irresistible, because it embodied jurisprudential principles which with some adaptation could be utilised for the service of the Western Roman emperors in their function as universal lords (*domini mundi*). In its traditional expression, the unity of the law is the result of its unitary source, *unum esse ius, cum unum sit imperium*' (Ullmann, 1975, p. 85).

The first law schools of the twelfth century existed to study the manu-script sources of law and were called the schools of glossators. The specific purpose of the glossators was to initiate the medieval students of law into the great books of Roman law, the name itself being a reference to a particular method and technique for studying and teaching the written law, that of the scholarly lectures (*lecturae*) providing 'glosses', word-by-word and line-by-line interpretations of the statutory texts or the *Corpus Iuris*. The glosses would explain unusual words, and more generally they would summarize passages of the text, state broad legal rules established by the text and would further annotate, classify and subdivide the text into titles. The paramount aim of the glossators was that of 'explaining the Roman law from within itself in purely legalistic terms. Their work was an exegetical analysis' (Ullmann, 1946, p. 1). The work of the glossators lies very clearly at the basis of the later developments of the western legal tradition. It was in the minute analysis of the categories of Roman law that the most basic techniques of legal method were decided and established. It is consequently broadly justifiable to define the basic categories of legal exegesis by refer-ence to the work of the glossators and these will be briefly analysed next. First, however, a brief mention should be made of the history and extensive influence of the school itself. In the first instance their work is to be associated with the law school at Bologna.

Bologna became the centre of legal studies in Italy in the twelfth century and soon attracted law students from all over Europe, though particularly from France and Germany. Scholars and lawyers trained in Italy went on to found and teach at law schools throughout Europe in the twelfth and thirteenth centuries and major centres of the new legal study were founded by Roman lawyers in France at Paris, Montpellier and Provence, in Ger-many at Cologne, Heidelberg and Leipzig, and in England at Oxford and later at Cambridge. In each case the Roman code was to be treated as the primary source of legal categories, rules and principles. It was, by virtue of its conceptual sophistication, to be treated as superior to local law and was to be studied, systematized and applied as the model or paradigm of legal method, even in those jurisdictions where it was not a directly applicable source of legal argument or substantive law.

The techniques of legal exegesis together constitute a very specific manner of approach or logic of reading and interpretation based upon certain crucial doctrinal assumptions as to the nature and character of written law. First, the statutory text or code is to be treated both as a complete and as a consistent source of law. These two assumptions are fundamental to legal doctrine. That the code is a *complete* source of law has various meanings. It means that the code or written law is to be read as containing the solution to all legal problems: it is either unnecessary or forbidden to look before or outside the code for the answers to legal questions. Here can be located one of the most fundamental of legal principles, that of legality itself as a series of texts to which all problems of law are referred. We can further associate with the completeness of the code all those techniques of legal interpretation which, basing themselves on rules and principles established by the written law, proceed to extend and apply those rules to new situations. The justification for such techniques is the completeness of the written law and the obedient exposition of the scope of the norms which it contains in the light of the will of the sovereign legislator. No interpretation can go beyond the written law but it is permissible to interpret and develop its meaning according to analogies, similarities (inductions) and deductions concerned with the logical entailments of a norm and with questions of degree (the greater includes the lesser etc.). The formal principle of completeness governing all these techniques of interpretation gives support to legal belief in the rule of law and in the mechanical role or function of the interpreters of that law. The law is written and is there to be applied and obeyed. The Roman law had become, in the view of the glossators, the universal law governing all humanity; it was *ius commune* or the common law and was of universal effect; by virtue of its completeness it was in principle to be obeyed in all situations.

The *consistency* of the code follows from and lends support to its completeness. The completeness of the code is a feature of its authoritative status (its sovereign source) and its consistency was also, originally, an aspect of its authority or of the ascription of authority to it. The code as a whole is a complete source of law; it is written reason, sacred and in logical terms a unity, a closed system of binding rules. The system of rules contained in the code is seen as a rational set of ordering principles; they come from the sovereign and they define and regulate social life: these rules cannot contradict each other, they cannot conflict or provide incompatible

answers to the same question, and, in the words of one of the most famous
of the thirteenth-century glossators, Accursius, the author of the monumental *Glossa Ordinaria*, no two statements in the *Corpus* are either 'con-
traria' (conflicting) or 'similia' (the same). In short, to understand the law is
to read and systematize it in such a way as will provide a single, coherent,
legal answer to any dispute or accusation. The belief that there is a legal
answer to legal problems and that this answer is to be found in the
professional knowledge of the written law is a profound characteristic of
legal technique or of the way in which the law is read. The belief that the
law is certain and predictable, that the judge or indeed the affected citizen
merely needs to find the relevant law in an impartial or objective manner, is
a belief based upon the assertion of the written consistency of the law seen
as a logical unity. The legal code is a written discourse which is separate
from and superior to other discourses and practices (economic, political,
ethical, religious and so on); it provides distinctive answers to problems
which arise initially in other spheres of social life.

The concept of the code as a complete and consistent embodiment of
legal reason and of legal rules is tied to a series of techniques for reading the
code and for commentary upon it. The exegetical techniques developed by
the glossators were entirely concerned to reduce the statutory texts of the
Corpus Iuris to a coherent system of rules, to a harmonious set of general
propositions or norms which could be logically applied, as a set of governing
principles or general norms, to the problems of the day. First, in broad
terms, the framework of interpretation of statutory texts proposed by the
glossators and later incorporated into other traditions of legal analysis can
be summarized as follows. The written law (or statute) is authoritative; no
legal resolution to a problem is justified unless it can be shown to be based
upon or derived from the written code. The code establishes the legality of
the rules applied in legal judgment. This legality is best described and
understood as a feature of the rationality of the legislator. The written law is
ultimately to be seen as the written representation of the rational will of its
sovereign source: understood as 'intended meaning', the rationality of the
law, its coherence and consistency, dictates that legal meaning does not
change over time. There is a single source for written legal rules and those
rules have a single meaning. The last point can be generalized as the
proposition that there is a unity to legal meaning; legal exegesis seeks to
discover the correct meaning of legal rules and to this end it elaborates a
series of techniques which will provide, more than anything else, a correct
standard of interpretation. The techniques which we shall now briefly
associate with the interpretation of statutory texts and illustrate more fully in
the next two sections of this chapter are techniques concerned with reading

the law in terms of its sources and the hierarchy of interpreters of those sources.

The techniques of legal exegesis are techniques of commentary which universally endeavour to control or restrict the reading of legal texts. Very generally, the exegete reads the law to discover solutions to legal problems. The first move in this scholastic procedure is to find a provisional legal classification for the issue raised. One or several texts must be read in terms of a search for a relevant classification or general category or categories of law which will apply to the instant issue. Once the general classification has been made it is next necessary to ascribe authority to the classification in terms of textual sources which establish it and the various rules relevant to it. The texts should be cited according to their degree of authority (of coercive power) and in many cases the citation alone will serve to resolve the problem. Where the meaning of the relevant authority is not clear or where its application is in doubt, further quotation from authority is needed to establish the correct interpretation by presenting authoritative commentary. The task here is a difficult one where the point of law at issue is disputed or where the factual situation or relation in issue is a novel one. Here the techniques of commentary, of control over the meaning of the text, are most elaborate and contentious. The law must provide a solution to the question of law and the statutory text must be read and interpreted so as to produce this solution as an authorized, textually established, legal answer to a legally formulated question. The techniques relevant to the procedure of commentary and interpretation are techniques which work from the text and restrict or generalize the scope of the law by means of a variety of discursive devices. These are aimed at creating what theologians termed concordances, agreed meanings which will unite different usages of the same term, the rule at issue with the text as a whole as a set of rules. In short, the text is elaborated so as to justify a general principle which will allow for the application or non-application of the particular rule to be seen as authoritative and justified.

4.1.2 *Exegesis and legal traditions*

The illustration of the actual workings of such techniques will be provided in the next two sections of the present chapter. To conclude the present broadly historical considerations, however, we will merely point to the development of the legal method of exegesis within the later history of the western legal tradition. The school of glossators, as has already been stated, had a foundational impact upon legal studies in Europe. It provided for the first time a science of law based upon the *Corpus Iuris*; it established an independent discipline of legal study and provided it with a meticulously worked-out set of legal techniques. The later history of those techniques has, of course, to be divided along the geographical and historical line which separates the civil-law and common-law traditions. In general terms it may be observed that the civil law is defined originally by the exegesis of the Justinian Code and for several centuries the *Corpus Iuris* was treated as being in principle the law in force throughout most of continental Europe (Watson, 1981), taking precedence over local law and local languages. The school of glossators itself survived until the mid-thirteenth century when it was replaced by the school of post-glossators or the commentators based originally in France. In broad terms the commentators wished to return legal study to the text of the *Corpus Iuris* itself and they argued that the text should be freed from the glosses – the interpretations and commentaries – provided by the earlier glossators; that it should be studied directly rather than through the vast apparatus of the Accursian *Glossa Ordinaria*. They did not challenge the exegetical doctrine or method but rather wished to reinforce it by returning to the original text and the original (historical) meaning of that text. Their aim was not to diminish but rather to increase the universal authority of the original manuscripts and to that end they developed even further those techniques of exegetical analysis that subordinated interpretation of the law to the rational will of the original source or legislator of that law. It was still Roman law and the Latin language which dominated the study and the practice of law within the civil-law countries up until the seventeenth century. The change which then occurred was gradual and a change less of technique than of the content of the law. The sixteenth century saw the rise of humanism within the major European universities (Ong, 1958), a movement which was again concerned to return learning to the classics of Greek and Roman civilization. In legal studies this meant a return to the original sources of Roman law where these had survived and a corresponding weakening of the authority of the *Corpus Iuris*, which had of course always been a secondary source of knowledge of Roman law. The change in orientation was not a dramatic one as far as the method of legal study was concerned and when the first studies of local law (*Institutes*) were produced in seventeenth-century France, Germany and Scotland in particular, they were organized very closely upon the basis of the divisions, classifications and categories of Roman law. Their model was that of the earlier law and they did not represent any great change in the fundamentally exegetical method of legal study.

While each of the civilian legal systems has a complex history of its own it can nonetheless be observed that the later development of modern codes throughout Europe in the eighteenth and nineteenth centuries follows a broadly similar pattern. The most famous and common example is that of the

French *Code Napoléon*, published in 1804. The *Code Napoléon* was a product of the French Revolution and its avowed purpose was, like that of the XII Tables (Stein, 1966), that of clarifying the law and of writing it down in as general and complete a form as possible. The *Code Napoléon* shares many of the features of the earlier codes and in several respects Napoleon can be compared to Justinian and his medieval western successors in stature, authority and role in relation to the Code he ordered and supervised. Further, the Code was clearly organized and divided according to the Roman legal classifications and it sought to provide the same level of generality and systematization as Justinian's *Institutes* in particular. The *Code Napoléon* was to provide a complete and consistent body of statute law in written form. The Code was indeed to become the fundamental basis of legal study and teaching in France and it gave rise to a new school of legal exegesis (*l'école de l'exégèse*) which defined the method of legal study in France right up until the beginning of the twentieth century. The work of the new exegetical school was that of reducing legality to statute law, and of reducing civil law to the *Code Napoléon*. Writing in 1857, the dean of the faculty of law at Paris wrote that, 'the whole body of statute law, the spirit as well as the letter of the law, with a broad account of its principles and the most complete treatment of the consequences which flow from it, *but nothing but statute law*: such has been the motto of the teachers of the *Code Napoléon*' (Perelman, 1976, p. 23). Nothing, in other words, was to be left to the discretion of the interpreter, and legal doctrine, in restricting itself to translating the exact meaning and implications of the legislation, by and large repeated the earlier glossatorial assumptions as to the nature, rationality and unity of the Code as a whole. All law emanated from the sovereign and exegesis was to provide the means of obedience to and application of that sovereign will.

Finally, the common-law tradition. We have seen in an earlier chapter (chapter 3, s. 3.1) that, historically at least, the development of the common law is a complex and distinctive legal tradition based upon a system of custom and precedent rather than upon a code. In origin at least the common law is unwritten law which is discovered and declared by judges as and when the particular case requires (Dawson, 1968). Its basis lies in custom rather than in any systematic code, its language was law French rather than Latin and when a legal profession began to emerge in the twelfth century the training in and teaching of law rested in the hands of the Inns of Court rather than in the universities. Allowing, however, for these and other distinguishing features of the common law, it is still possible to point to an extensive role played by Roman law even though that role is less direct than on the Continent and has a lasting significance in relation to legal method rather than a direct, substantive application. The influence of

Roman law on the English legal tradition dates back to the founding of the law school at Oxford University in the twelfth century and specifically to the work of one of its founders, Vacarius, who established the study of Roman law (the school of legists) in England. From Oxford and in the thirteenth century from Cambridge, the model and categories of Roman law spread into the English legal system, although the *Corpus Iuris* never became the law in force in a manner comparable to that on the Continent. Its main direct influence was upon the law of the Church (canon law) which had jurisdiction in questions of status, marriage and succession and upon the courts of Admiralty and Chancery. In broader terms, Roman law had an important indirect influence upon the vocabulary and categories of the early systematizers of the common law: upon Ranulf de Glanvill's work *On the Laws and Customs of England* written at the end of the twelfth century; upon William of Drogheda's *Golden Text Book* of the thirteenth century, and most importantly of all upon Henry de Bracton's *Laws and Customs of England*, a work written specifically for practising lawyers and based both in terms of its division of subject-matter (treating of the law of persons, of things and of obligations and actions) and in terms of its substantive content (particularly the distinction between real and personal property) upon Justinian's *Institutes* and *Code*. In the later medieval and post-medieval (sixteenth- and seventeenth-century) periods, the common lawyers and literary exponents of the common law jealously guarded it from continental influence but the formalism of the English legal system (particularly with regard to the forms of action and to the concept of problems of law or *disputatio*) and the development of a concept of the written law (the *Year Books* and common-law authorities) together with customary practice from time immemorial (1189) provides for the development of a binding system of precedent in the second half of the nineteenth century and owes much to the methods of legal exegesis as a doctrine. The work of the influential legal scholar William Blackstone in the eighteenth century again indicates the authority of the general categories of Roman law, although it was only in the nineteenth century that the doctrine of binding precedent as a system of legal texts and the modern concepts of codification and legislation really took hold.

The coming into force of the *Code Napoléon* in nineteenth-century France has no parallel in the common-law world. Nineteenth-century England was, however, the homeland of the Industrial Revolution, and English society and its legal system were subject to many of the same pressures and influences as their continental counterparts. The newly emerging modern state, new markets and forms of industrial commerce were bound to affect the legal systems throughout Europe and did so generally in the form of a new movement towards codification. On the Continent one of the major influences was the eighteenth-century work of Montesquieu, *L'Esprit des lois* (1748), a work which first fully set out the constitutional doctrine of the separation of powers, the doctrinal statement of the separation of law from politics. Law was the expression of the will of the sovereign and was to be impersonally and mechanically applied by a subservient judiciary. Judges should be 'no more than the mouth which states the words of the law: impersonal beings which can moderate neither its force nor its rigour'. In England – where Montesquieu's work was extremely popular and ran through several translated editions – a comparable tradition of legal thought develops from the work of Thomas Hobbes, *Leviathan*, and equally asserts the supremacy of the sovereign and later the value of the 'rule of law' as impersonal and objective regulation based upon the mechanical application of known general rules. The law was to be certain and predictable in its form and in its application and according to the nineteenth-century legal reformers the best manner in which this could be achieved was through codification. For John Austin and for Jeremy Bentham in nineteenth-century England, that all law emanated from the sovereign was a logical truth; judge-made law was merely the indirect or 'tacit' expression of the sovereign will whose most direct and desirable mode of expression was the statutory rule or legislation. It was in this context that the common law came to be seen as a system of binding precedent, as a quasi-code or harmonious and logically united set of written rules. The judge was to declare the law as already written and established in statutes and binding.precedents. The sovereign's laws were for the sovereign to change and a literal approach to statute law and a strict view of binding precedent were the consequences of this view. The doctrine of the sovereignty of Parliament reasserted the exegetical nature of legal studies which we find expressed both in England and also in the United States in the nineteenth century attempts to rationalize and systematize the common law and the corresponding endeavour to concentrate upon the formal features of law – the exact exegesis of the language of the rules – rather than upon issues of the content or value of legal rules.

4.2   TECHNIQUES OF STATUTORY INTERPRETATION

The principal motivating force behind codifications both ancient and modern has generally been seen by the political and legal professions alike as being that of rationalizing and making known the law. The sovereign will or legislative rule is put down in writing with the intention that those affected by or subject to the rule are able to order their affairs and predict their future commitments upon the basis of their understanding of those rules. The code or codification is aimed, in other words, at achieving a high degree of certainty and predictability within the law and it aims to achieve those ends by means of a written language. From first to last the code is a linguistic entity and the interpreters of the law, the legal profession, just as much as the subjects of the law, the citizens, must approach the statutory text and language by means of linguistic techniques of construction and interpretation or reading. Here, however, certain central paradoxes emerge. First and most significantly, it is generally the case that although we are all commanded, in civil- and common-law systems alike, to 'know the law', the language of the law is a specialized, archaic or ancient and frequently impenetrable language. While there are certain notable exceptions to this rule – the *Code Napoléon* as originally drafted or the contemporary East German Penal Code, for instance, are both expressed in a relatively comprehensible non-technical but extremely general language – it is generally the case that modern codes have either collected existing law into a permanent written form or have, in common-law countries, sought to intervene in a piecemeal way in a legal system and body of case-law concepts already expressed in a language peculiarly of the law's own making. The categories and concepts of code and legislation alike form a specialized or technical language and they are to be construed in a highly specific, professionally controlled manner. Neither the enactments themselves nor the exegetical techniques by which they are read and elaborated could be said to be immediately accessible to those unversed in the language or method of the law. Second and perhaps even more curiously, lawyers themselves are not provided with any explicit training in the linguistic techniques or linguistic background to legal analysis. While certain elementary rules of interpretation and certain specific technical legal meanings are part of the common stock of legal knowledge, the bulk of the lawyer's expertise in techniques of reading and in the vocabulary of the law is learnt 'in motion' or in the course of learning the rules of substantive law themselves. It is to the explicit formulation of that language and those techniques that we shall now turn.

4.2.1 *Language*

Even in its most modern expression, legal language is a technical and professional language. A large part of the legal vocabulary has simply to be learnt as a foreign language, as Latin, law French or medieval usages of a national language. The vocabulary of English law, for example, frequently dates back to the thirteenth century and in several areas of common law the basic legal terms for designating legal relations have remained unchanged over the intervening seven centuries. Even where legal language has become a part of everyday language, where the English dictionary contains legal words such as specialty, deed, trespass, obligation and so on, the ordinary usage is frequently incompatible or irrelevant to the legal usage. Thus, for instance, we may use the word trespass to mean wrong-doing generally, intrusion or transgression. In theological terms a trespass is a sin, while to the lawyer a trespass is a very specific kind of unlawful act. In contemporary law it is either trespass to property, a civil wrong, or trespass to the person, a wrong which has its origins in an archaic legal form of action claiming harm done with force and arms (*vi et armis*) against the king's peace. Legally, one can trespass upon land or upon the person; one cannot, for example, trespass upon someone's time, nor can one be prosecuted for a trespass for the simple reason that trespass is a civil wrong and not a crime. More broadly, it can be observed that much of the vocabulary of the law of contract has passed into everyday usage: contract, consideration, privity, misrepresentation, mistake, breach of contract and so on are all words found in the natural language. Each of those words, however, has a highly specific legal meaning and is defined by a large number of legal rules, and even a word as common as obligation has a special legal meaning, that of writing under seal.

Legal language is not ordinary language; it is a language that must be learnt and a language to which special attention must be paid in the construction of legal documents and of statutory texts alike. While problems of vocabulary (the meaning of words and phrases such as 'enfeoff', 'cestui que trust', 'vouch to warranty' and so on) are only part of the problem of legal language, they form a useful starting point for examining the general characteristics of the language of legal texts and the techniques applicable to them. We shall begin by examining the vocabulary (lexicon) of statutes and the techniques relating to literal meaning and shall subsequently proceed to examine further syntactic and grammatical features to legislative language.

4.2.2 *Literalism*

Contemporary legal assumptions as to the nature of language and specifically of statutory language do not differ greatly from the historical attitude towards the language of codes documented earlier in this chapter. The statute is to be seen and construed as the general and permanent representation of legislative intentions. The statutory rule is the final written form of expression of the sovereign will and it is to be interpreted and obeyed as such. Like any sacred or semi-sacred (professional) language, the words of the document or instrument are to be treated as binding and in the first instance it is to the specific words – to the letter of the law – that attention should be paid.

The first technique of statutory construction is that of literalism: the sovereign is assumed to have intended what the text says and equally to have intended the verbal form of that text. In the first instance the words of the statute will be given their *literal* meaning: 'it is to be borne in mind that the office of the Judge is not to legislate but to declare the expressed intention of the Legislature even if that intention appears to the Court to be injudicious' (*River Wear Commissioners* v *Adamson* [1877] 2 AC 743). If a Road Traffic Act states that travelling in excess of 70 miles per hour is to be an offence, travelling at 71 miles per hour constitutes an offence: the literal meaning of 70 m.p.h. being, among other things, *not* 71 m.p.h. Similarly if a rule prohibits passengers from boarding trains accompanied by a dog, it would not be an infraction of the rule to board the train accompanied by a bear. A bear, among other things, is *not* a dog. The point to be made is that, as a general first principle, the law assumes that words have a literal meaning, which is loosely describable as their lexical or dictionary definition. That meaning is a conventional meaning established by usage and it is the first meaning to which statutory words will be referred. If only because literalism is the most frequently cited rule of statutory interpretation, it is worth looking at its linguistic aspects in rather more detail.

We have already seen that a large number of legal words have a highly technical meaning, that they belong to a legal dictionary of meanings rather than to the general or natural vocabulary. Nonetheless, the linguistic problem of lexical or literal meaning applies equally to both dictionary and legal-dictionary meanings. In the broadest of terms, the literal meaning is defined linguistically as its 'value' within the system of lexical meanings (language code) that constitute the basic rules of the language being spoken or written. Two points should be noted. First, the literal meaning is a potential meaning rather than an actual usage; it is a conventional meaning within a system of such meanings (dictionary) rather than an actual use of the word in combination with other words. The dictionary definition of a word is independent of any linguistic or empirical context and is generally a negative definition in the sense of the examples given above; the word is to be differentiated from similar words and indeed from all other words in the form, for example, of male = *not female*. The technical lexical principle of definition does not, however, fully accord with the legal use of literal meanings. The more usual definition of literal meaning is as a correlation or equivalence between a word and its referent, between a phonetic entity (a series of sounds) and the object or idea which that combination of sounds conventionally refers to or represents. Such an equivalence is defined negatively only in the secondary sense that the scope of reference is the strictly lexical meaning of the word: its place within the dictionary or system of lexical rather than actual meanings. What the dictionary supplies is what the word ought to mean which is not necessarily what it gets used as meaning. Second, words do not generally or necessarily have any single literal meaning; they tend, as the dictionary shows, to have several. Words are not normally defined by a single synonym but by reference to several, a feature of the dictionary which illustrates that in terms of usage, the literal meaning will depend upon the context in which it is used. The future tense of the verb 'shall', for example, may have an imperative meaning within a set of instructions, while it is likely to have a predictive meaning in other contexts where it is used as a future tense, and in further contexts still may have a permissive meaning. The point is not simply that general terms in everyday use, common statutory terms such as reasonable, fair, careless and so on, have no very specific literal meaning but rather that no word has a single simple literal meaning except in certain instances in the dictionary itself or more frequently in the mind of the judge.

A literal meaning is, at the end of the day, always an interpretative meaning. A selection or choice has to be made – consciously or unconsciously – to prefer one of several possible literal meanings in the context of the phrase or clause or statutory rule to be interpreted. In legal terms it is only possible to suggest certain guidelines as to the manner in which literal meanings are established. There are no general rules of standard application at the level of the lexicon but there are a limited number of 'internal aids' to literal interpretation and also certain regularities of practice. Of the regularities of practice it is a reasonable generalization to say that the court will look favourably upon the etymology of words, their derivation from Greek, Latin, French or Anglo-Saxon. The modern use of the word may not accord with its derivation but possible meanings or extensions can be restricted by the etymology of the word: the word 'ethnic' in the Race Relations Act 1976, for example, comes from the Greek 'ethnos' whose most basic meaning is 'group'. In the light of that derivation the word should not be extended to include the definition of a group by reference to specific racial characteristics (*Mandla* v *Dowell Lee* [1983] 1 AER 1062, 1067).

The last point raises another general principle, that which restricts the extension of general terms; the court will not in general interpret a word in a statute as including more than its primary reference or denotative meaning. To some extent the reason for this is historical as well as doctrinal. The courts have frequently expressed a willingness to limit the scope and force of statutory rules, as for instance in the words of Winn LJ in *Allen* v *Thorn Electrical Industries* [1968] 1 QB 487 at 507:

I must reject as quite untenable any submission that, if in any case one finds a) that a statute is worded ambiguously in any particular respect, and b) finds also clear indications *aliunde* that Parliament intended that they should have the strictest and most stringent meaning possible, the court is therefore compelled to construe the section in the sense in which Parliament would have desired it to take effect, by giving the words their most stringent possible meaning. On the contrary I think the right view is, and as I understand it always has been, that in such a case of ambiguity, it is resolved in such a way as to make the statute less onerous for the general public and so to cause less interference, than the more stringent sense would, with such rights and liberties as existing contractual obligations.

Several of the 'internal aids' to construction provide a less extreme means to this effect of literalism and although they are strictly speaking syntactic and semantic rules, they are lexical in their outcome or effect. The rule *expressio unius est exclusio alterius* (to state one thing is to exclude others) effectively limits the meaning of a word to the thing or category named and silently (or by implication) excludes all other potential references and extensions. Similarly, authority can also be found in terms of the rule *ejusdem generis* (things of the same class) for the construction of the meaning of general words in a restrictive manner where the general words follow on a list of particular words. The general word is limited in meaning to the same class or type of thing as the preceding list; 'cars, vans, lorries and other *vehicles*' would be limited to vehicles of the kind illustrated in the preceding list and would be unlikely to include either bicycles, ships or airplanes although the latter are certainly vehicles. While it would be possible to give other examples of restrictive rules most explicitly formulated in common-law systems of statutory interpretation, the point to be made is that where possible the law will select a narrow, 'intensional', meaning of a word. The 'intensional' meaning refers to the lexical meaning of a term viewed as being defined by the meanings which it excludes – that residual meaning which differentiates the word from other words within the lexicon or dictionary is thus taken as the primary or literal meaning.

The rules of literal construction are persuasive rather than authoritative and we have indicated that the sense in which a word actually has *a* literal meaning is linguistically dubious. For reasons of which the law is well aware, the problem of the meaning of statutory words is seldom satisfactorily solved by recourse to literal meaning alone. The problems normally revolve around the context in which words are used and a primary observation to be made is that the immediate context is a legal one and that the important meanings are legal meanings. Here we encounter the fact already mentioned that the great number of everyday terms in legal use have a specific and special legal meaning and that this technical meaning will be privileged or preferred in most cases. The literal meaning of a legal word or 'term of art' is quite simply that meaning which has been established by legal authority. We earlier used the examples of trespass, obligation and contract. Of other possible examples dramatic instances are to be found in the interpretation of the 1919 Sex Disqualification Removal Act or the 1959 Restriction of Offensive Weapons Act. In the former case a question arose as to the meaning of the term 'disqualification' in s. 1 (i) of the 1919 Act which stated that no one shall be disqualified on grounds of sex or marriage from the exercise of any public office or function. A woman who in her own right inherited a peerage but was not invited (issued a writ) to sit in the House of Lords brought an action under s. 1 (i) but failed because the legal meaning of the term disqualification was held to be suspension of a right; one could only be disqualified from something or some activity to which one had a potential right. A woman, the court declared, was a woman for the entirety of her natural life and so could not be regarded as being disqualified from a public function which women had never had a right to exercise (*Viscountess Rhondda's Claim* [1922] 2 AC 389). More simply, in the 1959 Act the words 'offer for sale' had a strict contractual meaning which excluded 'displaying' an offensive weapon in a shop window from being an 'offer for sale' within the meaning of the Act (*Fisher* v *Bell* [1961] 1 QB 394).

The meaning of a word within the legal dictionary is primarily to be treated in terms of legal etymology – the legal derivation of the meaning of a word. In the case of both natural and legal etymologies a number of further techniques of construction are necessary and take the form of a progressive set of contextualizing techniques. If the literal meaning of a term is not definitive of its meaning – if legal common sense fails to prescribe a literal meaning – then it is necessary to draw upon a series of further stages of linguistic construction, upon syntax, grammar, rhetorical reference, register and finally legislative intention or intended meaning. Each of these categories may be briefly elaborated.

4.2.3 *Syntax*

Syntax aids construction by looking beyond the lexical meaning of a word to its meaning within a sentence and specifically within the correct construction of the sentence according to the basic rules of syntax and grammar. Little need be said as to the use of syntax save that it is frequently referred to and utilized as a secondary step in construction. The place or role of the word or phrase in the sentence in which it is used is analysed for the purpose of ascertaining its likely import: is it the subject of the sentence? What part of speech is it – noun, verb, adjective, conjunction and so on? What form of clause is the word found in? The questions asked are not linguistically sophisticated nor do they generally take account of contemporary work in other disciplines, particularly in linguistics, literary criticism and communication studies, where very detailed research on the lexical and syntactic forms of discourse has been carried out recently with especial reference to the various species of linguistic co-reference phenomena or 'intradiscourse'. On occasion indeed, the judiciary explicitly reject too great a degree of linguistic sophistication in relation to the construction of legal meanings.

> I protest against subjecting the English language and more particularly a simple English phrase to this kind of philology and semasiology, English words derive their colour from those which surround them. Sentences are not mere collections of words to be taken out of the sentence, defined separately by reference to a dictionary or decided cases and then put back again into the sentence with the meaning which you have assigned to them as separate words, so as to give the sentence or phrase a meaning which as a sentence or phrase it cannot bear without distortion of the English language. That one must construe a word or phrase in the setting of an Act of Parliament with all the assistance one can from decided cases and if one will from a dictionary, is not in doubt; but having obtained all that assistance one must not at the end of the day distort that which has to be construed and give it a meaning which in its context one does not think it can possibly bear. (*Bourne* v *Norwich Crematorium* [1967] 2 AER 376)

Leaving aside the judicial dismissal of philological and semiotic techniques of linguistic analysis which are precisely designed to facilitate the reading of the word in its linguistic and discursive contexts, it seems true to say that legal analysis stops with the syntactic rule of *noscitur a sociis*, the rule meaning simply that words take their 'colour' from their surroundings. Generally this is taken to mean that the word to be construed is analysed by reference to surrounding words rather than in terms of those more specific syntactic relations which linguists have analysed in terms of co-reference, cohesion, progression and localization. The word 'economic', for instance, in a provision requiring an 'integrated, efficient and economic transport facility' in a 1969 Transport Act would in principle be read in *conjunction* with the words integrated and efficient (*Bromley London Borough Council* v *Greater London Council* [1982] 2 WLR 62). A similar example can be taken from a Refreshment Houses Act of 1860 which states that 'all houses, rooms, shops or buildings kept open for public refreshment, resort and entertainment' during certain hours of the night were for legal purposes deemed to be refreshment houses and required a licence. The defendant owned premises called 'The Cafe' which opened during the stated hours and sold coffee, cigars and ginger beer. The owner did not have a licence. Blackburn J stated: 'the word public must be read with each of the three words that follow it . . . I do not think that entertainment need be something in the nature of refreshment. It is rather the correlative of resort – the reception and accommodation of the public who resort to the place in question' (*Muir* v *Keay* [1875] LR 10 QB 594). While the judiciary may on occasion rise to the heights of analysing noun clauses or of restricting the scope of reference of specific adjectival clauses, no real attempt is made to analyse the frequently peculiar syntax of legislative drafting. Generally the purpose of recourse to syntactic rules is that of creating a literal meaning: an agreed or unitary meaning is produced by reducing highly complex and repetitious syntactic constructions to univocality or singularity of meaning. Most broadly, such constructions are made to appear legitimate or acceptable by virtue of the use of particular forms of modality; modal auxiliaries (might, could, can, etc.), adjectives expressing certainty, and particularly verbs expressing mental or logical processes (seems that, thinks that, is evident that) are used to complement in an interpretative manner statutory constructions that are, in modal terms, predominantly imperative and axiomatic.

4.2.4 *Grammar*

Where syntactic construction fails to produce an adequate solution to the meaning of a word or rule a further technique to be called into aid is that which might be termed recourse to legal grammar. The legal technique of grammatical construction does not correspond to the linguistic sense of grammar simply meaning syntax. In terms of statutory construction the grammar referred to is that of the Act or legislative text as a whole. Grammatical technique refers to the attempt to make the whole text (viewed as a set of rules) consistent or grammatical in the sense of logically coherent. A word or phrase in a statutory provision may well refer to or be repeated in other sections of the enactment and the grammatical reading of that phrase or word will be one which produces a single meaning for *all* the instances where the word or phrase occurs. The technique is one which we earlier designated that of unity of meaning, such that a correct understanding or interpretation of the text is one which produces concordances, that is a reading which will control and regulate the text internally, that will produce a unity of meaning within the code and reaffirm the essentially authoritative character of the text as a harmonious set of rules.

In the above sense of grammatical technique it may be observed first that the statute will on occasion provide explicit instructions as to how it should be read. The Preamble to the Act, the long title, cross-headings and statutory definitions of terms within the enactment itself, may all be turned to as legitimate aids to construction of the meaning of a word or phrase in the legislative provisions of the code. The reasoning behind such recourse is simply that where the legislature expressly states the intention or purpose of the enactment it would be foolish to ignore such a statement of intent. Such a principle does not, however, extend to any of the non-statutory indications of the sovereign intention. The English court is not entitled to look to the reports of Parliamentary debates on legislative provisions, the reports of Hansard, for the reason that these essentially political facets to the legislation are extrinsic to the Act itself and would in all probability throw doubt upon the assumed univocality if not upon the rationality of the sovereign. At the same time, however, it is necessary to observe that the judicial interpreters of the statute will have a more general access to the climate of political debate surrounding contemporary legislation and even where this is not taken into account by means of reference to academic or literary sources which discuss such issues, it would be surprising if the general political atmosphere surrounding an enactment were not to affect the court either consciously or unconsciously. As we shall observe later, however, the ability of the court to assess the political intentions behind a piece of legislation is more a facet of doctrinal assumptions and allegiances than it is of any real or empirical assessment of the legislature's reasons and intentions.

Finally, where explicit aids to grammatical construction are not available, grammatical technique is to be understood in the broader sense of logical coherence. The whole text is presumed to be reducible to a rational or unitary propositional content. The logic involved and the propositions produced are not here governed by any account of the actual sovereign or legislative intention; they are rather the outcome of doctrinal consider- ations. The law – conceived as the sum total of existing legal rules – has generally to be viewed as the embodiment of a peculiarly legal form of rationality. Grammatical construction is not philosophy of law and legal interpretation generally pursues – at this stage of construction – an internal logic to specific bodies of legal rules. Separate provisions dealing with similar subject-matter must be interpreted together in such a manner as will result in a satisfactory and coherent meaning for both or all instances of a word or phrase or rule. The specific logic involved is hard to characterize for the simple reason that it is not used consistently or systematically. It is not a technical philosophical logic (deontic, semiotic or other) and it would seem to be most accurately described as a concern with presupposition, implication and reference – the last term being taken to mean both scope of reference (extension) and technical legal context of reference (intension/ associative field). An interesting example can be taken from an 1889 case governing the interpretation of an 1882 statute. By section 63 of the Act: 'for all purposes connected with . . . the right to vote at municipal elections words in this Act importing the masculine gender include women.' By section 11 (3): 'every person shall be qualified to be elected and to be a councillor who is, at the time in question, qualified to elect to the office of councillor.' Taken together or read grammatically it was held that the reference of s. 63 is 'voting' and consequently the word 'person' in s. 11 (3) should retain its traditional legal meaning, that of male person, and women were consequently held not to be qualified under the Act to be elected councillors (*Beresford Hope* v *Lady Sandhurst* [1889] 23 QB 79). Syntactic and grammatical techniques of reading were used together to restrict the meaning of the Act to an extremely narrow or literal one, an artistic meaning which coincidentally reaffirmed the much-litigated Victorian social principle of viewing women as lesser beings than males.

4.2.5 *Rhetorical reference (register)*

A technique of construction or interpretation which is often given greater weight than is acknowledged is that of rhetorical reference: the analysis of the meaning of words by reference to their intended audience. In common-sense terms it is obvious that if a speaker is addressing a French-speaking audience it is best to speak in French. On the face of it, it is appropriate, in other words, to take account of the language group to which the audience belongs and also, in rhetorical terms, to take account of the likely beliefs and attitudes that such a group will have. For instance, it would be difficult to praise the economic and political organization of Soviet Russia or communist China if speaking to an American audience. To take the matter further, however, rhetoricians and sociologists of language accept the fact that even within a national language there are numerous different speech-communities or categories of audience. The national language is *heteroglot* or stratified: different social, ethnic and generational groups have different vocabularies and different semantic fields and linguistic studies suggest that the range of potential expression and comprehension varies as between such groups. First, a national language is divided into social dialects:

> The internal stratification of any single national language into social dialects, characteristic group behaviour, professional jargons, generic languages, languages of generations and age groups, tendentious languages, languages of the authorities, of various circles and passing fashions, languages that serve the specific socio-political purposes of the day, even of the hour (each day has its own slogan, its own vocabulary, its own emphases) – this internal stratification [is] present in every language at any given moment of its historical existence. (Bakhtin, 1981, p. 259)

Second, each social dialect can be defined as a register of the national language, that is, defined in terms of its semantic content. A dialect is primarily a phonetic and lexical stratification of a language but it is also a pragmatic and semantic level of the language: socio-linguistic groups can be differentiated in terms of their specific semantic range, their shared knowledge, attitudes and beliefs and these should be referred to or kept in mind when evaluating the meaning of a language or discourse for those groups.

The legal construction of the meaning of a piece of legislation frequently takes into account the register or audience which the legislation is aimed at or intended for. So far as the interpretation of a statute is concerned, the range of audiences or registers extends from that of the legal institution itself through various other professional and technical languages to ordinary language or the putatively universal audience of common sense. The way in which the judiciary construe these audiences and the extent of their reference to them varies over time. In recent years, for example, explicit reference to the religious meanings of terms or acts (deeds) referred to in legislative provisions has tended to decrease while there has been a greater acceptance of psychiatric evidence of terms and meanings relating to mental processes and responsibility for acts. The categories and the content of audiences and registers change over time but it is possible briefly to list and comment upon the various groupings of registers.

(i) *The legal audience.* The most obvious, frequent and socio-linguistically the most powerful of audiences is that of the law itself, or more particularly the various strata of officials of the legal system. The law has a virtually unlimited capacity for and strong economic interest in rewriting language and speech in a legal register. The legal audience is the primary audience for all legislation in the sense that it is the legal profession which interprets and applies the law with the aid of the various law-enforcement agencies. What a piece of legislation means is in the final analysis always a question of what it means for the legal profession and specifically its most elite branch, the judiciary. In a sense such a principle is even true of the interpretations of legislative language which are referred to other audiences and particularly those of the national language itself. Reference to the ordinary or natural meaning of a word tends, as we have already seen, to be intuitive or introspective: in deciding what a general word such as 'reasonable' means the court will often refer to everyday perceptions of reasonableness but will not substantiate the actual meaning of the word in the various social registers. The judiciary are 'armchair' linguists and the common-sense meaning of a term will be a reference more to the common sense of the judge interpreting it than to any extraneously existent common-sense or 'ordinary' meaning. The legal register, in other words, is a restricted, atypical and professionalized register and there is little reason to suppose that it is socio-linguistically representative; while the judiciary may occasionally express the pious hope that the law is intelligible to the non-lawyer (Paterson, 1982), the better view is expressed in a work of semi-doctrinal authority: 'the reality of the situation is that a great proportion of ordinary citizens – perhaps a majority – have no general conception of the legal structure or of its criteria of validity' (Hart, 1962, p. 111). In other words, the primary legal audience is composed of lawyers and legal officials; it is they who in the first instance must obey and apply the law, and it is reasonable to suppose that the law is to a large extent formulated to that end; 'the lawyers' characteristic and specific practice is *translation* into a discourse which they both use and create' (Dingwall and Lewis, 1983, p. 129).

Reference to the legal audience also has a more specific meaning or role. The legal audience takes the form of other legislative provisions dealing with the same or similar subject-matter, texts *in pari materia* to the word or provision being interpreted, and also previously decided cases on the provision in question or on those *in pari materia*. Both such techniques of interpretation recognize that legislation is always an intervention into an existing system of law or code and they seek, by looking at the legal effects of an enactment upon existing law, to produce a coherence or unity of meaning between the restatement or reform of the law given in the Act and the prior system of rules. The statute is always to be viewed as part of a larger unity, that of the written law as a whole, and the techniques used to construct the statute itself will frequently recognize the need to account for and to systematize the legal effects of the new law and will generally only recognize fundamental changes in the existing law where these are expressly made in the new legislation. Finally, the techniques taken together form a large part of what is known as the Mischief Rule, the rule that when a provision is ambiguous or obscure and cannot be satisfactorily construed by reference to its literal meaning nor by reference to syntactic or grammatical aids to construction, then the court is free to look at the mischief which the provision is intended to eradicate. The mischief in question is broadly to be taken as a legal mischief, as a gap or conflict, ambiguity or irrationality in the prior law rather than as an empirical defect in the operation or application of the legal rules affected.

The rule that statutes *in pari materia*, statutes dealing with similar subject-matter, be construed together, is well established. It is based on the doctrinal assumption that the sovereign cannot make mutually incompatible commands or statements. There has, in other words, to be a propositional unity of meaning as between different legislative rules and it is the task or 'art' of statutory interpretation to discover this unity or coherence. Linguistically the most interesting feature to this technique is that it assumes not only the rationality of the legislator but also a unity of intention or meaning over time. The law is always to be treated as an existent system, as a coherent system or harmonious body of rules existing together as a unity at any given moment in time. The law or code as a whole is to be construed synchronically rather than diachronically, logically rather than historically, and this requires that as a general rule previous usage or conventionally established meaning will determine present forms of meaning unless there are strong reasons to the contrary. Similarly, previously decided cases determinative of the meaning of a statutory provision will be binding upon the later court construing that same provision or similar provisions.

(ii) *Professional and technical registers.* The common-law tradition has always recognized customary practice as an important aid in determining the meaning and application of legal rules that affect the practice. For example, a contract between specialist traders in chemical products will, where terms of the contract are ambiguous and need to be interpreted, be construed in the light of the normal practice or standard form of transaction *within that trade.* In *Geo Mitchell Ltd* v *Finney Lock* [1983] 2 AC 803, for example, the contract to be interpreted by the court related to the sale of seed cabbages. The question before the court was whether a specific exemption clause in the contract was 'reasonable and fair' as originally required by s. 11 of the Unfair Contract Terms Act 1977. The 'reasonableness' of the exclusion term was to be determined by reference to the trade in which the clause was operative and Lord Bridge concluded that the 'evidence indicated a clear recognition by seedsmen in general, and the appellants in particular, that reliance on the limitation of liability imposed by the relevant condition would not be fair or reasonable.' The law will accept specialist evidence on customary meanings and practices relevant to recognized trades. Similarly, in construing statutes which are designed to regulate specialized activities the court accepts the standard meaning of terms within the social register or specialist language of the profession concerned to be the 'true' meaning. It is assumed that in drafting a piece of legislation intended to affect or alter the rules relating to a specialized activity, it is the technical language of the intended audience, of those directly affected, which will determine the meaning of the words and language used in the statute. As noted earlier, in looking at the linguistic register of a piece of legislation the view of the court construing the legislative provisions as to what constitutes a specialized register or indeed as to what weight ought to be allowed to that register changes over time. New professions and new trades emerge and are slowly recognized by the law as expert endeavours, but the point to be stressed is that such new languages or linguistic registers are not accepted instantaneously and are sometimes not accepted at all. The issue is interestingly commented upon in the case of *McLoughlin* v *O'Brian* [1982] 2 AER 298, 311–12, where Lord Bridge observes, in the context of a case concerning negligently caused psychiatric damage to the plaintiff (nervous shock), that 'for too long earlier generations of judges have regarded psychiatry and psychiatrists with suspicion, if not hostility . . . Now, I venture to hope, that attitude has quite disappeared', although he admits that 'it is in relatively recent times that these insights have come to be generally accepted by the judiciary' and judges should now, wherever relevant, accept psychiatric evidence 'as to the degree of probability that the particular cause would produce the particular effect'. In a comparable fashion, professional and technical languages also fall into disuse and it would be illogical to suppose that statutory construction would not recognize such disuse or desuetude.

(iii) *Ordinary language.* The command to know the law or the maxim that ignorance of the law is no defence to civil or criminal liability has a linguistic correlate in the construction of statutory provisions. Where general words are used in a statute or, more importantly, where a statute is intended to be of general effect and is designed to regulate everyday activities, then the language of the Act will be interpreted as common or ordinary language. The logic behind this interpretative rule is simply that if 'ordinary' people are affected by the Act then the language of the Act itself should, where possible, be given its ordinary meaning. In linguistic terms, however, this assumption is a debatable one: it is neither an accurate description of the practice of modern legislation and codes, nor is it a linguistically justifiable approach to statutory provisions; it is rather a common-sense justificatory argument which lacks any very clear linguistic substance or support.

The argument concerning ordinary meaning is descriptively inaccurate. The point is one of simple observation; the practice of contemporary legislative drafting is immensely complicated and it is simply untrue that generally effective provisions are comprehensible to the major portion of the population. The reasons underlying such a statement are numerous. The vast majority of the population do not know where to find the law, neither is it likely that if they did have access to the statutory instruments they would be able accurately to assess the legal meaning of a contemporary statute, irrespective of its intended audience. At the end of the day, statutes are addressed to lawyers or on occasion to other professional bodies but hardly ever to the general populace. To understand even such generally applicable legislation as that concerning theft or taxation is a notoriously complex professional task and is not always even particularly easy for lawyers or the judiciary themselves. These statutes are drafted in a professional register, they are frequently litigated and amended, and even in the case of seemingly simple provisions their proper interpretation requires a knowledge of prior law, principles of interpretation and legal procedure generally. Such knowledge is by definition professional knowledge; it is not generally available and the task of the professional bodies is precisely that of translating legal language into ordinary language, for which task they are richly rewarded.

When judges refer to the need for general provisions to be interpreted in terms of ordinary meaning they are best understood as putting forward a prescriptive argument as to what the wording *ought* to mean; they are certainly not describing any actual meaning as far as the statute itself is concerned. Even in prescriptive terms, however, the argument is a dubious one. First, it is dubious because it fails to recognize the specifically legal register of statutory language as practised, a language which even in its simplest forms is frequently archaic, specialized in its use of categories and concepts and finally, peculiar in its syntactic and semantic forms: statutory drafting is repetitious, prolix (lengthy and exhaustive) and frequently indexical. Indexicality refers to the sense in which any given provision of an Act is likely to assume or refer to other provisions and the Act as a whole. As has been seen, it is only infrequently that a legislative provision can be taken in itself as a singular rule. It is more usually the case that the word or phrase or rule to be interpreted will imply other aspects of the code. Linguistically we may observe further that the associative field, the connotations and synonyms of legal terms, are not those of other registers of the natural language and again it must be pointed out that they require a specialist knowledge for their interpretation. Second, it is socio-linguistically and indeed rhetorically dubious to assume that there is any single ordinary register or common and 'true' meaning of words. We refer here to the earlier argument that words do not have a literal or ordinary meaning: the sociology of language clearly indicates that no two forms of ordinary usage are the same; there are as many social registers and as many differing usages as there are independently definable social groups within any given national language. It is simply untrue to assert that there is a single standard, correct or true usage. Standard English, for example, is generally definable simply as the register of an economically, ethnically and sexually dominant group within English political society, a language register which may seem 'ordinary' or 'natural' to the legal profession but is in fact restricted to a limited number of groups within the society as a whole (Morley, 1980). Finally, we would stress that even though the recourse to 'ordinary' meaning is linguistically contestable, it is nonetheless a technique that is frequently invoked by the interpreters of statutes and can be simply understood and utilized as a reference to the common sense and standard English of the judiciary itself.

(iv) *Factual contexts*. A final brief but extremely important context to the interpretation of statutory language is an empirical one. The language of the Act, for legal purposes, only becomes the object of explicit interpretative techniques when litigation under the Act comes before the courts. Much of what has been said previously must be looked at in the light of, or subject to, the rider that the language of legislative provisions is only ever interpreted on the basis of its application to a particular set of facts. The point is not quite as obvious as it might at first sight seem: what are regarded as relevant are the legally abstracted facts of the case before the court and the manner of fact-finding or of the *instancing* of the case at law are again considerably more technical than commonsensical. A whole series of assumptions and devices is to be attached to the legal instancing of a decision and the facts thus discovered by the court are highly relevant to the meaning attributed to any particular provision. As we shall have occasion to look at this issue in greater detail in the next chapter, it is sufficient merely to note the existence of this problem. It affects statutory interpretation in a manner comparable to its role within the system of precedent: the legal facts of a case are normative generalizations abstracted from the empirical details of the dispute or allegation. In general terms, for example, a dispute between an individual and a multinational company is to be instanced in terms of legally relevant rights and duties. The law does not in general examine the human or social characteristics of the dispute but rather looks at the relevant legal categories involved. It is not a singular and unique individual, a person with a biography and with a specific class and gender, ethnic background and psychological characteristics with whom the court is concerned, but rather a consumer with the rights and duties obtaining to all consumers. Similarly, the company involved is viewed as a corporate legal subject and a manufacturer; the law will not analyse the economic and social status and political role of the company but simply its generic characteristics. In such circumstances it may be observed that a major part of the interpretative task of construing statutory provisions takes the form of the legal designation of the facts of the case. The instancing of the case is a rhetorically charged process; the categories under which the actors in a dispute are subsumed play an important part in the outcome of the dispute itself – the meaning given to the legislative provision (Goodrich, 1984, p. 194 ff).

4.3 CONCLUSION: DOCTRINE AND STATUTORY MEANING

We have used the term doctrine as a reference to a clearly definable set of legal beliefs as to the nature and characteristics of legal meaning. In general terms, legal doctrine is that set of prior adherences or allegiances that constitute the legal code as validated discourse. Doctrine assumes certain 'truths' as to legally authoritative utterances, truths as to the sources and methods and content of legal statements. With regard to statutory texts we have argued that their authoritative status has a historical basis in the exegetical tradition of religious and later legal codifications, in which the sovereign will is represented in the permanent written form of the code and later the statute. The word of the statutory text was originally conceived to be the divine word and later became the word of reason, a language which was assumed, for doctrinal purposes, to be rational and imperative. The statutory text is first and foremost to be understood so as to be obeyed, and the techniques of statutory interpretation work so as to secure the doctrinal requirement of obedience and to make this submission appear reasonable and justified.

More than anything else, the techniques here elicited and analysed work to the effect of making the legislative will appear logical and reasonable, impersonal and impartial. They work to create the image of the *rule of law*, an image of justice under the law in which the application of the statutory text is to be seen as the literal or the logical consequence of the language of its expression. What we have further suggested is that the basis of that image is open to question or to doubt. At the level of doctrine and of technique the linguistic assumptions of exegesis are peculiar or specific to the social registers of religious and legal institutions. While we would not argue that legal training or education – the acquisition of linguistic competence in the reading of legal texts – necessarily requires a detailed knowledge of legal doctrine or of beliefs underlying the techniques of interpretative construction, we would argue that doctrinal considerations are the necessary basis of the techniques analysed and further that it is only possible fully to understand the method of legal textual practice by looking further at doctrinal factors. To comprehend the role of legal doctrine is to read the law more closely and more critically than would otherwise be the case and it consequently seems appropriate to present in conclusion two further considerations of doctrine as it affects technique.

4.3.1   *The decision to interpret*

In discussing the history and general characteristics of the code within the western legal tradition we have on several occasions observed that the authoritative status of the statutory text is closely allied to the doctrinal assumption that the code forms a rational unity. In general terms this unity and rationality of the code – the belief that it forms a complete and coherent statement of the law – lies at the basis both of the literal approach to legal language and of the techniques of interpretation that seek, by lexical, syntactic, grammatical and rhetorical means to render the statute univocal or singular in its meaning. The function of the reader or the judge in relation to the statutory text is one of obedience rather than of evaluation or choice – the law is written so that it may be found and applied. Following the consequences of this approach, it may be observed that when techniques of interpretation are resorted to by the judiciary they are primarily techniques that are internal to the statute viewed as a code and a genre with specific rules of its own. The principle is one which may be described as that of *legal pertinence*: the decision to interpret is triggered by the assumption that anything the sovereign has stated in the written legal form of the statute is rational and relevant to the regulation of legal disputes or prosecutions. Where, however, this pertinence is not immediately apparent, some manipulation of the language of the statement or provision may be necessary to discover its 'true' or underlying meaning – the meaning which legal doctrine requires that it be given, and which it will, if necessary, actively create under the various guises of 'faithful' interpretation. While strictly exegetical approaches to the legal text have frequently denied that interpretation is ever necessary – no matter how absurd the consequences of the statutory rule it must nonetheless be applied – there is also a lengthy history to an apparently contradictory view, which admits that it may on occasion be necessary to look behind the words of the statute to find the real intentions or rationale for a particular statement.

The rule referred to earlier as the Mischief Rule is best described as allowing for interpretative recourse to the sovereign's intended meaning where the literal construction of the rule is absurd in its effects. The decision to interpret is here seemingly triggered by the desire to take account of the extra-linguistic or extra-textual consequences of a rule, but if it is examined closely it is clear that this rule does not in fact look outside the legal text but rather subjects the text to a concept of *doctrinal implausibility*. The view that a facet of the statutory text is absurd does not connote a critical evaluation of the text from outside the legal textual culture and professional competence, but rather invokes the categories of legal doctrine, of the rationality and justice of the law, to secure an acceptable meaning for the text within the wider legal genre to which it belongs. Recourse to the intended meaning of the utterance, to what it meant to say rather than to what it did (apparently) say, does not break the contract between legal speaker (sovereign) and legal reader (judge). The intentions are not actual intentions but rather they are normative intentions; they are confrontations between the literal text and legal doctrine as the text of interpretative rules. The isolation of the legal code is not threatened but is rather confirmed.

4.3.2   *The isolation of the code*

In the last analysis, professional expertise in the legal reading of statutory texts is comprised precisely of the ability to separate questions of legal meaning from wider questions of the value, utility or effects of legal rules, questions of the social and political import of the legislative text and the mode of its application. Doctrine teaches that the law is rational, logical and desirable and the contract underlying the legal genre, that between legal speaker and legal audience, between text and reading, is the agreement that the symbolism of rationality and justice remains unchallenged by any extrinsic factors, by any examination or questioning of the code in its context, in its non-normative and extra-textual dimensions and effects. While this contract between government and its legal arm is occasionally broken, the overwhelming weight of legal doctrine as well as of explicit legal authority continues to support it.

The isolation of the code is first a temporal phenomenon: the law is to be treated as a system of norms, as a synchronic object of study having a complete and consistent existence at any one moment in time. Generally, there is no historical dimension to the law in force: provided the rules pass the legal institutions' tests of validity they are thenceforward unquestionable in terms of their genesis or origin. What is presupposed, in other words, is the unity of the sovereign intention over time – the unchanging reason of the legislative will. The presumption of rationality over time cannot be challenged in terms of extra-legal considerations although certain internal legal rules relating to disuse or desuetude do exist, at least nominally, in most systems. In particular the maxim *cessante ratione cessat ipsa lex*, which is taken to mean that a rule of law which has lost its underlying rationale is itself no longer a valid rule of law, is occasionally invoked to resist the application of a statutory rule which, by virtue of its origin, can no longer be given effect without inconsistency or conflict with more recent provisions or rules. The principle is not, however, a substantive one; it is normally used, if at all, to challenge procedural and formal aspects to the rule and its application, its relation to or role within the isolated code.

Finally, a more explicit doctrinal significance is to be attributed to the isolation of the code from other discourses and particularly from political influence or interest. The principle of the separation of powers, the separation of law from politics, will be encountered in more explicit and interesting forms in the subsequent chapters. As regards the interpretation of statutes, the independence of the judiciary is an axiomatic and incontestable doctrinal requirement. The techniques by which the judge pronounces the law as the will of the sovereign are based upon the ascription of authority first to the statutory text and second and importantly to the subordinate sovereignty of the judge. In the end the construction of statutes devolves upon the authority of the judge and it is with consideration of the status and role of the judiciary that the next chapter will be concerned.

REFERENCES AND FURTHER READING

Augustine, St: *On Christian Doctrine* (ed. Robertson) 1958. Liberal Arts Press. Indianapolis.
Bakhtin, M. 1981: *The Dialogic Imagination*. Austin, Texas.
Berman, H. 1977: 'The origins of western legal science'. 90 *Harvard Law Review* 894.
Berman, H. 1983: *Law and Revolution*. Cambridge, Mass.
Dawson, J. 1968: *The Oracles of the Law*. Ann Arbor, Michigan.
Dingwall, R. and Lewis, P. 1983: *The Sociology of the Professions*. London.
Eco, U. 1984: *Semiotics and the Philosophy of Language*. London.
Foucault, M. 1976: *The Birth of the Clinic*. Tavistock, Devon.
Franklin, J. 1966: *Jean Bodin*. New York.
Goodrich, P. 1984: 'Law and language'. 11 *Journal of Law and Society* 173.
Goodrich, P. 1985: in B. S. Jackson and D. Carzo (eds) *Semiotics, Law and Social Science*. Gangemi Editore, Rome.
Halliday, M.A.K. 1978: *Language as Social Semiotic*. London.
Hart, H. 1962: *The Concept of Law*. Oxford.
Hayes, J. and Holladay, C. 1982: *Biblical Exegesis*. London.
Morley, D. 1980: *The Nationwide Audience*. London.
Ong, W. 1958: *Ramus: Method and the Decay of Dialogue*. Cambridge, Mass.
Paterson, A. 1982: *The Law Lords*. London.
Perelman, C. 1976: *Logique Juridique; Nouvelle Rhetorique*. Dalloz, Paris.
Robinson, O. 1985: *European Legal History*. Abingdon.
Stein, P. 1966: *Regulae Iuris*. Edinburgh.
Ullmann, W. 1946: *The Medieval Idea of Law*. London.
Ullmann, W. 1975: *Law and Politics in the Middle Ages*. London.
Vinogradoff, P. 1929: *Roman Law in Medieval Europe*. Oxford.
Watson, A. 1981: *The Making of the Civil Law*. Cambridge, Mass.

5

Hermeneutics:
Precedent and Interpretation

> If law be a science, and really deserve so sublime a name, it must be founded on and claim an exalted rank in the empire of *reason*; but if it be merely an unconnected series of decrees and ordinances, its use may remain, though its dignity is lessened, and he will become the greatest lawyer who has the strongest habitual, or artificial *memory*.
>
> (Sir William Jones, 1781)

5.1 INTRODUCTION

It was an organizing theme of the previous chapter that one can only fully understand the way in which lawyers and courts approach and apply statutory texts by looking at the lengthy history of religious and legal codifications. The techniques of statutory interpretation, just as much in common-law as in civil-law jurisdictions, are ultimately to be understood in terms of an exegetical concept of legal method or legal reading which has its origins in biblical law and, somewhat later, in the development of western legal science around the reception of the *Corpus Iuris Civilis* in twelfth-century Italy. In terms of contemporary techniques of statutory interpretation there are differences of style, emphasis and of degree between the common-law and civil-law traditions but the hierarchical status and mode of application of the codified text are fundamentally comparable within the two systems. When it comes to case law and to the concept or system of precedent, however, it is generally supposed that the differences between civilian and common-law systems of legal regulation are extensive, qualitative and in all probability absolute. In dear insular England the legal profession has long been jealously protective and fiercely proud of the independence and uniqueness of the common law. While the past century and a half may have witnessed a massive increase in the quality and scope of legislative rules and may also have seen a distinct restriction in the constitutional role of the judiciary and thus in the concept of the rule of law, it is still often argued that the common-law system as a whole is the unique historical achievement of an extremely small legal elite – the English judiciary. It will be one of the principal arguments of the present and subsequent chapters that while there are certainly a number of important distinguishing features to the common-law system of precedent, it is neither historically nor conceptually accurate to view it simply as an isolated or discrete national legal achievement. The case-law techniques developed over several centuries of Anglo-American legal experience are historically considerably more diverse and conceptually much broader than the claim to uniqueness or insularity would allow. A brief outline of these two arguments – historical and conceptual – will form the introduction to the analysis of the discursive techniques relevant to the construction and application of precedent, techniques which will be grouped in the present chapter under the label of *hermeneutics*, and in the subsequent chapter under that of *rhetoric*.

5.1.1 *Historical context*

First, the historical context of precedent. In its broadest sense the term 'precedent' means 'something which goes before' and as legal precedent it refers to the priority of previous decisions over the judgment of the contemporary instance of dispute or accusation. In this early, general, sense precedent is the privileging of the past over the present, a respect for continuity or tradition as justifications for the exercise of religious, political or legal power. Thus defined, precedent plays a role within all of the classical and medieval western legal traditions. Even where the law is predominantly oral and unwritten – in pre-classical Greece, in the early Roman Republic or in pre-Renaissance Europe – those responsible for taking decisions or arriving at judgments would almost invariably invoke pre-existent rules and principles. In early Germanic law, for instance:

> When a case arises for which no valid law can be adduced, then the lawful men or doomsmen will make new law in the belief that what they are making is good old law, not indeed expressly handed-down but tacitly existent . . . a law hidden but already existing is discovered, not created. There is, in the Middle Ages, no such thing as 'the first application of a legal rule'. Law is old; new law is a contradiction in terms; for either new law is derived explicitly or implicitly from the old, or it conflicts with the old, in which case it is not lawful. The fundamental idea remains the same; the old law is the true law, and the true law is the old law. (Stein, 1966, pp. 5–6)

The principle depicted is only too familiar to the English common law which has traditionally regarded the law as a permanent set of unchanging rules which are discovered, declared and applied to new cases. In its broadest sense precedent is based not so much upon logic or reason as upon the repetition of a discourse or way of life and mode of belonging. In this sense there is nothing unique to the system of legal precedent; a similar principle of the repetition of formulas and of ritualized texts can be found in the development of religious, scientific and literary traditions as well. In its widest formulation, it has been persuasively argued that most societies make a distinction between 'primary' and 'secondary' texts, between 'discourse uttered in the course of the day and in casual meetings, which disappears with the very act which gave rise to it; and those forms of discourse that lie at the origins of a certain number of new verbal acts, which are reiterated, transformed or discussed; in short discourse which *is spoken* and *remains spoken . . .* and *remains to be spoken*' (Foucault, 1981, p. 220).

The principle of repetition, the claim to find the law in prior practices, statements, judgments or statutory texts, is clearly much broader than the system of precedent itself as a system of case law. At the same time, however, it is clear that in broad historical terms the overriding principle of the common law is far from unique. All legal systems embody some element of precedent, nor is the actual historical development of the common law peculiar to England. Very briefly, the common law as a national legal system developed during the reign of Henry II and its main institutions were devised before his death in 1189. In its earliest form, as a system of royal remedies available either from the Court of Common Pleas or from the itinerant royal justices, it was based upon a mixture of civil and local law, while its proceedings were at first conducted virtually exclusively in Latin. The royal judges themselves were originally churchmen trained in canon (religious) law and Roman law. It was churchmen trained in civil law who originally fashioned the common law as a system based upon royal writs. If we look at the literary sources for the common law of the twelfth and thirteenth centuries, we see that its methods and categories were strongly influenced by Roman law and it is really only towards the end of the fourteenth and the beginning of the fifteenth century that the exponents of the common law began explicitly to resist the influence of the Papacy and of canon law (*Corpus Iuris Canonici*) while also objecting ever more vehemently to the role of civil law within the common-law jurisdiction. Thus, for instance, Sir John Fortescue in a work entitled *Praise of the Laws of England*, written around the mid-fifteenth century, argues that civil law is irrelevant to the needs of the English and that only a system of customary law can adequately meet the requirements of the English political constitution or Parliament (Skinner, 1978).

The most peculiar or distinctive feature of the English legal system at this stage of its growth was that it had severed its ties with the university law schools of Europe and of England. Its language was now law French rather than Latin, its judges were selected from the emergent legal profession –

the order of the coif and later of serjeants-at-law – rather than from the Church, and education or training in the law was restricted to the Inns of Court and to the unsystematic learning by experience of apprenticeship. The period in question, from 1256 when Bracton stopped writing to 1758 when Blackstone began his lectures, has been fittingly described as 'nearly five hundred years of vacuum' during which period the common lawyers were hermetically sealed off from the outer world and especially from the needs of their own society (Dawson, 1968, p. 48). The period constitutes what could be termed the prehistory of the English system of precedent. In terms of substantive law, the case law of the *Year Books*, it was constituted by a highly technical system of writs and procedural rules conducted in a foreign language and only partially, and frequently poorly, reported. The development of the common law as a series of cases decided by reference to custom and customary, highly technical, procedures is not markedly different from the local law in other parts of Europe. Cases were decided most frequently by reference to prior decisions or to 'ancient ways', traditions emerged by strength of repeated applications of judgments, but there is no sense in which prior decisions or practices were viewed either as binding in and of themselves or as together forming a coherent or complete system of laws. Citation of precedents was a powerful rhetorical or argumentative tool from as early as the mid-fourteenth century, but the lawyers of the period were clear that 'no precedent is as persuasive as reason.' The attitude is one which can be traced without difficulty through the subsequent four centuries. In 1554, for example, Dwyer comments that 'precedents and usage do not rule the law, but the law them' and as late as 1774 Lord Mansfield was still able to assert that 'the law of England would be a strange science indeed if it were decided upon precedents only. Precedents serve to illustrate principles, and to give them a fixed certainty' (*Jones* v *Rendall* [1774] 1 Cowp. 37, 39).

The crucial period for the modern development of the concept of a system of precedent, as a rational body of case-law rules stating in advance the law applicable to any given instance of dispute or accusation, is that between 1758, when the first lectures on the common law were delivered by Blackstone at Oxford, and 1861, when the House of Lords, sitting as a purely legal body, first clearly elaborated the doctrine of binding precedent in *Beamish* v *Beamish* [1861] 9 HLC, 274. Of the many conditions for the emergence of a doctrine of precedent, we shall at this stage note only those that relate directly to the present introductory argument. First, there was the emergence of an authoritative system of law reports, dating from Burrow's Reports of 1756 to the system of judicially approved and authorized reports which developed from the early 1800s onwards. The significance of reliable written reports both in England and, interestingly, on the

Continent at roughly the same time, can scarcely be overstated. As early as 1765 Lord Campbell had stated, 'if it is law, it will be found in our books. If it is not to be found there, it is not law' (*Entick* v *Carrington* [1765] 10 St. Tr. 1030), the view, in short, that the only law is textual law to which should be added the observation that not only is the written law now deemed to be comprehensive but it is also now reasoned in an explicit and publicly available vernacular, English-language, manner. Underlying or concurrent with the development of official reports is the crucial re-emergence of literary expositions of the law based principally in the universities. What occurred in the mid-eighteenth century in England was the reawakening of academic and disciplinary or doctrinal interest in the common law and even to some extent an interest in the political purpose that the law should pursue and the social needs that it should endeavour to meet. At any event, the new juristic attitude sees the first major attempts to produce legal textbooks, systematically and logically ordered accounts of the substantive law, very much based upon continental (civilian) models of jurisprudence and of legal 'institutes' – the first native-language accounts of local law – which were called 'institutes' precisely because their inspiration and conceptual ordering derived from Justinian's *Institutes* (see chapter 4, s. 4.1; also Cairns, 1984). Even in terms of the developments and innovations in common-law doctrine itself, Roman law categories and influence were of extreme importance and, as we shall argue in more detail later in this chapter, the supposed peculiarity or distinctness of the common law is more apparent than real.

5.1.2 *Conceptual context*

The attempt to develop the common law into a logically coherent system of rules enshrining binding precedents occurred extremely late in its history and was more a response to the political and ideological pressures of nationalism and representative Parliamentary democracy than it was in any genuine sense an expression of an internal logic to the common law itself. The development of institutional writings was a *European* phenomenon connected to the rise of the nation-state in the eighteenth and nineteenth centuries (Poggie, 1978, pp. 60–85). Throughout Europe the eighteenth century saw the decline of civil law (*ius commune*) and of Latin as the language of the legal system and their replacement by the study of local law. As early as 1679, for example, Louis XIV had ordered the creation of professorships in French law at the French universities. Similar developments occur in Spain, Germany and Scotland and indeed in England except that England lagged somewhat behind – Charles Viner's endowment of the first university lectureship in common law at Oxford University was not until 1755 – although it is important to note that the arguments in favour of local law and language can be traced back much earlier, to Coke's *Institutes* (*Commentary on Littleton*, 1628) and to disputes as to the relevant language of the law which had become frequent and heated by the first half of the eighteenth century.

The point we wish to emphasize is that the context of the development of the common law as a unified system of law is European and not simply English. The two principal tendencies within the common law during the seventeenth and eighteenth centuries – the tendency to stress English law as *national* law to the exclusion of other jurisdictions (the civilian jurisdictions of canon law and admiralty), and the promotion of the study of English common law in the universities – have their exact equivalents in the development of continental legal systems during the same period (Skinner, 1978). On the Continent, of course, the outcome of these developments were the major eighteenth- and nineteenth-century codifications of national law rather than the creation of a system of local or customary law unified by a doctrine of binding precedent. The bases of the codifications in question, however, are comparable to those of the unification of the common law. Essentially the same institutional systematizations of local law and the same doctrinal emphases on comprehensiveness and clarity of exposition for teaching purposes lay behind both the civilian and the common-law developments. The point is a crucial one because it defines not only the conceptual culture to which the unification of the English system of precedent belongs but also and more importantly in the present context, the way in which the products of this development, the texts of the common law, are to be approached and read.

The fierce nationalism of the common law and the inflated claims as to the historical unity and uniqueness of the English system of precedent should not be allowed to blind the student of the common law to the broader tradition to which it belongs. The tradition within which the common-law texts should eventually be placed and read is that of European legal humanism, the tradition which the common law re-encountered directly when law teaching and legal doctrine returned to the universities and to the essentially European culture and curriculum that the university represented. Humanism, of which legal humanism is but one branch, is not an easy tradition to define and some historians have suggested that the term cease to be used altogether. For our purposes, however, it refers to the development of a particular method of teaching and of study in the universities of Europe from the mid-sixteenth century until the rise of rationalism in the nineteenth century. The humanists organized the university arts curriculum (which included law) around the study of logic (and logical grammar), rhetoric and history, which methods they applied to the study of the reason and traditions of antiquity. While it is true that the humanists were principally concerned with antiquity, with the classics and the proper appreciation and transmission of the classics, their concerns and methods were very much broader than those of the preceding, more strictly exegetical school of scholasticism. What the legal humanists in particular developed was first a specific method for the reconstruction of the classical texts of Roman law and second a fervent concern with the teaching (*doctrina*) of that tradition and its texts, with their integration into local law and life, in short their dissemination as a tradition, as a mode of belonging to the community and as a culture. In the present chapter we shall concentrate upon the techniques for reading precedent that derive most directly from the humanist tradition and are grouped under the heading of *hermeneutics*: the discipline that studies the rules of interpretation and understanding of recorded expression or texts (Dilthey, 1976, p. 249), the discipline whose task is that of interpreting transmitted texts (Gadamer, 1979, p. 486). We shall reserve for the next chapter the analysis of that wider and more critical set of case-law techniques that derive from a much older, *rhetorical* tradition of analysis which, in origin at least, was concerned with the techniques of persuasion or 'speaking well in civil matters'. We would at this stage merely note that the distinction is a somewhat artificial one in so far as rhetoric and hermeneutics both study the rules relating to probable arguments and both equally formed part of the humanist tradition of textual interpretation as it was taught and studied in the arts syllabus of the late medieval and post-medieval universities.

5.2   THE HERMENEUTIC TRADITION

The word hermeneutic derives ultimately from the name of Hermes, the son of Zeus, who in Greek mythology acted as the messenger or herald of the gods. In its broadest and most ancient meaning, hermeneutics thus refers to a form of communication which takes place across the gulf that separates the mortal from the immortal, the human from the divine. What is involved is essentially an act of translation in which an original, foreign or alien language and meaning is unlocked and communicated: the signs and symbols of the gods are rendered intelligible and familiar by the interpreter, Hermes. In brief, it could be said that the task of the earliest hermeneutics was that of translating the foreign and strange into the familiar and recognizable, the distant and written into the present and spoken; in the words of a leading contemporary proponent of the tradition, 'the word hermeneutics points back to the task of the interpreter, which is that of interpreting and communicating something that is unintelligible because it is spoken in a foreign language' to which is added that 'everything that is set down in writing is to some extent foreign and strange, and hence it poses the same task of understanding as what is spoken in a foreign language' (Gadamer, 1979, p. 487).

In its earliest forms the methods and techniques of hermeneutics were applied to a wide variety of mythological, religious and legal traditions and texts. Hermeneutics covered all forms of interpretation, including the strictly regulated procedures of biblical and legal exegesis. For the purposes of the present chapter it is therefore necessary to emphasize that we shall be using the term hermeneutics in a historically limited way. In talking of hermeneutics and hermeneutic techniques of interpretation, we are referring specifically to that branch of textual criticism that developed, primarily in the European universities, in the eighteenth and nineteenth centuries and is associated with post-medieval humanism and the development of scientific methodologies for the reconstruction and interpretation of classical Greek and Roman literature. In this section we shall examine the context and content of humanistic hermeneutics and then move in the following section (s. 5.3) to analyse legal hermeneutics and the techniques of interpretation that such a discipline suggests.

5.2.1 *History and tradition*

The key to any form of hermeneutics is its sense of history or of tradition. Throughout the various stages of its development, from the Renaissance to the nineteenth century, the consistent concern of hermeneutics has been with the recovery and reconstruction of ancient texts and alien meanings. Hermeneutics (or by its earlier name philology or philological interpretation) is best comprehended as 'historical consciousness', as a method which reflects upon and draws up the rules for recollecting and interpreting documents deemed to be of historical significance, 'all that no longer expresses itself in and through its own world – that is, everything that is handed down, whether art or other spiritual creations of the past, law, religion, philosophy and so forth – is estranged from its original meaning and depends for its unlocking and communication upon hermeneutics' (Gadamer, 1979, p. 147). The two elements to this description of hermeneutics are of equal significance. First, there is the sense of the importance, the authority and value, of tradition as a way of life or form of community and of communal belonging. The historical texts or monuments of the past are to be treated as models of an exemplary, classical existence which the interpreters of the tradition would have us, the reader, follow. Second is the assumption that tradition and the texts in which it is contained bear a 'true' meaning which is their original meaning. The task of hermeneutics is that

of elaborating the rules or techniques that will uncover that original meaning and will reinstate it: the purpose of reconstructing a tradition is ultimately to relive it or at least to continue it, to place oneself within a tradition
that has been made (by the rules of hermeneutic method) to speak to the
present. These two aspects to hermeneutics are clearly parts of the same
problem – that of interpretation – and in the following account of the key
elements of the discipline our concern is precisely to evidence the necessary
dependence of techniques of interpretation upon conceptions of community, authority and value.

5.2.2   *Community and morality*

Hermeneutics was never an innocent discipline. Its concerns with tradition,
with the custody and handing-down of 'correct' or 'standardized' textual
meanings, was never simply an exercise in scholarship or historical science
alone. It was also always an exercise in the furtherance and teaching of the
tradition being preserved and interpreted. The early religious hermeneutics, for example, was concerned not simply with the historically correct
meanings of the Scriptures but also, and perhaps more fundamentally, with
preaching the scriptural message and maintaining the unity of the Christian
way of life. Similarly, the later humanist hermeneutics was inspired by the
active desire to recapture what was termed the 'spirit of antiquity'. Its
principal goal was that of transplanting the Greek and Roman textual
heritage into the present, 'it is the study of the classical world in the totality
of its life – artistic and scientific, public and private. The centre of this study
is the spirit of Antiquity, which is reflected in the purest manner in the
works of the ancient writers' (F. Ast, 1808, in Bleicher, 1980). Humanism
was a revival which wished to imitate a classical culture which was perceived
as being superior to local culture; it wished to give the distant past priority
over the present. In short, the aim of this humanistic hermeneutics was that
of using the classics to create and to cohere a specific sense of community or
common sense (*sensus communis*), the sense of a pregiven communal value or
a morality seen as tradition.

The sense of community as transmitted through the classical texts was a
strongly ethical one. The spirit of antiquity represented an ideal of moral
well-being, a tradition of community in which the common good represented not merely the sense of collective belonging but also the judgment of
right and wrong in particular cases. Tradition created community as common sense, as a set of accepted standards and beliefs, as a totality of values
and a sense of the whole which precedes the present and by which the
present is judged. Community for the hermeneutic interpreter is based
upon classical tradition, and this tradition is to provide the interpreter with

the 'authorized' point of view, the prejudice or prejudgment, from which interpretation begins. It is thus possible to observe that for hermeneutics understanding and interpretation always take place within the context of tradition and as an elaboration of the values of tradition, themselves perceived as the community and common sense of the historically prior culture. We may further observe that common sense here begins to take on certain of the meanings which we associate with it today. Common sense represents a series of accepted values, values which it is claimed are held in common and consequently do not need justification or explanation; they are simply generalizations as to value from which argument or interpretation can begin. Common sense is here the communal expression of agreement as to value, as to right and wrong; in short, it is a consensus as to meaning which provides the authority for individual judgments based upon and justified by appeals to reason and reasonableness, to the 'common sense' (in legal terms the '*communis opinio*') of moral standards.

5.2.3 *Authority and doctrine*

Common sense and reasonableness as the standards of right and wrong are clearly somewhat vague categories. The important point, however, is not the general and somewhat abstract nature of community as a set of shared beliefs but rather the way in which the categories of common sense and reasonableness can be put to work in creating justifications for interpretation. In its broadest sense, an interpretation is justified if it can be shown to accord with or to be derived from traditional usage and values. The basis of this argument takes the form of saying that tradition establishes community, tradition is the cement of community and that consequently what contributes to the maintenance, the continuity, of community is self-evidently good. Values, particular judgments as to right and wrong, are always to be referred back to the context of the value, that of the pre-existent whole, whether that whole or totality be that of community or in more specific circumstances, that of a religious, political or legal tradition.

The demands of continuity expressed above provide for a very specific sense of authority and doctrine within the hermeneutic tradition. Authority takes the form of a canon of accepted texts, from which all arguments and interpretations are to be drawn. The canonical or authoritative texts are the 'sole rule and depository for faith and morals'. The written traditions, the texts and great books of antiquity are the source or spring of all science; they are canonical in the sense of being authoritative as precedents, as justifications based upon prior community (Ong, 1958, pp. 121–3). The point to be stressed is that authority is historical and textual, authority is a particular kind of knowledge rather than simple subjection; it is in the hermeneutic view pedagogic reason rather than simple domination: 'the recognition of authority is always connected with the idea that what authority states is not irrational and arbitrary, but can be seen, in principle, to be true; it is the authority of the teacher, the superior and the expert' (Gadamer, 1979, p. 248).

Authority as the validity of what has been transmitted lies at the basis of doctrine. The derivation of the word doctrine is itself instructive, the Latin *doctrina* meaning teaching and corresponding to the word *disciplina*, meaning learning. The hermeneutic joining of authority and reason has its extension in the belief that knowledge is something transmitted and taught. Every educational discipline has its field of doctrine which may be broadly defined as its principles and classifications, its accepted truths, its authors and authorities. We would note finally that the relation between doctrine and teaching is one in which doctrine is defined by and remains within the hands of the teachers or in more contemporary terms, the teaching institutions. Doctrine consists of the truths handed down by educators – by priests, judges, politicians, scholars and so on – all of whom are experts in the classics, custodians of ancient truths which are preserved for and presented to their contemporary audiences.

5.2.4 *Judgment and interpretation*

So far our account of the central elements of hermeneutics has concentrated upon the sense in which the hermeneutic tradition reconstructs and preserves ancient texts and ancient meanings. This task of the reconstruction and teaching of traditions has frequently been the primary and only goal of the theory of hermeneutics. Practitioners of the discipline have simply been historians who have laboured by philological (strictly linguistic) means to discover the original meaning of the classical texts and who have then, as teachers, sought to promulgate or pass on that knowledge. Such an attitude towards hermeneutics was predominant, for example, during the period of the Reformation when for Luther and his followers the biblical texts were to speak for themselves (*sola scriptura*) as purely historical records of God's truth. Much of the criticism that has been directed at hermeneutics as a discipline has been directed at this conception of it as a purely historical methodology, and as a wholly uncritical philology or activity of reconstruction. Such an enterprise has frequently and justifiably been attacked as being passive, inactive and submissive, as wholly failing to judge the classics and so merely safeguarding and handing down an elitist tradition and its ideological meanings.[1] While we shall return to these arguments and criticisms when we come to look at questions of rhetoric and hegemony in the next chapter, it may nonetheless be observed at this stage that however it is evaluated, hermeneutics necessarily implies an involvement in, a practice or application of, the teachings it transmits. The point is made by Dilthey when he observes the 'strange fate of hermeneutics' which is that 'it only gains recognition when there is a movement among historians which considers understanding individual historical manifestations an urgent matter for scholarship' (Dilthey, 1976, p. 261).

It is to some extent only when traditions have become questionable that hermeneutics, the rules whereby tradition is consolidated and handed on, becomes an explicit object of study, for example: for St Augustine in relation to the Old Testament in the face of the threat of the break up of the early Church; for Luther and the Reformation in relation to the decadence of the Roman Church; for contemporary critical legal studies even, in relation to the increasing archaism of dogmatic jurisprudence. What is centrally at issue is the relevance of tradition, a question both of under-standing tradition and its context but also of becoming critically aware of the fact that the values of a tradition are only as good as their interpretation and application to present contexts. Hermeneutics is in this sense always a contemporary discipline and in its strongest form it has always been con-cerned not simply with the reconstruction of historical meanings but also and equally with the present integration of the historical knowledge that it has acquired. For religious and legal hermeneutics in particular, the classi-cal texts were not simply there to be imitated but were also to be adapted to their contemporary situation, the context in which the text was being proclaimed, announced or read. Very simply, hermeneutics has long recog-nized that the concrete instance is itself never wholly rule governed, that the principles of morality or law are never complete or unambiguous in the individual situation, that it is always necessary to 'creatively supplement' or develop the law, to make a judgment that will apply the rule to the particular case or preaching.

The art of interpretation or of understanding the full significance of the text involves what the humanists termed *subtilitas applicandi*: the fusion of the concept of understanding with that of the application of the text to be understood, its applicability or relevance to the present situation of the interpreter. Understanding and application were parts of a single process or, in a more recent formulation, 'there is in theological and religious hermeneutics an essential tension between the text set down ... and the sense arrived at by its application, either in a judgment or a preaching. A law is not there to be understood historically, but to be made concretely valid through being interpreted ... The understanding of texts, of law or gospel, is always new and different according to the particular situation' (Gadamer, 1979, p. 275).

5.2.5 *Canons of textual interpretation*

One of the more interesting implications of the last point made – the assertion that understanding and application are parts of a unified process – is that it becomes very difficult indeed to regard the process of interpretation as a strictly logical operation. If there is always something unique to the interpretation of a text, namely its relation to the particular instance or circumstance of its interpretation and application, then it is not possible to view interpretation as producing meanings that are wholly necessary or indisputably binding. The point is one which has been the subject of numerous recent theories of interpretation and of reading which have argued that any instance of interpretation always involves a choice and a motive, an element of the 'play of meanings' which denies that there can ever be a single 'correct' or valid interpretation.

Humanist hermeneutics, however, has always tended to claim that there is either an original or a correct meaning to the text and that this can be discovered, if not by logic alone, at least by the careful application of the rules or canons of interpretation. Humanism 'dreams of deciphering a truth or an origin which escapes play and the order of the sign' (Derrida, 1978, p. 292) and in an earlier formulation of Dilthey's, 'the final goal of the hermeneutic procedure is to understand the author better than he understood himself' (Dilthey, 1976, pp. 259–60). What is at issue in such statements is clearly the question of the existence of standards of correct interpretation, the question of how one verifies a meaning or reading or judgment as being, in the circumstances, the correct one, the best available. To conclude the present introduction to the hermeneutic tradition we shall look in very broad terms at the more important of the canons of interpretation, the rules of what Schleiermacher, one of the most famous of the nineteenth-century exponents of theological hermeneutics, had called the 'art of avoiding misunderstandings'. We would stress, however, that the rules or guidelines that we select themselves constitute a simplification and indeed an interpretation drawn from the hermeneutic theories both of the nineteenth-century re-organization of the discipline and from contemporary exponents of textual interpretation:

(i) *Autonomy of the text.* Although the nineteenth century and Schleiermacher in particular developed hermeneutics into a philosophy of 'understanding' which was concerned with all questions of shared meaning and communication, hermeneutics has remained primarily a textual discipline. The problem of meaning is a textual problem for Dilthey and it remains so in the contemporary works of Gadamer, Ricoeur and others. Very simply, hermeneutics is concerned with what has been transmitted in tradition, and our access to tradition and its meanings is through the language and texts of the tradition in question. Tradition is language and the 'full hermeneutical significance of the fact that tradition is linguistic is clearly revealed when the tradition is a written one . . . The written text represents the real hermeneutical task' (Gadamer, 1979, pp. 351–2). The problem of interpretation is thus always to be conceived in terms of the problem of the meaning of a text; the text is taken to express a whole (totality) and is consequently a complete object of study.

(ii) *Historical meaning.* The text is to be approached first as a historical object. It has a physical form, author, and time and place of appearance. A full appreciation of the meaning of the text will take account of these factors; it will examine where and when and by whom the text was written, in what language it was written and how it was received, transcribed or read. While many of the historical techniques consist of extremely technical philological procedures for eliminating errors of textual transmission, the general issue can be formulated more simply. Words and texts change their meaning over time and one important stage in the process of interpretation is consequently to relate the text to the meanings and ideas that were prevalent at the time it first appeared. For Dilthey indeed 'history is the great dark book, the collected work of the human spirit, written in the languages of the past.'

(iii) *Grammatical meaning.* The grammatical meaning of the text originally tended to refer to the pure linguistic (lexical and syntactic) meaning that the words themselves were capable of bearing. That one takes account of the grammar of the text would merely require that attention be paid to its language, that one analyse the meaning of the sentences in themselves. Somewhat later a further meaning was added to the term grammar in hermeneutics: the canon of grammatical meaning came to be associated with the unity or coherence of meaning. Following on from the assumption of the autonomy of the text is the assumption that the text is a 'structured totality': 'the meaning of the whole has to be derived from its individual elements, and an individual element has to be understood by reference to the comprehensive, penetrating whole of which it is a part' (E. Betti, p. 58, in Bleicher, 1980). It is never sufficient, in other words, to treat the individual element of the text as being self-contained; it must be integrated into the text or speech or work as a whole.

(iv) *Institutional and intentional meanings.* The canons of interpretation outlined above show the hermeneutic method to be one which isolates the text – interpretative work is wholly committed to textual meanings – and then applies a series of integrative (intratextual) techniques to the segments of the text so as to isolate further the correct meaning of both part and whole. There are generally speaking only two forms of integration and these can be broadly described as institutional and intentional, objective and subjective. In the terminology of more recent philosophies of language, to understand an utterance requires that we understand it as a speech-act, that is, as an intentional utterance which makes use of a variety of institutional or conventional means to achieve its purposes. The meaning of the uttterance or speech-act is to be sought in a combination of factors: first, to say something is to act intentionally, it is to do something, and hermeneutics had generally sought what it is that is intended to be done in the mind of the speaker. The problem of intention is thus seen as a psychological one – who is the author of the words, what did the author intend? Second, the meaning intended may not always be the meaning successfully realized in the speech-act: our intentions are mediated through the institution of language; we cannot create meanings which the words or syntactic constructions used cannot bear, nor can we do things through language which our social institutions or speech-community cannot recognize or tolerate. It could be said that meaning always has a social dimension and that the meaning of an utterance will be sought not simply in the mind of the speaker but also in the conventions of the speech-community or 'language game' to which the speaker belongs; 'you must obey', for example, will have very different meanings when spoken by a citizen, a parent, a police constable or a court of law. If we now turn to the question of how the common law is to be read doctrinally as a system of precedent, it is very clearly the case that the meanings we attribute to the law reports are principally institutional meanings and it has indeed been the age-old task of legal hermeneutics to elaborate the techniques by which such institutional meanings are to be discovered and applied.

5.3 LEGAL HERMENEUTICS

The study of legal texts and legal meanings is a branch of the discipline of hermeneutics as a whole. Our reason for spending some considerable time setting out the elements of the broader discipline of interpretation or hermeneutics and for looking in some depth at the categories of tradition, community, authority and judgment was simply that those concepts and categories themselves constitute the basic elements of legal hermeneutics and of the system of precedent as a particular species of the discipline of interpretation. The law is indeed an exemplary object for hermeneutic study: it is in the strongest of senses a tradition and community concerned with handing down specialized knowledge and meanings which will be authoritatively interpreted and applied to the judgment of particular cases. As was observed earlier (s. 5.1.2) the strongest version of the legal tradition as a system of precedent – as a coherent set of rules – is one of relatively recent origin, but the tradition itself and the appropriate methods of reading it are much older and are in the main shared (as hermeneutics) by the civil-law and common-law traditions. Our principal argument in the following account of legal hermeneutics and of the techniques relevant to the reading of precedent is indeed to the effect that there is no radical break or qualitative change in the nature of precedent or legal decision-making in the nineteenth century when precedent first comes to be seen or at least represented as being a system of binding rules. The doctrine of *stare decisis* and the elaboration of the principle of the rule of law in which the function of the judge is simply that of logically applying predetermined legal rules both have their counterparts in European legal doctrine and both can be found existent in different formulations much earlier in the history of the common law. Innovations in ideology, changes in the manner in which the legal community represents and justifies its social and political roles, should not blind the student of legal texts to the fact that the claim (declarative) that there is a strict logic of legal interpretation or the belief that 'legal reason' can alone provide 'correct' answers to legal problems are no more than exaggerated (dogmatic) assertions of the hermeneutic requirement that the law be respected and obeyed (imperative). Because the claim to a logic of law and of law-application is still frequent within law teaching and within the textbook tradition of jurisprudence, as well as forming an important part of the media representation of law, we shall return to this issue repeatedly in the following sections.

5.3.1 *Law and tradition*

First and most obviously, legal method stipulates that the common law be read historically, that is, that it should be read in terms of its continuity and as a tradition. This requirement has several implications. In a very general sense reading the law as a tradition is a mechanism for creating a sense of legal identity: legal meanings develop over time, they are handed down in carefully preserved and reported formulations and most important of all, the legally transmitted meaning is part of a tradition of interrelated legal meanings. The historians of the common law, Maitland, Pollock, Holdsworth, Plucknett and others, have tended to stress the latter feature to the development and expansion of the common law – it forms a 'seamless web' or an 'uncut cloth', it moves forward as a tradition in an inexorable and coherent fashion as a set of meanings and as a way of life. The great antiquity of the law is matched only by the slow, boring logic of its adaptation to contemporary circumstances. The law goes back beyond memory; 'time immemorial' has elapsed since the law was made and it is thereby recognized that legal change always lags behind social change – the law is a force for conservation, it is measured and majestic in its attitude towards change and the legal tradition has always to some extent maintained an image of distance and seriousness which separates legal problems from the interests and conflicts of everyday life.

The texts of the common law lay considerable stress upon the tradition and the age of legal meanings and the sources of law. To some extent this stress upon history as the antiquity and continuity of legal rules is simply a way of justifying legal judgments which might otherwise be seen to raise contemporary issues of a political and ideological character: because the legal issue has been decided before, it can be answered without reference to any factors other than those of legal history. In the case of *R* v *Miller* [1954] 2 AER 529, for example, the defendant was prosecuted for rape of his estranged wife. The wife had left her husband a year before the incident in question and had filed a petition for divorce. Before the petition was heard, the husband had sexual intercourse with her against her will. In the absence of any direct authority on the question of whether or not a husband can be convicted of rape of his wife, the court was faced with the need to construct a legal answer to a question which carried with it a number of important ethical, social and political or policy implications. Instead of looking directly at the policy issues involved – at issues of the status and rights of married women, at problems of evidence and of legal policy towards the institution of marriage, or indeed at the character of the husband's conduct in the case to be decided – the court returned to the seventeenth century and a literary exposition of the common law by the judge Sir Matthew Hale, who had remarked rather tersely that 'a husband cannot be guilty of rape ... upon his lawful wife, for by their mutual consent and contract the wife hath given up herself in this kind unto her husband, which she cannot retract.' The contract of marriage, in other words, constitutes a general consent by the wife to sexual use by the husband, which consent cannot be negatived by the wife's refusal on a particular occasion. Suffice it to say that the marriage contract is seen, in this respect, as a permanent conveyance in which the wife becomes the sexual property of the husband and renounces or loses the 'right or power to refuse her consent'. In terms of the use of tradition, the example evidences the priority of historical meanings over any more direct justification of a particular value commitment or policy judgment on the part of the court. The technique involved belongs, in the first instance, to the 'empire of memory', to the realm of recollection although, as we shall argue in the subsequent section, its role as repetition is eventually much less important than its symbolic or doctrinal functions.

One moment in the process of reading the case law can thus be designated as the search for traditional or historical sources and meanings. As much as anything else, the technique involved is one of memory, that of the ability to recall and presumably repeat ancient and highly technical usages. While it would not be helpful to proliferate the examples, it can be usefully observed that the exercise of remembering the law has always been a feature of the legal tradition and it remains so – perhaps somewhat irrationally or anachronistically – in the form of legal professional exams quite as much as in the continued judicial stress upon time-honoured principles and the historical authority of the common law. The substance of what is to be remembered has obviously changed. Initially, the common lawyer needed a knowledge of the law administered at Westminster Hall, of a highly technical and difficult system of oral pleadings. Later, it was the *Year Books* which would provide information and clues as to pleadings and writs, 'the book moves in abstruse games of legal chess' (Dawson, 1968, p. 54). In the later development of named Reporters (1550–1790) and eventually of the authorized law reports, the use of memory is frequently tempered by the claim to reason or to doctrinal rationality. The legal meanings remembered are always related to other legal meanings and to the principles and reasoning of the law as a whole. It remains the case, however, that past authority or precedent is generally required in the justification of a decision – reason alone is insufficient – and that if the judge believes that there is no authority for deciding a case then the plaintiff must be non-suited or a verdict of no case to answer entered. In terms of a relatively recent example, the dissenting judgment of Viscount Dilhorne in the much-cited case of *Home Office* v *Dorset Yacht* [1970] AC 1004 at 1051, is instructive. The question at issue in the case was that of whether or not the Home Office were liable in negligence for damage caused to property by a party of boys from a borstal, who had escaped from the supervision of borstal officers employed by the Home Office. It was the view of Viscount Dilhorne that the point at issue – that of liability in damages for escaped prisoners – had never been decided before and that consequently 'there is no authority for claiming a duty of care exists with respect to custodians of persons lawfully in custody to anyone suffering damage consequent upon their escape. We are, therefore, here being asked to create a *novel* duty . . . no doubt very powerful arguments can be advanced that there should be such a duty'; but in Viscount Dilhorne's view it is not the function of the judge to alter or to create law: 'the facts of a particular case may be a wholly inadequate basis for a far reaching change of the law. We have not to decide what the law should be and then to alter the existing law. That is the function of Parliament.' In brief, the law always already exists and it is the constitutional function of the judge to declare that law. The principal tool or technique for aiding in such declarations is clarity, in the above view at least, that of memory or textual tradition and nothing more.

The concept of law as something that is there to be recollected or remembered and declared from the existing sources or law in force at any given time is generally to be related to a variety of other images and values of the legal process, principally those which emphasize the desirability of a law which is certain, predictable and rational. We would note first that the view remains a prevalent one, 'in the vast majority of cases there is very little doubt . . . the life of the law consists to a very large extent in the guidance of officials and private individuals by determinate rules which . . . do not require . . . a fresh judgment from case to case' (Hart, 1962, pp. 131–2). Second, however, we would note that the issues raised by this concept of precedent are considerably more complex than those of the nature of traditions and memory alone. The problem of precedent is next to be related to problems of reason and value within the legal community.

5.3.2   Law and community

Tradition is never solely or only memory. Hermeneutics has generally recognized that the transmission of a tradition is not simply the mechanical task of accurately transcribing earlier meanings, it is also the recollection of the 'spirit' or 'idea' of a past era and of classical texts. The tradition has to be understood before it can be fully used as a model for present relations and actions, before it can speak to the present. In legal hermeneutics too it has consistently been argued that precedent is more than simple repetition, that it has its basis in reason or principle or what has been described as the 'legal idea' which the particular case exemplifies and makes live again in the new surroundings of the contemporary case.[2] In other words, the legal tradition represents considerably more than just the record of prior decisions; it represents also a particular way of reading those decisions so as to discover within them a rationality – a sense of value and commitment to community – which will be carried forward in future decisions. In the present section we shall examine what this 'rationality' consists of by looking more closely at the concept or concepts of legal community. We shall first very briefly analyse the *community of lawyers* or legal profession itself as the interpreters of the law, and second consider the more important though essentially related concept of legal community as a *community of doctrine* or value, legal community or legal order here being seen much more broadly as the basis of the social order and of the moral and political community itself.

While it may seem somewhat trivial or irrelevant to look at the nature and constitution of the legal profession when trying to understand how precedent texts are to be construed or read, there is, we would argue, much to be gained from such an analysis. In several senses, the law is only as good as its interpreters: the law is always to some extent a set of future possibilities and it is to the composition and values of the legal community that one should initially look to estimate how possibility and choice are likely to be exercised. At the same time, it can be observed that membership of the legal community is always something more than a purely technical qualification; it is a way of life and mode of belonging – a set of habits, beliefs and values which can be briefly illustrated by looking at the history and stages of professional qualification in the law. From its beginnings in the twelfth century to the present day, the legal profession both in Britain and on the Continent can consistently be described as being as much a political body with varying religious, ethical and political functions as simply a group with a particular form of expertise or specialized knowledge. A brief historical review of the development of the profession will serve to introduce the point.

The origins of the legal profession within the Roman, continental and English legal systems have all been to some degree religious. The *Digest* of Justinian refers to lawyers as the 'priests of the law' (*sacerdotes legum*) and a comparable religious status and function can be discerned in most of the other early legal communities. In France, for example, a royal ordinance of 1274 established the oath and rules of the lawyers' guild which is well described as a quasi-religious fraternity 'whose members swore a lifelong oath to uphold standards of truth, to remain orthodox and never to cheat or to overcharge clients. If they fell short of these goals, it was not for lack of good intentions. They heard mass every day and attached extraordinary significance to ceremonial . . . (Kelley, 1982, pp. 178–93). Classically, law was defined as 'knowledge of things divine and human'; it was the equivalent of wisdom or 'true philosophy' and it entitled its practitioners to involve themselves in the widest variety of legislative, administrative and intellectual pursuits. By the sixteenth century lawyers were legislators, political theorists, lay defenders of the Christian faith, social reformers, custodians of tradition and even philosophers. Similar developments can also be observed within the history of the profession of the common law from the mid-thirteenth century onwards. While we have already dealt with many of the relevant details, we would here stress the hierarchical social status of the early legal profession and secondly the significance of the development of the common law from the thirteenth century to the present day.

The English legal profession grew up in the late thirteenth century around groups of experts – attorneys and narrators or oral pleaders – in the technicalities of litigation before the royal courts. Their services were offered to the public at large but were centred in London at Westminster Hall and their art has been described as resembling something of an 'occult science' or magical knowledge of forms of pleading. Only somewhat later, around the mid-fourteenth century, did the oral pleaders become what we would now recognize as the precursors of the contemporary profession, the holders of a monopoly over appearance in the higher courts and the sole source of candidates for appointment to the judiciary. From *c.*1400 the legal profession was organized around the Inns of Court which provided a degree of vocational training and apprenticeship as well as a limited amount of formal schooling for the student of the common law. From the sources available it would appear that the legal training was as much a social education in morality, manners and reverence for authority and the 'ancient ways' as it was directly the study of legal pleadings. Sir John Fortescue, writing in the 1460s, describes a curriculum at the Inns of Court which included, 'in addition to the study of law a kind of academy of all the manners that the nobles learn. They there learn to sing and to practice all kinds of harmony. They are also taught there to dance and engage in pastimes that are proper for nobles' (Dawson, 1968, pp. 39–45). The student of the common law gained a very diffuse or general education at the Inns of Court and in the law courts themselves, where the apprentices would watch proceedings and on occasion receive direct instruction from the bench. By the sixteenth century these forms of education had matured into a training in disputation or in mooting of questions of law, while the Inns themselves were now organized into a much more formal hierarchy of student apprentices, utter (outer) barristers, readers, benchers (the governing body of the Inn) and serjeants of law from whom the judiciary were selected.

The social and political prestige of the Inns of Court was at its height during the fifteenth and sixteenth centuries. The Inns themselves attracted their members virtually exclusively from the nobility and their clientele was also drawn by and large from the governing families or ruling class. In brief, the social character and composition of the upper tier of the English legal profession and judiciary was now settled 'in all its audacity and ingenuity, with its subtleties and its formalism, its prejudices and repetitions, its deliberate obscurities, and its mysticism, in short, with all its qualities and faults ... Nothing more was needed to create a legal system and to surround it with the atmosphere of religion' (Levy-Ullman, 1935, pp. 84–5). It would be surprising in the extreme if such a tightly knit professional elite with a monopolistic control of the legal arm of government and already, in the sixteenth century, the bearer of several centuries of tradition, did not adhere to, protect and promulgate a clear and highly specific sense of community and of communal values. Legal education in the sixteenth century, and in most general forms today as well, was and is a training in values and community, a training in deference to authority and hierarchy which will qualify the student for membership of a social and political professional body, a privileged class and a predominantly male institution. It will also teach the student that law is a part of the natural order, that it is the embodiment of justice and the foundation of social life itself. In the words of Sir Thomas Wilson, a sixteenth-century English canon lawyer, 'take away the Law, and take away our lives, for nothing maintains our wealth, our health, and the safeguard of our bodies, but the Law of the Realm, whereby the wicked are condemned, and the Godly defended ... By an order we are borne, by an order we live, and by an order we make our end ... By an order Realms stand, and Laws take their force.'

The law is not to be viewed, however, simply as the source of community; it is also in major part the definition and arbiter of community morality or social value, the content of community. The law of the realm referred to above – the order by which we live and die – is also a community of doctrine (of teachings) and of values expressed explicitly and also implicitly in the texts of the common law. The values enshrined in and protected by the common law obviously change over time and so also to some extent does the nature or at least the boldness of the judicial role in enforcing the legal conception of community and morality. What remains constant, however, is the fact that any common-law text belongs to a wider tradition and community of texts and that it should consequently be read in the light of that community of texts (intertextuality) and the values that such texts espouse. In more formal terms we would introduce the observation that the major portion of any legal judgment consists of what are traditionally defined as *obiter dicta* – general justifications and contextual argument which point to the values and principles underlying a particular body of law and serve to indicate not simply what the court considers the law to be but also why it is right that it should be taken as such. The decision is shown, in other words, by way of general argument as to attitudes, desired modes of behaviour and wider social and legal values and relations, to be necessary and to be the best that can be reached in the circumstances. To a very great extent the so-called 'logic of the common law' is precisely this tireless elaboration and affirmation of the values of legal community and legal order – the text is as much a sermon and an exhortation as it is in any strict sense an exercise of logical subsumption. To understand legal community and legal value we thus need to learn to read the legal text as a whole, we need to know what it is that leads to and justifies the purported statement of the rule (*ratio*), and we need to understand the moral significance of the legal text as a form of

life. In terms of reading precedent we can now move to formulate some of
the layers of the legal meaning to be found in the legal text and to outline
the techniques of interpretation relevant to them.

(i) *Reading legal structure.* A lengthy and continuing tradition of judicial
precedent sees it as an essential task of the common law to define and
enforce community values in an explicit and direct way. A number of very
basic beliefs as to the nature of social life and relations, as to social cohesion
or the social bond and as to the moral standards or correct forms of
conduct, inform and determine legal decisions. The major categories of the
common-law disciplines are closely related to fundamental legal values of
the kind referred to, values of consensus or cohesion, and the legal categories should be read and understood in such a way as to highlight the social
values underpinning or structuring the law. Obviously we cannot here detail
all the fundamental values relevant to the various domains of the common
law. To make the task of reading such values even more difficult, the values
espoused are frequently presupposed or assumed rather than explicitly
stated. In the following outline account we shall merely illustrate the legal
conception of basic values by reference to a few simple and explicit
examples.

In the first years of the eighteenth century in the case of *Ashby* v *White*
[1703] 2 Ld Raym 938, a returning officer at Parliamentary elections had
refused to allow the plaintiff, a fully qualified voter, to register his vote. The
plaintiff sued the returning officer for damages and although there was no
precedent for such an action the then Lord Chief Justice Holt found no
difficulty in allowing the action on the simple grounds that 'a right that a
man has to give his vote at the election of a person to represent him in
Parliament there to concur to the making of laws, which are to bind his
liberty and property, is a most transcendent thing, and of a high nature . . . it
is a great privilege to choose such persons.' Granted the 'transcendent'
nature of this right the common law must provide a remedy where no
remedy previously existed – liberty and property are values which were of
sufficient strength in 1703 to create new law, and could be termed struc-
tural values. Similarly, in 1765 in the case of *Entick* v *Carrington* [1765]
Si Tr 1030, Lord Camden CJ observes that 'the great end for which men
entered society, was to secure their property. That right is preserved sacred
and incommunicable in all instances, where it has not been taken away or
abridged by some public law for the good of the whole.'

The values of private property and of individual liberty are sufficiently
intrinsic to the legal view of the social fabric to create new law and new
rights. Two years before *Entick* v *Carrington*, in *R* v *Deleval* [1763] 3 Burr
1434, Lord Mansfield had stated that over and above the protection of such

explicitly formulated values as those of property and liberty, the courts were equally charged with protecting society from moral outrage, behaviour 'contra bonos mores'. The court was in his view the 'custodian' or 'censor' of moral values and where necessary would use the criminal law to superintend the moral welfare of society as a whole. In a celebrated case in 1962, *Shaw* v *DPP* [1962] AC 220, Viscount Simmonds entertained 'no doubt that there remains in the courts of law a residual power to enforce the supreme and fundamental purpose of the law, to conserve not only the safety and order but also the moral welfare of the state'.[3] In short, the common law embodies certain basic values or purposes with regard to the nature of the social order and whatever the manner or degree of their explicit judicial recognition it would be impossible to read the development of the common law without reference to them. The context of legal decision-making is that of the legal community and the values that legal order exists to protect. To those of freedom, private property and moral order already touched upon could be added a much longer list incorporating the most salient of the judiciary's historical and collective political and moral stances as they affect the legal vision of social cohesion. They would include all the major heads of public policy and national security where the courts acquiesce in or actively further interests of the State as they perceive them to be. In 1977, for instance, in *R* v *Secretary of State for the Home Department, ex parte Hosenball* [1977] 1 WLR 766, Lord Denning commented in a case concerning a deportation order that 'there is a conflict between the interests of national security on the one hand and the freedom of the individual on the other. The balance between these two is not for a court of law. It is for the Home Secretary.' The legal vision of social order is to be understood and read, in the first instance, in terms of those values that are axiomatic to legal judgments – values that are often explicitly related to law-creating acts but which require no justification because they are integral to the legal perception of social reality or what might be termed the judicial attitude. Thus Lord Diplock remarks in a discussion of 'reasonableness' of administrative decisions, that 'whether a decision falls within this category is a question that judges by their training and experience should be well equipped to answer or else there would be something badly wrong with the judicial system' (*CCSU* v *Minister for the Civil Service* [1984] 3 AER 935). We shall move now to look more closely at how those effortless legal answers are arrived at.

(ii) *Reading legal categories.* To read the law in terms of legal assumptions as to how society works and the interests it works for is to concentrate initially upon certain very general hermeneutic features of the legal conception of community and value. The basic legal values referred to here are extremely abstract and largely symbolic in their functioning. They are referred to simply on the grounds that they represent in a magnified form the basic structure of case-law development and argument. When we move from reading the reports in terms of the fundamental values of community underlying major areas of the common law, to reading substantive legal categories, it might appear that there is a transition not only of scale but also of quality or kind of reasoning. It might be thought that while it is always possible to refer to historical legal relics, to major innovations in the law which used a somewhat radical political and moral vocabulary, the same could not be said to be true of the everyday workings of legal regulation. When it comes to technical questions of, say, the validity of a contract, of liability in damages for negligently caused economic loss or indeed the possibility of obtaining judicial review of administrative decisions, the issues and techniques of reading would leave the realms of a humanistically conceived common sense for the dispassionate terrain of the logic of rule governed behaviour. The opposite, however, proves to be the case.

The vocabulary of the common law and the categories through which the various legal disciplines operate are striking for their generality and for what one legal commentator has termed their 'illusory reference' (Stone, 1947). As can be ascertained from even the briefest acquaintance with any legal textbook, the substantive disciplines of the common law consist of broad legal categories which are not only extremely vaguely defined but are also subject to constant revision, counter-examples, exceptions and exclusions. Legal categories are resources for legal justificatory argument; they create possibilities but will not definitively exclude any specific desired options. Legal categories will enforce a particular vocabulary and will also provide a particular way of correctly posing and arguing legal questions, but nobody could be expected to read the case reports as in any sense containing mathematically precise formulations of legal rules. As Jeremy Bentham, the nineteenth-century liberal legal reformer expressed it, the common law works rather 'just as a man makes law for his dog. When your dog does anything you wish to break him of, you wait till he does it and then beat him. This is the way you make laws for your dog, and this is the way the judges make law for you and me.' There is always room, in other words, to arrive at a decision and then to find in the available vocabulary and categories an acceptable legal justification for the solution chosen. We shall examine the characteristics of the legal vocabulary and categories in the present section and then move in the next section to look at the relationship between abstract categories and concrete outcomes, between argument and decision.

Descriptive accounts of the language and concepts of the common law have tended to agree that it is distinctive by virtue, amongst other things, of being a generic or connotative lexicon. While there is considerable disagreement as to the significance of this characteristic – some argue that it renders the law impenetrable or incomprehensible, others that it is necessary to legal precision – the fact that it is a connotative code or language does not seem to be disputed. In crude terms, the principal feature of a connotative code may be listed as follows.[4] First, the language of connotation is not a referential language: words such as right, duty, obligation, corporation, contract and so on do not refer to or stand for real entities but instead refer to specific legal functions or relations. Connotations can thus be said to refer to the manner in which a term or phrase belongs to an associative field or paradigm – the term is associated with or connotes numerous other legal terms within a field or paradigm of lexical and semantic associations. It is in some respects precisely because legal language does not directly refer to empirical processes or social relations that it is frequently argued for this reason to be a distanced and specialized language: it is self-referring or auto-referential, it is technical in the sense of being wholly conceptual rather than in the sense that other professional or scientific languages are technical primarily because of their need to classify extralinguistic processes and relations – as, for instance, in medicine, psychiatry, business or education. Categories such as that of 'consideration' in the law of contract, for example, do not have any simple or literal meaning but are rather to be defined in terms of their connotations, by reference to their relation to a wide variety of associated legal terms relating to adequacy, intention, duress, privity and so on. The concept of consideration simply does not have a single definition or denotation; it merely has a number of functions or uses which will be understood best not by studying the category of consideration in the abstract but rather by looking at how it is manipulated within the community of legal values. The second characteristic of connotation relates precisely to the freedom that a very general conceptual vocabulary allows. The connotative code is a symbolic vocabulary – it is in very loose terms a second order of language, a series of indirect (relexicalized) meanings which require contextual clarification and interpretation. While it can be argued that all language is symbolic[5] and in need of interpretation, our point here is more simple. A generic professional language such as that of the common law is intrinsically an intentional vocabulary; it is open to intentional manipulation, that is to multiple possible usages in a way that a classificatory or denotative code would appear not to be, at least not so obviously, precisely because the intentional vocabulary or generic language is always free of particular reference or denotative restrictions on usage. We shall return to this point slightly later in looking at how the legal category is made concrete or applied to the particular facts of the case. For the moment we shall look more closely at the generic characteristics of the legal lexicon.

The general categories of the common-law disciplines are resources for argument and for justification rather than being precise classifications of social relations. It would not be possible, for example, to formulate the tortious category of negligence in such a way as would accurately determine or even greatly illuminate the countless instances in which the category applies. The specific vocabulary of negligence presents countless limitations, exceptions, extensions, multiplications and contradictions of the basic moral principle expressed in *Donoghue* v *Stevenson* [1932] AC 562, to the effect that there was a 'general public sentiment of moral wrong-doing for which the offender must pay' on some if not all occasions. When, as a matter of law, the defendant must pay is regulated by a complex terminology which has grown up over the intervening fifty years and purports to specify and govern legal issues concerning, for example, the existence and breach of duties of care, standards of care, remoteness of damage, kind and quantum (amount) of damage and so on. All such categories claim to specify, in terms of professionally construed concepts, when liability will be occasioned. If we turn to see what these categories in fact mean we discover, in 1981, in a case purportedly concerning remoteness of damage and causation, that ultimately 'a robust and sensible approach . . . will more often than not produce an instinctive feeling' and that Watkins LJ had on the facts before him 'the instinctive feeling that the squatting damage here is too remote' (*Lamb* v *Camden London BC* [1981] 2 WLR 1038). Elsewhere, reference to instinctive feelings, to 'common sense' or to the legal view of what is reasonable or fair, is only slightly more oblique. In 1984 the test for a duty of care in a negligence action concerning, among other things, the recoverability of economic loss, was formulated by a unanimous House of Lords in the case of *Governors of the Peabody Donation Fund* v *Sir Lindsay Parkinson and Co Ltd* [1984] 3 AER 529, in the following stages. The court moved first from a general principle, the view that it was 'advantageous if the law is in accordance with sound *common sense*'. Next the court canvassed views from an earlier decision of the House (*Dorset Yacht* p. 143) where the court had concluded that 'in the situation stipulated in the present case it would not only be *fair* and *reasonable* that a duty of care should exist but it would be contrary to the *fitness of things* were it not so . . . Policy need not be invoked where *reason and good sense* will at once point the way.' Mentioning finally that the court is the 'spokesman of the *fair and reasonable man*' it was concluded that 'in determining whether or not a duty of care of particular scope was incumbent on the defendant it is material to take into consideration whether it is *fair and reasonable* that it should be so' (emphases added). Time and again the court invokes the categories of reason, justice, fairness, fitness, good sense and common sense as in the end determining the existence or non-existence of a legal duty. In short, its reference is to the traditional legal hermeneutic sense of community, ethos and value by which to judge the 'true meaning' of a given category.

There are of course considerable problems with the procedure just outlined. Not least one might argue that the benign humanism of ageing members of the legal profession is not the most rational of methods for resolving social conflict. What cannot be doubted, however, is that far from decreasing, the judicial recourse to general sentiments of social value can be found in all branches of the common law. The hermeneutic issue of what is 'reasonable in all the circumstances' pervades both public and private law and is increasingly acknowledged and identified in areas of law where previously legal doctrine had claimed to operate upon the basis of more precise and technical categories. Increasingly the courts are explicitly prepared to recognize and to discuss the policy factors relevant to the determination of legal values and in that sense they provide at least some explicit guidance as to the application of the legal categories. In crude terms, however, the invocation of a very few broad heads of policy and of public policy does not arrive at the heart of the issue, which is rather that there still remains considerable latitude for using the legal categories in any of a number of ways. To understand how the categories are in fact used or how the policy constraints are implemented involves looking behind their explicit formulation to the values of the legal community and doctrinal commitments by whom and by reference to which they are administered. The categories themselves, in other words, have no single or settled meanings; their reference is illusory in the simple sense that, for example, whether or not a particular bargain was struck as the result of 'economic duress' (*Universe Tankships of Monrovia* v *Int. Transport Federation* [1982] 2 WLR 803), whether or not a particular breach of contract will result in the contract coming to an end (*Hong Kong Fir Shipping Co* v *Kawasaki* [1962] 2 QB 26), whether a particular naturally occurring hazard constitutes a legal nuisance (*Leakey* v *National Trust* [1980] 1 AER 17), or whether or not a particular administrative decision was contrary to the principles of 'natural justice' (*Bushall* v *Secretary of State for the Environment* [1980] 2 AER 608), all eventually revolve around the judicial view of social propriety or reasonableness in the circumstances of the case.

Precedent and our reading of the categories of precedent as the expression of legal community is at its most basic an exploration of the institutional bases of legal decision. Hermeneutics teaches that an adequate reading of legal texts will pay less attention to the self-conscious formulations of method and of rules to be found in the text itself than to the methods of interpretation, to the tradition and values of which the text is evidence. That tradition and values change is indisputable and Parliament will itself frequently intervene to remove the more obviously archaic elements of the common law. Nonetheless, the point remains that the interpretation of legal categories is an exercise in moral reasoning and that lawyers can predict the outcome of that enterprise not by means of mathematically precise rules but rather by virtue of a knowledge of legal values and legal community in which rules play only a very general and really very limited role. Thus, by way of final example, a lawyer might well have been able to predict in 1968 that an action for damages in negligence brought against a barrister would be unlikely to succeed but he or she could certainly not have pointed to any rule or rules which would preclude such an action. In the event the House of Lords in *Rondel* v *Worsley* [1969] 1 AC 191, decided that in so far as the negligence complained of occurred during the preparation or conduct of litigation the barrister owes no duty of care. Of the various justifications offered for this outcome the court discovered:

 (i) an overriding value in the form of a duty owed by the barrister to the court and to the 'administration of justice', which duty should be fulfilled free of the possibility of negligence actions brought by clients;
 (ii) that the House felt it undesirable that aggrieved clients might reopen issues already tried and decided by the court in the original action;
 (iii) that it was thought undesirable that a barrister be open to the potential damage to professional reputation that an action for negligence would incur.

We would observe very briefly that barristers are not alone in having professional reputations to protect, nor are they alone in owing a duty to a principle of broader scope than that of their clients' interests (the most obvious example being the medical profession and the Hippocratic oath), yet other professional bodies do not have the same immunity. As to the issue of retrial, the opening up again of issues already decided by the court, it is misleading in the sense that a negligence action claims that the barrister – or doctor or accountant – acted in an unprofessional manner, that he or she fell below the standard of care owed by persons of that profession, and not necessarily that the outcome of the trial would have been different or that life or limb or company could have been saved.[6] In short, the House of Lords to some degree evidenced in that case a view that the legal profession (barristers at least) is special or privileged as compared to other professions, that it has a mission that transcends the coarse self-interest and the prejudices of everyday social conflicts, and it is to this claim that we shall now turn.

5.3.3 *Authority and legal reason as doctrine*

In hermeneutic terms and so also in terms of common sense it would be quite permissible and indeed accurate to say that the decision in *Rondel* v *Worsley* made new law. The broad argument of the previous section was precisely to the effect that it is a general truth that in imposing their own particular conceptions of community the judicial interpreters of precedent necessarily create new law. The vocabulary of the common law is a connotative lexicon, a generic language which, even where it resists explicit use of ethical standards of reasonableness, fitness, justice, fairness and the like, is sufficiently broad or context-independent to allow for any of several meanings to its key terms. The judiciary do indeed from time to time explicitly acknowledge their role as protectors of the community and of communal standards. In such instances they recognize and declare the traditional hermeneutic task of the humanistic lawyers, the task of interpretations that create law by building upon a textual past and the values that such texts are understood to have transmitted. In short, the hermeneutic task is not one of algebraic or purely logical precision, but a much broader endeavour aimed at moral or ethical interpretations and at the constant evaluation and implementation of tradition and community. The question remains, however, of whose traditions and which community.

The concept of legal authority within the hermeneutic tradition described above resides in the recognition that its interpretations of the legal categories, its creations of legal meanings and rules, are founded upon moral knowledge or ethical insight. The authoritative legal interpretation implements the traditional values in a scholarly and morally justified way. It is moreover the supreme paradox of the past century or more of common-law development that in almost direct proportion to the increase in the interpretative and creative role of the law, both the judiciary and the textbook theories of legal reasoning and adjudication have denied and attempted to banish the hermeneutic philosophy and techniques. In the standard account of the system of precedent from the mid-nineteenth century to the present decade, hermeneutics has been forced to take second place in the professional accounts of legal method and technique; it has been supplanted by an ideal, the rationalist concept of the rule of law. For the professional lawyer – academic or practising – it has been convenient to make use of a variety of theories which explicitly deny that legal authority is founded upon value and interpretation. Obviously such theories are debated and their more exaggerated claims are challenged but the governing ethic of the legal profession and of the study of law is one which straightforwardly states that lawyers simply apply rules, that they are mechanics or technicians of an obscure but practical knowledge. In such a context of value-freedom the lawyer has only one technique of interpretation, that of reason, and only one community, the universal community of rationality. The authority of law becomes the authority of logical truths. More importantly in terms of reading the law, the doctrine of the rule of law operates to stipulate a particular style to legal judgments and a particular form to the presentation of legal arguments in terms of rules.

While the concept of the rule of law is expressed in a variety of different ways and is explained in terms of very different logical and interpretative implications, it is itself a relatively simple political or constitutional principle. The rule of law refers in very broad terms to the ideal that the legal regulation of social relations is to take place through general rules applied in an impartial fashion to all persons alike. The rules are to be known in advance, they are to apply equally to all persons, and their application is therefore to be placed in the hands of a disinterested and distinct profession of official rule specialists: lawyers and more particularly the judiciary. The important point to be recognized in all the different formulations of the rule of law is that it proposes as a doctrinal truth the separation of the validity of law or the question of legal authority from political or moral or even social justifications. The rule of law as the government of rules and not of individual or group interests is presented as an exercise in the logic of rules – the judge is the neutral instrument of rules that come from outside the community of lawyers and are merely impartially applied by the legal institution. For present purposes we may summarize the rule-of-law doctrine as the source of a particular conception of judgment or adjudication according to the logical entailments of rules as opposed to the political or moral preferences of the rule-interpreters.

In many respects the nineteenth century was the heyday of the doctrine of the rule of law as a political and constitutional principle. In 1861, for example, it is in essence the rule of law which is very simplistically referred to by the Lord Chancellor, Lord Campbell, in the case of *Beamish* v *Beamish* [1861] 9 HL Cases 274, as justifying the adherence of the House of Lords to its own previous decisions: 'the law laid down by ratio decidendi being clearly binding on all inferior tribunals and on all the rest of the Queen's subjects, if it were not considered as equally binding upon your lordships, this House would be arrogating to itself the right of altering the law and legislating by its own separate authority.' In terms of the manner in which cases are to be decided and by implication also the manner in which they are to be read, the decision restricts the House of Lords in very simplified terms to examining the meaning of rules and resisting the temptation to legislate. A century and just over two decades later, in the curious context of a House of Lords decision concerning the scope of liability in negligence for nervous shock, Lord Scarman reformulated the doctrine in terms of principles – in terms of generalizations that are broader than any specific justification required for the case in hand. In its actual usage, a principle would appear to be either a broad rule derived from a major House of Lords decision and lent dignity or authority by continued usage, or a rule or generalization of the legal value that underlies a related series of cases. In the case in question, Lord Scarman argued that the constitutional function of the court, the House of Lords, was to decide the case before it on the basis of legal principle: 'by concentrating on principle the judges can keep the common law alive, flexible and consistent, and keep the legal system clear of policy problems which neither they nor the forensic [legal] process which it is their duty to operate, are equipped to resolve. If principle leads to results that are thought to be socially unacceptable, Parliament can legislate to draw a line or map out a new path.' Social, economic and administrative policy issues raised by the case were to be ignored because such issues could not be handled by the court process (*McLoughlin* v *O'Brian* [1982] 2 AER 298). By 1982, however, it is arguable that the proposition put forward by Lord Scarman is a residual one and of a relatively limited symbolic application even within the area of law then under consideration. Whatever the practical or substantive limitations of the concept of the rule of law, however, it remains the case that legal doctrine still requires legal argument to be formulated in terms of rules and legal principles and the system of precedent is still most often taught in terms of *stare decisis* or rule-following. Rules, we are told by the judiciary and by the textbooks, are still the guardians of our freedom and the rule of law is our protection against arbitrariness of government or misuse of power.

No one would deny that the various forms of rules and principles operative within the system of precedent are of great significance as a language for stating or describing the major available legal arguments relevant to specific issues or areas of law. The language of rules also has an important role to play in maintaining the legal vision of ethical community: rules are aligned to the value of the legal profession as a source of continuity, of precedent or repetition, in that rules are said to render the decision-making process certain and predictable, calculable and knowable. It is undoubtedly important to the legal profession to maintain the image of the rule of law or of the law of rules as part of the legitimating function of legal community, particularly in areas of political conflict. However, as the hermeneutics of legal community shows, legal rules are resources, or the means of legal argument; they are not the iron cage of certitude that the judiciary or the textbook will sometimes suggest. On the contrary, 'whatever the importance of the rule of law as ideology, as a legitimation of government, it can be doubted whether a comprehensive system of legal rules binding state agencies and citizens alike has ever been a primary basis of social order' (Cotterrell, 1984, p. 169; also Unger, 1978, pp. 176–81). We have tried to show that the system of precedent does not and cannot depend upon any literal (or strict) concept of a logic of legal rules. While it is important to keep the doctrine of the rule of law and of the separation of powers in mind when reading legal texts, the language in which legal judgments are formulated should not hide the essential ethical, political and social choices that interpreters of the law are inevitably involved in making. We shall review some of the principal hermeneutic reasons for treating the concept of rule-following and the value of legal certainty with caution and conclude in the final section by analysing the most fundamental reason of all, that relating to the mode or the techniques of law-application – the question of reading legal outcomes.

We would observe very briefly that:

(a) The common law is professional knowledge. Case law is seldom reported in the national media aside from the occasional sensational trials and even if routine legal decisions were available outside the specialist reports, they would be largely incomprehensible to non-lawyers. It is not general knowledge that case law makes or develops the law and it can be forcefully argued that 'the convoluted and archaic style in which it is presented, the volumes and volumes in which it is contained, the labyrinth of courts from which it is reported all contrive to keep it in the hands of a profession rather than the layman' (McBarnet, 1982, p. 412).

(b) The concept of the rule of law vastly overestimates the importance of formal legal rules in economic and social life. Even during the period of the Industrial Revolution when the impersonality and predictability of the law was often said to be essential to the security of economic transactions and developments, 'in fact it is neither clear that industry and trade wanted or needed the law, nor that the law did, or could have provided, the predictability so often asserted' (Rubin and Sugarman, 1984, pp. 4–5). More contemporary social studies clearly indicate that formal law is only one of many sources of discipline and control in modern states. To a large extent, national and multinational business will regulate itself, while 'the hierarchies that affect most directly and deeply the individual's situation are those of the family, the workplace and the market' (Unger, 1978, p. 180; Henry, 1984).

(c) Where the legal system is the direct source of authority and decision, it is again not always clear that the legal community in its entirety follows the rules set down in the reported precedents. The law reports are accounts of the decisions of the upper courts and are written by professional lawyers for professional lawyers. The bulk of the law's contact with the public is, however, in the courts of first instance, particularly the magistrate's court, as well as various tribunals. Trial in the magistrate's court does not often involve formal legal argument – the overriding majority in criminal cases are unrepresented by lawyers, are institutionally directed towards pleading guilty and are judged and sentenced by a lay magistrature which is not required to provide any formal or written justification for decisions that will seldom if ever be widely reported. There is, in short, an inequality between individual and institution which is most marked in the lower courts where the unrepresented individual will take on the financial resources, fact-gathering capacity and institutionalized knowledge of officials of the State and its enforcement agencies (McBarnet, 1981; Carlen, 1976).

(d) Even where the formal rules are invoked, their role is a questionable one. The generality of the legal categories is such that there will always be a number of categories or rules or even policies that will be relevant and available to argument in any given situation. The case reports will provide a wealth of competing rules covering similar situations, competing interpretations of the same rule in different contexts and competing references to factors or values that will negative or support a rule-application. Thus we see precedent dramatically at work in the hands of the Lord Chief Justice in interpreting the generic authority on the English administrative-law category of natural justice:

> Of course there is a wealth of authority on what are and what are not the rules of natural justice. The rules have been described in various ways, as 'an unruly horse', I think, in one decision, and there is no doubt that what may be the rules of natural justice in one case may very well not be the rules of natural justice in another. As has frequently been said, and there is no harm in repeating it, all that the rules of natural justice mean is that the proceedings must be conducted in a way which is fair to the firm in this case, fair in all the circumstances. (*R* v *Commissioner for Racial Equality, ex parte Cottrell and Another* [1980] 3 AER, 265)

What is 'fair' in law is intimately a hermeneutic question, it asks precisely how 'all the circumstances' are to be constructed and how policy, value, community and tradition are to be interpreted in the particular case.

5.3.4 *Legal judgment and legal technique*

The most important contribution of hermeneutics to legal studies has undoubtedly been its insistence upon the relationship between interpretation, understanding and application (*subtilitas applicandi*) of legal rules. All three elements are parts of the same process, such that it is meaningless to talk of the validity or sense of a text, or rule, gospel or law, outside the moment and situation of its application in a concrete judgment or preaching. Everything set down in law exists in a positive tension with definite action or decisions. There is, in the hermeneutic viewpoint, an ambiguity in the law which is centred upon the relation between generality or rule and practical reality: 'it is the work of interpretation to make the law concrete in each specific case, i.e. it is a work of application . . . The application of the law is not simply a matter of knowing the law – the dogmatic existence of law is of less importance than hermeneutics, the creative supplementing of the law' (Gadamer, 1979, pp. 295–6). In short, the essential task of legal hermeneutics is formulated time and again as being that of applying the historical or traditional meanings of the law to the contemporary case. The task is a practical one; it involves adapting the transmitted law to the needs of the present, as the legal community conceives them to be, it involves linking the 'legal idea' to a concrete reality (Betti, in Bleicher, 1980) in such a way as to mediate what was previously understood with what is currently required or desirable. Again it is Gadamer who provides the most sophisticated account of the task of legal hermeneutics:

> It is not its task to understand valid legal propositions, but to discover law, i.e. so to interpret the law that the legal order fully penetrates reality . . . That an interpretation of the law is, in a juridical sense, an act that creates law cannot be contested. The different principles that are applied in this act, for example the principle of analogy or the principle of filling in gaps in the law, or finally the productive principle that lies in the legal decision itself, i.e. that depends on the particular legal case – reach deeply into the material of the law itself. (Gadamer, 1979, pp. 470–1)

Of the 'principles' of law-application which Gadamer mentions – those of analogy, filling gaps (lacunae) and reaching a decision – it is the last which is the most significant. The general propositions that the court invokes in deciding a case, the analogies (resemblances, likenesses) that the court cares to summon up, the gaps that it seeks to fill in the abstract framework of the law, are all resources or means by which the court can arrive at the decision that is deemed to be most suitable to the case before it. Gadamer even goes so far as to comment that 'the distance between the universality (generality) of the law and the concrete legal situation of a particular case is essentially indissoluble' (Gadamer, 1979, p. 471). There is, in other words, no way in which abstractly formulated rules can fully determine in advance how the particular case is to be decided and the reason for this is not simply that the general rule is sometimes ambiguous, nor that the particular case was unforeseen or unforeseeable at the time that the rule was stated. The reason is much more simple and pervasive: it is that the system of case law operates not at the level of the general rule or the legal principle but at that of the concrete case, that is at the unique level of the facts of the particular case. Once such a circumstance is recognized and the individual case is seen for what it is, as being always to some extent an individual decision, then it becomes much clearer that to understand the law is to understand a process of judgment: the exercise of the judicial choice or discretion in relation to particular facts. The choice inherent in law-application is not an arbitrary or necessarily an extensive one. It is a choice – as we have seen earlier – that is firmly embedded in legal community and legal values, it is a discretion that is exercised in the language of rules and generally with explicit regard to the legally recognizable consequences of decisions; but it is nonetheless always a discretion and it is always logically possible, on the facts of the case, to exclude the general rule or to find that another rule or principle will override the apparent rule. In concluding our discussion of hermeneutics we will look at two crucial facets to law application and will reserve for the next chapter the more extended discussion of the rhetorical face of legal rules.

(i) *Facts and rules – instancing the case.* The general description of how case-law precedent works has tended to be given in terms of the obligation imposed upon later courts to follow the rules set down in earlier cases. The earlier case states a rule or several rules which are to be defined as, for example, a combination of the facts treated as material by the judge and the decision based on and related to those facts (Prof. A. L. Goodhart) or as any rule of law treated by the judge as a necessary step in reaching a conclusion (Prof. R. Cross), the conclusion being the decision on the facts of the case before the court and as found or categorized by the court. The legal rule is always to be related to what is 'decided' or 'concluded' in the particular case being used as a precedent. Such a requirement invests even the definition of a legal rule with the duality of legal hermeneutics as a whole, the peculiar result of such a duality – that between the general and the particular – being that it is logically impossible to state what the law is. The very definition of the legal rule renders it unknowable, if only for the very simple reason that it will never be possible to state in advance how a rule enunciated in relation to one set of facts will be treated in relation to a later – and never identical – factual context.

The first, relatively trivial, point to be made is that 'in mere logic there are as many general propositions extractable from a decision as there are possible combinations of distinguishable facts in it' (Stone, 1966). Further, those distinguishable facts may be stated at any of a number of levels of generality, thereby allowing the judge to include or distinguish the future case according to factors outside the logical or linguistic meaning of any given rule, a position which leads one commentator to observe that:

the mystique of case law lies not only in the esoteric nature of professional knowledge; it lies in the very particularistic and *post-hoc* form it takes ... Since every case is, or can be made out to be, unique, this means that what the law is in relation to that case, whether it will continue an established line of reasoning or establish a new refinement, cannot be definitely known in advance. The case by case method means that you literally never know what the law is. (McBarnet, 1982, pp. 412–13)

Each case, in other words, will refine and reformulate the rule according to the legal definition and evaluation of the facts before the court.

Take, for example, two loosely comparable situations. In *case A* a landowner C employs D to construct a reservoir to supply a mill on C's land with water. Through no fault of C's the water collected on the land escapes and causes damage to the property of an adjoining landowner, who sues for damages in tort. In *case B* a landowner L builds a munitions factory on L's land and, without any proven fault on L's part, causes severe injury to a third party who was visiting the factory when a number of shells exploded. In *case A*, decided in 1868, it was held that the plaintiff could succeed in an action for damages on the basis of a generically established legal principle which became known by the name of the case, the rule in *Rylands* v *Fletcher* [1868] LR 3 HL 330. The rule or rules that allowed recovery in that case have generally been formulated in terms of the proposition that where someone brings on to their own land, for their own purposes, and collects there something which was not naturally there and is likely to do mischief if it escapes, they must keep it there at their peril. If they fail to do so they are liable for all the natural consequences of its escape irrespective of whether or not they had been at fault in allowing the escape. *Case B* was decided in 1947 (*Read* v *Lyons* [1947] AC 156) and refused to apply the so-called rule in *Rylands* v *Fletcher* on the grounds, among others, of factual differences between the two cases. Even a brief analysis of the judgments in *Read* v *Lyons* shows

(i) that the rule in *Rylands* v *Fletcher* was only one of several rules potentially applicable to the case;

(ii) that the rule in *Rylands* v *Fletcher* itself could be formulated at any of a number of different levels of generality;

(iii) that in the event the rule, however formulated, did not apply and several different justifications for this non-application could be provided.

Of the factual differences between the two cases, the following appeared to be amongst the legally more significant: *case A* involved damage to property (*alienum*) and consequently harmed proprietary interests, *case B* involved injury to a person (*alium*) and consequently harmed personal interests only;

the distinction in question being a doctrinal one for which no direct authority was cited. *Case A* involved an escape from the land in question while in *case B* there was no such escape; the distinction here being based upon the formulation of the rule in *Rylands* stressing the relation between a term of the rule (escape) in the case and the facts on which it was based. The facts of *case A* were decided during peacetime while the facts of *case B* were decided in wartime – a difference strictly extrinsic to the earlier case but relevant to the particularization, the contextualizing, of *case B*. Finally and perhaps most strikingly, the collection of water on the land in *case A* was a non-natural use of the land, the collection of explosives on the land in *case B* was held to be a natural use of the land; the distinction here being simple pragmatism or policy with little relation to the meaning of the original rule.

If, as is the position in American law, one possible formulation of the rule in *Rylands* was that ultra-hazardous activities will bring with them a tortious liability for any harm that they may cause, then it must be accepted that there is no immediately obvious reason for not applying that principle in *Read's* case. It is not for any logically compelling reason that the principle does not apply in the later case nor is there any overriding reason for regarding the two sets of facts as being distinguishable. In the end it simply has to be acknowledged that the very form of the case-law rule provides the judges in subsequent cases with any number of possible factual distinctions for the very reason given earlier, namely that no plausible theory of logic or of meaning can formally stipulate how the given legal rule – even granted there is simply one applicable rule – is to be related to the facts of the instant case. The judge must necessarily create the specific link between the general and the particular and, as traditional legal hermeneutics has long recognized, that is an unavoidable consequence of the act of interpretation as an act of judgment. Whatever the language used in describing the decision, and in *Read's* case it is that of principles and rules, there is always a choice as to how to instance the case or how to make it concrete in relation to the particular parties, groups, classes, interests and general policy factors and consequences involved in the decision. There is, in short, a further factual element to be considered, that of the social and economic reality to which the case is to be related, a question we shall formulate in terms of the legal 'outcome' to the case.

(ii) *Reading legal outcomes.* The possibility of distinguishing the facts of a case and so not always applying a rule of precedent, the ability to create exceptions to the rule, is clearly a powerful resource in the development of the common law. As the example above illustrates, however, the designation of legal similarities and differences is not simply a question of observed facts. Because every case is in principle unique it is always possible to distinguish it from prior cases. In consequence it is necessary to construct a legal reason for distinguishing the facts of a case from those of an earlier decision although the courts and legal doctrine more generally will frequently deny that any choice or significant choice has been exercised or any meaningful or novel departure from the pre-existent law has occurred. Many if not most cases are 'easy cases' in the eyes of legal doctrine and the facts presented are simply and logically subsumed under the pre-existent rule. Easy cases, however, are seldom as unproblematic as they are presented as being; what is easy about such cases is not that there is no element of choice in relating the rule to the facts of the case but rather that pre-existent legal values, common sense or legal sense of community clearly favour one outcome rather than another. Provided that the legally desired outcome is not in doubt then rules and facts can be made to produce such an outcome. There was no difficulty, for example, in the Scottish criminal case of *Hartley* v *HM Advocate* [1979] SLT 26; (McBarnet, 1982) in holding that a confession to murder was 'fair' and admissible as evidence on the facts of the case as found by the court of first instance. The facts were that a seventeen-year-old had been taken to a police station in Glasgow to aid police in a murder enquiry. He had been held in custody for twelve hours without sleep and without either legal or parental guidance or advice. Shortly after 2.30 a.m. he had, in the course of one of many interrogations, confessed to the murder of a five-year-old boy. The three Scottish Law Lords sitting in the appeal against conviction, had no doubt whatsoever that the confession had been 'voluntary' and that what had taken place had been fair. The court was able both to uphold the general rule of precedent that confessions be voluntary and fair as an essential principle of the relevant system of case law and also hold the appellant, on the facts of the case, to be clearly and correctly convicted. While it is clearly not possible to comment on the decision itself, it is possible to observe that the meaning of the rule that confessions be voluntary and that the confession be obtained by fair means is, in practice or in terms of the legal outcome to the case in question, somewhat less a matter of the abstract meaning of a clearly established civil right and more a question of policy and value or here expedience in the enforcement of law and order. 'The theoretical freedom to exercise a right', as an earlier Scottish court had described the 'right' to refuse police detention without a warrant, is not necessarily a right in practice or in fact (*Swankie* v *Miller* [1973] SLT 28) and it would be inaccurate or at the very least naïve to read the case reports or the development of precedent without careful attention to the details of outcomes.

To read the legal outcome is to examine the content of the legal decision and to analyse the narrative it contains: how did the dispute or prosecution occur, how was it presented and how did its resolution affect the pre-existing state of both legal and extralegal affairs? To some extent, in other words, the legal decision represents an inquiry into social conflict and one approach to analysing cases is to look at the way that such judicial inquiries endeavour to resolve those conflicts. We have already observed several features of how such decisions are reached – they are conducted professionally and are consequently somewhat opaque or secretive, both in terms of the professional language used, and in terms of publicly available knowledge of the law created in legal decisions. More important still, the structure of legal argument is concerned with rules and not with facts. Where the facts of a case are discussed in any detail they are addressed primarily in terms of the individual litigants and their conduct and only secondarily, if at all, in terms of the social as opposed to the legal significance of the decision arrived at. The courts 'do things' with rules and as a community or institution they have specific functions to perform and goals to achieve within the wider social and political context of the decision-making process. Precisely because the factual elements of a decision are treated in terms of individuals, however, and because the justification of the decision will be presented in the language of legal rules, in terms of generalized categories, the case report makes it extremely difficult to read the narrative basis of the legal outcome or to assess fully the content of the case in terms of its material context and its social, economic and other policy implications.

The decision arrived at in a specific case and the justification given for that decision in the reported judgments do not simply reflect the individual content or narrative structure of the particular dispute and its resolution. Certain forms of argument or justification are inadmissible to the legal community. Legal doctrine also requires a particular form and language to be given to the judgment. On occasions where the case has attracted a wider audience than that of the legal profession itself, further consideration is likely to be given to the communication of the relevant legal values and attitudes, as well as to the requisite image of legal authority and rationality in providing an outcome. Hermeneutics, because it is concerned primarily with passing on or teaching a tradition, is not really equipped to examine these different levels of the construction and communication of legal meanings and messages to different audiences. Hermeneutics will tell us what a tradition is and it will also allow us to understand the historical character and spirit of a tradition, but it is the older discipline and techniques of rhetorical analysis that must be turned to if we are to approach the question of how legal texts achieve their different effects and work to communicate different meanings to different audiences. To put the same point in a slightly broader perspective, it could be said that hermeneutics preserves tradition and constantly endeavours to emulate or repeat the logic of a past culture, whereas rhetoric is broader than tradition and traditional disciplinary boundaries, and exists to describe and to question the received values. At its best it is a form of social and political criticism which constantly threatens the orthodox textual meanings and doctrines with the account of the administrative and political practices to which they are tied. Rhetorical analysis confronts the speaker not only with an account of what has been said but also with an account of what has been done and it is to this issue, that of the relation of legal text to legal practice, that the next chapter is addressed.

NOTES

1 The most elegant account is to be found in F. Nietzsche, *Homer and Classical Philology* (Edinburgh, 1903) idem, *We Philologists* (Edinburgh, 1911) More detailed linguistic arguments to the same effect are to be found in V. Volosinov, *Marxism and the Philosophy of Language* (London, 1973).
2 The occasional references to hermeneutics in contemporary, Anglo-American, jurisprudence have tended to use it in this sense. Following Wittgenstein's interpretation of rule usage in the *Philosophical Investigations* (Oxford, 1963) it has been observed that recognizing and interpreting rules involves a degree of commitment to them, an 'internal aspect' which allows the interpreter to understand the rule and to be able to distinguish following the rule from going against it in novel circumstances. See, for introductory analyses, D. N. MacCormick, *Legal Reasoning and Legal Theory* (Oxford, 1978), appendix 1; R. Dworkin, *A Matter of Principle* (Cambridge, Mass., 1984).
3 See also, *Knuller* v *DPP* [1973] AC 435; *R* v *Gray* [1982] 74 Crim App Reports 324. For extrajudicial debate, see Lord Devlin, *The Enforcement of Morals* (Oxford, 1965); J. A. G. Griffith, *The Politics of the Judiciary* (London, 1985). For private-law examples see *Miller* v *Taylor* [1769] 4 Burr 2303; *Benyon* v *Nettlefield* [1850] 3 Mac & G 943; *Pearce* v *Brooks* [1866] LR 1 Ex 213. The most striking example of all is probably *Thompson* v *R* [1918] AC 221, 259.
4 More technical accounts of the distinction between connotation and denotation can be found in Hjemslev, *Prolegomenon to a Theory of Language* (London, 1962) for whom the connotative code is the purely expressive dimension of a language and it is this view which is borrowed and developed by Barthes, *Elements of Semiology* (London, 1967) for whom the connotative plane of a language is seen as being its purely ideological dimension.
5 The implications of this argument for the study of law and particularly for a critical legal studies will be examined in chapter 7. For the linguistic dimension of this issue see T. Todorov, *Theories of the Symbol* (Oxford, 1982); idem, *Symbolism and Interpretation* (London, 1983), J. Derrida, *Margins of Philosophy* (Brighton, 1982), pp. 207–73.
6 For the contemporary position, see *Saif Ali* v *Sydney Mitchell* [1980] AC 198. The points made, however, remain unchanged with regard to the conduct of litigation, provided that the peripheral issue of proof of damage is ignored. Granted the ability and willingness of the common law to estimate damage in terms of probabilities and percentages in relation, for example, to loss occasioned by breach of contract (as, for example, in *Chaplin* v *Hicks* [1911] 2 KB 786), or indeed in relation to other forms of tortious loss, especially physical injuries,

there would seem no compelling reason why such an approach could not, granted the motive, be applied to professional negligence. Further, where negligence was proven to the satisfaction of the court then there would seem to be no conceivable argument for *not* re-examining the original trial, always granted that the negligence was capable of having materially affected that trial.

REFERENCES AND FURTHER READING

Bleicher, J. 1980: *Contemporary Hermeneutics*. London.
Cairns, J. 1984: 'Blackstone, an English institutist'. 12 *Oxford Journal Studies* 318.
Carlen, P. 1976: *Magistrates' Justice*. Oxford.
Cotterell, R. 1984: *The Sociology of Law*. London.
Dawson, J. 1968: *The Oracles of the Law*. Ann Arbor, Michigan.
Derrida, J. 1978: *Writing and Difference*. London.
Dilthey, W. 1976: *Selected Writings*. Cambridge.
Foucault, M. 1981: *The Archaeology of Knowledge*. New York.
Gadamer, H. 1979: *Truth and Method*. London.
Hart, H. 1962: *The Concept of Law*. Oxford.
Henry, S. 1984: *Private Justice*. London.
Kelley, D.R. 1982: *The Beginning of Ideology*. Cambridge.
Kelley, D.R. 1984: *History, Law and the Human Sciences*. London.
Levy-Ullman, H. 1935: *The English Legal Tradition*. London.
McBarnet, D. 1982: 'Legal form and legal mystification'. 10 *Int. Journal of the Sociology of Law* 409.
McBarnet, D. 1983: *Conviction*. London.
Mueller-Vollmer, K. 1985: *The Hermeneutics Reader*. Oxford.
Ong, W. 1958: *Ramus: Method and the Decay of Dialogue*. Cambridge, Mass.
Poggi, G. 1978: *The Development of the Modern State*. London.
Rubin, G. and Sugarman, D. 1984: *Law, Economy and Society*. Abingdon.
Skinner, Q. 1978: *The Foundations of Modern Political Thought* (2 vols). Cambridge.
Stein, P. 1966: *Regulae Iuris*. Edinburgh.
Stone, J. 1947: *Social Dimensions of Law and Justice*. London.
Stone, J. 1966: *Legal System and Lawyers' Reasoning*. London.
Ullmann, W. 1975: *Law and Politics in the Middle Ages*. London.
Unger, R. M. 1978: *Law in Modern Society*. New York.

6

Rhetoric: Precedent and Argument

6.1   INTRODUCTION

The earliest records of trials – or more accurately of judgments – within the western literary tradition are to be found in the Greek epic poems which were first set down in writing around 750 BC by Homer. The *Iliad* of Homer provides numerous accounts of disputes that lead to killing and feuding, and it also gives several examples of self-help in defence of rights, which self-help would on occasion lead to monetary or other recompense for harm or wrongs done. More remarkable than the various accounts of war, feuding and payment of blood-money, however, are the detailed descriptions which Homer gives of disputes settled by judgment in front of the assembly of the people in the public square or *agora*. The most famous instance of such a judgment in the *Iliad* (Bk. 18) is that of the trial depicted on the shield of Achilles.

Homer reports that there was a dispute in the assembly place, in which two men were in loud disagreement as to the compensation payable for the killing of a third party. One of the disputants claimed that the full compensation had been paid, while the other refused to receive that compensation, for reasons that are not entirely clear. Both parties were presenting their arguments to the assembled people and both wanted their grievance to be tried at the hands of a judge. The passage continues: 'the people were cheering them both on, supporting both sides; and heralds quietened the people. The elders sat on polished stones in a sacred circle, and held in their hands sceptres from the loud-voiced heralds; with these they were then hurrying forward and giving their judgments in turn. And in the middle lay two talents of gold, to give to the one who delivered judgment most rightly among them' (*Iliad*, 18. 497–508). The details of this passage have given rise to considerable scholarly controversy but it is possible at least to comment upon some of the main features of the trial. The dispute itself concerns the amount of compensation payable for the death of a relative, the sum needing to be sufficient to prevent or put an end to blood feud (retaliation killings). The issue is addressed to the people and the speeches are explicitly made – both in the passage given and in other passages – in the presence of the people, public speaking being 'an essential concomitant of judicial procedure in Homer' (McDowell, 1978, p. 17). Public opinion is essential to each stage of the trial. When open argument in front of the assembled people has failed to resolve the dispute, it goes to judgment. The judges are elders of the community (literally 'knowers') and each of the elders present would give a judgment. The judge who settles the dispute is the judge whose opinion is best received by the assembled people: the elder presents an opinion directly to the people and that opinion which receives most applause, the most public support, is the one accepted. The two gold.talents are paid to the elder who provided the best judgment.

The most significant feature of the trial is the degree of public or democratic participation in it. The public assembly, the *agora*, was both the place of judgment in matters of politics and of law, and also representative of the manner of judgment: carefully constructed speeches would be made before the assembled public and the judges too would speak to the public in giving their opinion or solution to the disputed issues. The simple reason for this form of procedure was that the people were eventually the judges of the best solution or judgment proferred by the elders. The first point to be made is thus that the people act, at each stage of the dispute, as the forerunners of the later classical Greek (450–220 BC) jury trial. The trial is adversarial, a dispute is conducted in front of the assembly and its outcome is democratically adjudicated. The second point follows from the first. The most important skill for anyone in any way involved in either a legal dispute or in proposing a political policy to the people, would be that of 'speaking well' or 'persuasively' to the assembly. In the Homeric trial cited and in several other scenes in the *Iliad*, the heroic actors will be called upon to speak publicly or formally to harangue the crowd and they would receive training in the art of these verbal disputes or contests. Such training in successful public speaking was eventually set down systematically in hand-books and became the technical art of rhetoric or oratory, the study of public speech in terms of communication and persuasion or effect.

Long before the emergence of any distinct class of lawyers or legal professionals in the west, the manuals of the rhetoricians of classical Greece had set down and taught the art of effective presentation and argumentation in the law courts of Sicily and Greece. The handbook literature or manuals on rhetoric date from the work of Corax and his student Tisias in mid-fifth-century BC Syracuse. From then there develops a tradition of technical or forensic (legal) rhetoric best defined as the study of effective speech before the newly established law courts of the Greek and Sicilian democracies.

Trial in those assemblies or courts was before a jury, the minimum size of which was, in Athens for example, 201 members. The jury was empowered to decide issues both of fact and of law, and the procedure of trial would consist of a speech by the plaintiff and a reply by the defendant, each in the form of a continuous address to the jury. The forensic handbooks would summarize the basic principles or techniques of effective presentation or discourse in the primary legal setting of the early classical assembly. From the accounts available, the concern of the manuals was principally with the organization and structure of legal rhetoric: a speaker would begin with an introduction (*prooimion*), continue with a narration (*diegesis*), and should follow that with witnesses, evidence and probabilities – with proof and refutation – and finally move to a conclusion (*epilogos*). The handbooks would also examine issues of style and of linguistic devices (principally metaphors) relevant to persuasion, but the most important aspect of proof or of making a persuasive case was the elaboration of arguments based upon probabilities by which Tisias, for example, is said to have meant that which seems true to the multitude, as in the following example: 'If a weak and brave man, having beaten up a strong and cowardly man, is brought into court, neither must tell the truth. The coward must claim that he was not beaten by a single brave man: i.e., he must claim to have been attacked by two or more, whereas the other must refute this, insisting that the two were alone, in order to use the argument "how could a little one like me have attacked a big one like him?" ' (Plato, *Phaedrus*, 273 a–c).

From its legal beginnings rhetoric developed rapidly both in terms of the sophistication of its techniques as well as in terms of the range of its subject-matter. Of the classical theorists of rhetoric, Isocrates and later Aristotle in Greece, and the Roman forensic orators Cicero and Quintilian are the most important for an understanding of the later meaning and uses of rhetoric as a discipline which was to study all forms of public speaking and was increasingly to concentrate particularly upon religious and literary forms of persuasion. During the Middle Ages rhetoric as *ars dictaminis* – the art of composition or of letters – was frequently more important to preaching, to literature and to poetry than it was to law, but its relevance to legal education was never wholly forgotten. During the formative period of the common law, for example, the very first lay legal experts were orators or indeed rhetoricians, the oral pleaders (narrators) before the royal courts whose skill or expertise was precisely that of verbal precision and linguistic dexterity in presenting correctly formulated pleadings: 'no one could be a successful lawyer in those days unless he were a skilful pleader; and to be a skilful pleader exactness of expression, above all things, is essential' (Holdsworth, vol. V, pp. 457–8).

More generally, eloquence and indeed elegance of speech were clearly regarded as virtues by the medieval legal profession. The ability to argue forcefully before court or jury was obviously an essential element of legal skill and it lay very much at the basis of the common lawyer's training in hypothetical problems of law, the *disputatio*, which would form the object of prolonged debates or 'moots' (mock trials) at the Inns of Court in the fifteenth and sixteenth centuries in particular. Finally, as the discussion of hermeneutics in the previous chapter indicated, the legal art is an art of interpretation; it is concerned not with a necessary or scientific logic, but with probable arguments, with evaluative reasoning and not with absolute certainty. Rhetoric is the discipline which most explicitly studies the techniques relevant to presenting and evaluating, affirming or refuting, such probable arguments. It is concerned precisely with analysis of the available means of persuading an audience that a particular decision or course of action is likely to benefit the community or, where the issue is one of past facts, that a particular account of events is the most probable or the most likely to conform to the truth (what happened). In the course of this chapter we shall look first at the general principles and themes of the rhetorical tradition and then examine their relevance to legal (justificatory) argument and particularly to an understanding of the rhetoric of legal texts; rhetoric here is defined as the reading of legal texts as acts of communication, as discourses designed to influence, to persuade and to induce action.

6.2 THE RHETORICAL TRADITION

The meaning of the term rhetoric and the uses of the rhetorical discipline have changed dramatically and frequently over the course of their history and according to the different institutions (religious, legal, political, literary) in which they have played a significant role. The rhetorical discipline has experienced very fluctuating fortunes, numerous deaths and revivals, and only recently it has become something of a fashion again as the 'new rhetoric' (Perelman and Tyteca, 1958) or as semiotics (Todorov, 1982) or even as the critical discipline which unmasks or 'demystifies' ideologies (Eagleton, 1982). Aside from vague generalities of the kind which define rhetoric as simple persuasion or eloquence, any brief account of the purposes and techniques of rhetoric is likely to be extremely selective and will always be open to the charge of favouring one species of rhetoric over others. We therefore openly acknowledge that the following outline favours a critical rhetoric and concentrates on those aspects of the rhetorical tradition which come closest to political criticism in its classical sense of the study of arguments related to the historical situation and immediate needs of the community (*polis*) to which the speech or discourse is addressed.

A somewhat stronger version of the last-mentioned argument in favour of a critical rhetoric would emphasize the historical context of technical rhetoric and would equally observe the political circumstances or conditions under which the discipline has been significant. According to the classical authors, rhetoric was the invention of Corax of Syracuse and it was defined, as was observed earlier, as the art of speaking well before the law courts of the newly established democratic assemblies of Sicily and Greece. The most important factor to be noted from this claim to an origin is that rhetoric emerges as a discipline at the same time as the political form or system of democracy replaces the earlier monarchies and oligarchies of the heroic age. Speech and the science of 'speaking well in civil matters' (Quintilian), however, are not always politically or socially valuable traits, for 'what need is there for long expressions of opinion in the Senate when the best men quickly come to agreement? What is the need for many meetings before the people, when the ignorant multitude is not deciding a matter of political policy?' (Tacitus, *Dialogue*, p. 127). In broad terms, it can be argued that a discipline which teaches the art of persuasive speech is really only of value in a society where citizens are free to be persuaded or are capable of choosing between different courses of action. For eloquence to be important, speech must be socially meaningful; it must be imbued with some degree of social power – the ability to make a difference to events or actions and thus to find its place within an established public sphere. The incentive for a serious or technical rhetoric is thus the possibility of speech being publically or politically effective and the condition for this effective speech is a political system in which persuasion or dialogue are the means of decision-making rather than coercion or straightforward threat. Thus for the Roman Tacitus, discussing the conditions of the great oratory of the past, 'there was the high rank of the defendants and the importance of the issues, which of themselves are in the highest degree conducive to eloquence . . . For the power of genius grows with the importance of affairs, nor can anyone produce a speech that is brilliant and renowned unless he has found a case worthy of it' (Tacitus, *Dialogue*, p. 131). Rhetoric developed, in other words, because it served a purpose and it tended to flourish where it had the opportunity of being effective: 'great eloquence, like a flame, is fed by fuel, is excited by motion and grows bright as it burns' (Todorov, 1982, pp. 61–3).

The public sphere within which rhetoric flourished in classical Greece was a very limited one. It included the citizens of the individual city-state but it excluded the much larger number of non-citizens dwelling within the city – most notably women and slaves (Elshtain, 1981). With the later incorporation of Greece into the Macedonian Empire in the third century BC, that is with the destruction of the public sphere by virtue of the conquest of Greece by Alexander the Great, rhetoric virtually disappeared as a practical art in Greece. In the Roman Empire too, rhetoric and the public assemblies to which it was tied became progressively less significant as the emperors of imperial Rome expanded their power both at home and abroad. It is probably accurate to state that rhetoric was, from relatively early on, an elitist occupation and that it was tied to very limited democratic forms: it was taught to and was useful for the members of a fairly restricted ruling class who would use it in the assemblies to further their political or legal aims. The point remains, however, that within the fluctuating scope of the democratic public sphere that was available in Greece and Rome, rhetoric taught the rules of effective speech, of language as action tied to the functions of the various social institutions, that is to the religious, legal and political activities and decisions of the assembly. Rhetoric is defined by Aristotle in this spirit, as something useful, as a means of discovering the arguments available for proposing and carrying out a particular institutional or communal goal: rhetoric 'is useful; it functions not to persuade, but to discover the available means of persuasion in each case' (Aristotle, *Rhetoric*, I.I. 1355b). Slightly later Aristotle repeats the point in arguing that 'the speech has three elements – the speaker, the subject and the person addressed, and the end proposed has reference to this last, that is, to the hearer' (I.II. 1358b). We shall move now to examine the elements of the speech, those of speaker, subject and hearer, and look briefly at how the rhetoricians claimed to be able to influence their audiences.

6.2.1 *Speaker and institution*

The link between rhetoric and the democracy of the city-state or republic is an essential one. To understand speech, according to the rhetoricians, one must understand first its context and its purpose. Speech aims to communicate. It is always a dialogue – even inner speech is addressed to oneself – and it should therefore be understood analytically as a social activity or at least as an interaction between socially organized individuals. The speech is a process and the rhetoricians wanted to classify the various stages and contexts of that process. Obviously enough the speech begins with a speaker and it is consequently important to examine the qualities of the speaker and the effect that such qualities can have upon what is said and upon the influence or effectiveness of the statement.

The first rhetorical category is that of the speaker and it encompasses both the general and the particular attributes necessary for the successful orator. In general terms, there are various classes of speaker organized

according to thè institution to which they are tied or for which they speak.
For Aristotle and later rhetoricians there are three main institutional contexts of speech which are defined in terms of genre, those of the political
(deliberative), legal (forensic) and ceremonial (epideictic/panegyric) occasions of public speech. According to which institution or social context the
speaker belongs, she or he will inherit the vocabulary, style and purposes of
that institution. The political speaker, for example, will be concerned with the
future actions of the community or State, with diplomacy, war, legislation
and so on, and will attempt to exhort or dissuade the audience in terms of
the expediency of a particular course of conduct. Similarly, the legal speaker
will inherit the language and purpose of the legal assembly or the court. The
legal speaker will be concerned with accusation and defence in relation to
past actions; she or he will need to prove or to refute a cause of action and
will do so in terms of the justice or injustice of the proposed decision. The
point to be stressed is that there is always an institutional or social context to
both the speaker and the speech and this context is likely to affect not only
the terms and purposes that the speaker can refer to but also the status and
authority of what the speaker says.

In the assemblies of ancient (Homeric) Greece, the elders offering judgment to the people would hold a sceptre while they spoke. The sceptre
symbolized their judicial office and to some degree would have provided a
social or institutional authorization for their role and speech. Similarly, the
Roman forensic orators would wear special and, according to Tacitus,
highly restrictive robes when addressing the courts, and even today the
barristers and judiciary in the common-law courts wear wigs and gowns
which symbolize their social standing and their special role. In more general
terms, the point to be considered is that speaker and speech are socially
organized and authorized in carefully prepared rhetorical settings: the
medieval Church would jealously guard the right of priests alone to enter
the pulpit or to serve communion, in the same way that it is traditionally the
right of the academic to speak from the lecture podium, the right of the
judge to sit on the 'bench', of the Lord Chancellor to sit on the Woolsack in
the House of Lords and so on. What is signified is a rhetorical authority
which the institutional setting provides for the speaker and of which the
effective rhetorician will make full use.

While society or the prevailing political order will frequently determine
who may speak, on what occasions and with what likelihood of any great
effect, the rhetorical speech will also endeavour to establish its own authority or status. Rhetorical analysis will examine the 'circumstances' of a
statement and will consider 'who' said it, 'where, when, why, how and with
what assistance' (St Augustine, III. XII. 18–19) but will take greatest
account of the 'authorship' of what is said. The authority of the individual

speaker has traditionally been a matter of a mixture of qualities. Social position at birth was classically of great importance and statistically is still of considerable relevance, successful orators tending to be predominantly male and upper or upper-middle class in contemporary political, legal and academic institutions. In Britain in particular, noble birth of itself carries with it the opportunity of a rhetorical career in the House of Lords as a political body, the second of the two assemblies which make up the restricted forum of Parliamentary government. Where the authority of the speaker is not inherited or socially or legally prescribed, the rhetorician must endeavour to create it. In Aristotle's words, 'the speaker must not only see that the speech shall prove its point, or persuade, but must also develop a certain character in himself and in the judge, as it matters much for persuasiveness . . . that the speaker should appear a certain sort of person' (*Rhetoric*, II.I.1377b). It is important for the speaker to develop a personal authority based upon a display of a combination of knowledge, intelligence, virtue and good-will. Those qualities make the speaker trustworthy or credible, they lend weight to the speaker's pronouncements and increase the likely influence of the speech for the reason that the audience's 'estimate of a speech is not the same, but either wholly different or different in degree, according as we regard a person with feelings of affection or dislike, and are angrily or charitably disposed towards him' (II.I.1378a).

6.2.2 *Audience and argument*

In placing a considerable degree of importance upon who it is that is speaking, rhetoric comes to recognize that access to the public sphere or to politically and legally effective speech is often strictly regulated. Political society and more particularly the media will automatically provide the properly qualified speaker with an audience and the more strictly controlled access to the audience is, the less the personal qualities of the speaker matter. In strictly scientific contexts, for example, the quality of the speaker is supposed to be of little importance and it could indeed be said that the most rhetorically effective scientific speech will be one which gives itself the greatest appearance of impersonality or objectivity. The scientific speech should appear to instruct, to inform and to prove but if it performs the other offices of rhetoric connected with persuasion, with 'moving' or 'bending' (Cicero) the audience, this ought to appear to be on the strength of its rational content and not because of the persuasive power of the particular speaker. The conclusion to be drawn from this example of the rhetorical requirements of the contemporary scientific speech is a simple and crucial one. The rhetorical speech must be appropriate to its audience or, as Cicero explains it, the orator must 'adapt himself to occasions and persons. In my opinion one must not speak in the same style at all times, nor before all people, nor against all opponents, nor in defence of all clients, nor in partnership with all advocates. He, therefore, will be eloquent who can adapt his speech to fit all conceivable circumstances' (Cicero, *Orator*, 35–6). To classify the different kinds of audience and the arguments appropriate to them, to be rhetorically wise in Cicero's terms, was one of the major tasks of classical rhetoric and constituted its most long-lasting and significant contribution to the theory of argument – the concept of topics or places of argument (*loci communes*).

Just as rhetoric considers the speaker in terms of both general, institutional, characteristics and also in terms of individual virtues or peculiarities, the audience or hearer is also to be examined according to various different levels of appropriateness of the speech to its context. For Aristotle, rhetoric is defined as 'the faculty of observing what are, in every situation, the available means of persuasion' (I.I.1355b). Although different schools of rhetorical thought have set out very distinctive sets of criteria for discovering the arguments available and appropriate to each specific context of speech or audience, they have tended to agree at least that it is always a primary task of the rhetorical study to indicate the means of appearing relevant and convincing to different audiences and on different subjects. In very general terms we may observe that any rhetoric seeks to induce co-operation between speaker and audience. It aims to produce 'contact of minds', 'agreement' or 'identification': the audience is brought to recognize itself in the values, purposes and arguments that the speaker proposes and ideally the audience will then act upon the values or attitudes expounded. The question which receives very different answers is how this effect of identification is to be produced, by what techniques or by what method, and by what arguments a consensus can be reached between speaker and audience. In the following paragraphs we shall summarize certain of the more general features of appropriateness and merely note in passing the possible extensions or alternatives to the positions and attitudes set out.

First, the speaker must look to the type of audience and should adapt the speech to the generally known characteristics of the audience type. Traditionally, rhetoric has approached the question of audience type in two stages. Initially there is the already mentioned question of the genre or institution to which the speech is attached or addressed. Originally the issue here was that of the three different forms of assembly, the legal, the political and the ceremonial, each of which would require a different kind of address and a different style of argument. The subsequent history of public speech and public sphere would require that the different kinds of genre be greatly extended to include, for instance, literature, propaganda, advertising, newspapers, bureaucratic circulars and so on, as well as the genres of the contemporary media and new technologies. Each genre or institution will be characterized by a specific set of expectations as to the appropriate mode of address or speech and will dictate to a greater or lesser extent who may speak, what they are to say and how they are to say it. To the general features of audience type should be added the specific peculiarities of the particular audience and the particular occasion. To the general advice given by Cicero as to the adaptation of the speech to its audience can be added the detailed and meticulous advice offered by Aristotle. With a great degree of subtlety, Aristotle lists the relevant categories or features of audiences that require attention. Each audience will have its own characteristics and context. Thus, for example, account should be taken of the place of address: 'it is not hard to praise Athenians to Athenians. One must represent, as existing, that which is honoured by each set of people – as by Scythians, or Lacedaemonians or philosophers' (I.IX.1367b). Similarly, account should be taken of the age, sex, social class, wealth, power and fortune of the audience. While there is plenty of scope to disagree with the actual description of character given by the classical rhetorician, the principle is easy enough to grasp. For example, in Aristotle's view, 'young men are lustful in character, and apt to do what they lust after . . . They are changeable and fickle in their desires . . . They are passionate, quick to anger and apt to obey their impulse . . . All their mistakes are on the side of excess or vehemence . . . they do everything *too much* (II.XII.1389a–b). As to the rich audience and the character of wealth, 'rich men are insolent and overweening . . . for they feel as if they had all goods – wealth being a sort of measure of the whole worth of all else, so that it seems to command all things . . . It is characteristic of the rich to think themselves worthy to govern . . . the character of wealth is that of a prosperous fool' (II.XVI.1391a).

Having ascertained the genre, the type and character of the audience, the speaker must look for or discover (*inventio*) arguments appropriate to that particular context. Each genre and each type of audience is to be analysed in terms of the values, beliefs and attitudes that it is likely to adhere to, that are persuasive to it or that are of particular relevance for it. The point to be made is a relatively simple one. Any speech must select an argument or premise from which to start, the orator must choose a beginning and develop the theme of the speech from such a beginning. The classical rhetoricians provided two sets of techniques related to available arguments, which are best classified in terms of universal and particular topics or places. The universal topics can be treated swiftly. They are general truths that are available to all arguments and will appeal to any rational audience or any group of hearers concerned with truth or objectivity. The concept of universal topics is derived from Aristotle and refers to necessary truths of an extremely vague or general kind concerning things that are preferable or desirable – particularly happiness and things conducive to happiness, generally viewed in terms of quantity, of a greater or lesser amount of good things. For Aristotle, for example, 'that is more desirable which is most useful at every season or at most seasons, e.g. justice and temperance rather than courage: for they are always useful, while courage is useful only at times . . . If everyone were just, there would be no need for courage, whereas all might be courageous, and still justice would be of use' (*Topics*, III.2.117a–b). Universal topics or general truths of the kind illustrated can be multiplied indefinitely. From Cicero, for example, we learn that an 'efficient cause is superior to one that is not; those things which are complete in themselves are superior to those which stand in need of other things; those which are in our power are preferable to those which are in the power of another; those which are stable surpass those which are uncertain; those which cannot be taken from us are better than those that can' (Cicero, *Topics*, XVII.70). The more recent rhetoricians Perelman and Tyteca add several examples of their own: what is rare is preferable to that which is easily obtained, the timely or seasonable is more to be desired than the ill-timed, that which exists has superiority over the possible, that which has gone before is to be preferred to that which comes later and so on.

The universal topics should be looked at – as the examples, we hope, indicate – somewhat critically. They are too vague to be either true or false of themselves, and have to be related to specific arguments or situations. While they do provide general arguments or themes which can be usefully manipulated in a particular context, their tendency is conservative and banal, they are clichés or tautologies which only really take on meaning when related to specific argumentative situations. The particular topics are of greater interest as 'storehouses for arguments' of relevance either to a specific audience or to a specific subject-matter. Each subject or discipline or genre has its own audience or audiences. In many senses, rhetoric as a practice exists precisely to create or confirm the identity of the audience, whose feeling of belonging is reinforced by speech which affirms and extends the argument or topics it already adheres to, and which appeals to values it considers its own. As a way of analysing speech or discourse, rhetoric therefore concentrates on the 'speech act' or utterance as a way of doing something or of communicating with an audience. Rhetoric will analyse any discourse as a dialogue and will attempt to set down the values or arguments which identify the speaker and the audience as belonging to the same genre or discipline. Thus, for example, particular arguments and methods of arguing are common to lawyers and are deemed to suit the needs of the legal community or are viewed as likely to be effective when used in legal settings. Arguments as to justice and injustice are the ultimate aim of the legal genre in the opinion of Aristotle and the specific topics of the legal discourse will be primarily concerned with ways of asserting the justice or injustice of the actions or omissions before the court. In very general terms, the principles of equity and the maxims of the common law form the broad base of legal topics or commonplaces: it is always open to the legal speaker to appeal to arguments taking as their starting point, for example, the topic that 'no-one may profit from their own wrong-doing', that 'the law cannot demand the impossible', that 'the law will forbid the arbitrary exercise of discretion' and so on as the situation dictates.

The rhetorical point, however, is not so much to review the content of the specific topics of a particular field of argument but to observe the general character of the audience as the most important element in a discourse. Literary skill, legal expertise, successful preaching, victory at the political hustings and so on will all depend to a large degree upon making use of the conventions or topics of argument within their specialized field or discursive domain. The reason for this is simply that by recognizing the needs of the immediate audience and by formulating the speech in terms of arguments that are familiar to that audience, the speaker is far more likely to achieve the broad objective of persuading the audience, of leading it in the direction that the rhetorician wishes to advocate. In brief, speech is always speech in a concrete situation and before a variety of *established* audiences. Rhetoric will study the character and beliefs of that concrete audience and will attempt to understand both the structure of the audience and also its current needs, so as to provide the speech with such situational relevance or topicality as is likely to ensure a sympathetic reception.

6.2.3 *Probability and proof*

Rhetoric differs from other disciplines in that it refuses to privilege or to adhere to any one set of values or any one conception of truth. For the rhetorician, all speech, all discourse, is contingent: all discourse belongs to a context and is addressed to a particular audience at a particular time and place. Just because the speech happens to be a legal judgment, a philosophical address, a prime-ministerial or presidential broadcast, does not make it any less a rhetorically organized statement with its own historical limitations. For the rhetorical analysis, all speeches are the same in that they are all attempts to engage in dialogue and in so far as the discourse has a purpose, they endeavour to persuade, to make their point. For the rhetoricians, speech is always a process, action within a context, and it would be wrong to allow any one context a privileged claim to have access to truth or to objectivity; precisely because discourse is situational it is concerned not with truth but with probability and improbability (verisimilitude), with what seems to be true to a particular audience or with that which has the effect of truth in a given context. The rhetorical approach to speech is thus pragmatic or functional; it is concerned not with absolute truth or pure logic but with a quasi-logic, that of practical actions and affairs or with what is termed 'practical reasoning' in contemporary legal theory.

Arguments as to probability, like the topics already mentioned, are either general or specific. General probabilities were of the kind that debated whether truth was greater than wisdom and were termed *quaestiones* by the Roman rhetoricians. Specific probabilities were termed *causae* and were concerned with particular cases, for example with debates as to whether X did Y, an offence meriting punishment Z. A discussion of a factual situation and probabilities of guilt or innocence connected with it would normally, however, raise some issue of a more general nature concerning, for example, motives for action or relations of cause and effect. For Quintilian, for instance, the legal speech in particular is characterized by the need to relate the case in hand, the conflicting situation or *causa*, to the legal problem or general issue of human behaviour which it raises as its *quaestio*. In either case, however, the problem facing the rhetorician will simply be that of presenting an argument which will fit the circumstances of the case into the interpretation which the rhetorician favours. The argument will need to show that the favoured outcome is more probable, likely or normal than any opposing view of the case. A relatively simple example of this kind of argument can be taken from one of the earliest rhetorical handbooks, the *Tetralogies* of Antiphon. A man has been killed in a lonely spot. The slave accompanying him was also attacked and has died, but not before stating that the defendant was the murderer. The prosecutor begins his speech by arguing that it angers the Gods and pollutes the moral atmosphere of the city if murderers go free. He goes on to point out that a crime that is premeditated is always the most difficult to discover and convict, he comments that in such cases 'great trust has to be placed in probabilities' and continues:

> It is unlikely that muggers killed the man, for no one who ran the risk of his life would have abandoned the object of his robbery when he had it in his hands. Yet the victims were found with all their property intact. Nor did someone kill them in a drunken frenzy, for we would have information from his fellow drinkers. Nor did the murder result from an argument, for they wouldn't have been arguing in the middle of the night in a deserted spot. Nor did the murderer kill the victim in mistake for somebody else, for he would not have killed both him and his slave. Since these probabilities are dismissed, the fact of the death points to the man having died as a result of premeditation. And who is more likely to have set upon him than one who had already suffered great wrongs at his hands and was expecting to suffer still more? That man is the defendant.

The orator continues to develop these probabilities, then summarizes the argument and stresses again the religious importance of removing murderers from the State. The defendant then presents a series of opposite probabilities: that the victim might well not have been robbed because the assailants were disturbed and they wisely preferred safety to profit, that the slave in terror of his life is unlikely to have recognized the murderer and would be prone in that state to outside influences, and so on.

Arguments as to probability are never absolutely conclusive; they appeal rather to a sense of normality or likelihood which is based not upon logic but upon group experience, opinions and points of view. In the above example neither set of arguments or reasons is indisputable; they are best regarded as elements in a controversy whose resolution will be the responsibility of the judge – in the case of the example given, the judge being the democratic assembly of at least 100 jurors. It can thus be concluded that the probability concerns nothing more definite than the general rule; the accusation cannot be refuted outright but can only be shown to be more or less generally true than the objections to it – its probability can be sustained or disproved in argument. In legal speech particularly, proof of the probable is an essential ingredient of judgment and its importance is continuously stressed. It is nonetheless necessary to remember that proof based upon probability is always a 'relative conception'; it is always open to dispute and to argumentative disproof: only authority can resolve a dispute as to probabilities and that resolution is no better than the justifications which are offered for it as a decision or judgment.

6.2.4 *Rhetorical style and rhetorical devices*

Despite popular images of rhetoric as the manipulation of language and as a discipline which disregards the truth in favour of the ornate or flowery style of persuasion, rhetoric was classically much more concerned with proof and probability than it was with questions of mere style (*elocutio*). For religious and legal rhetoric in particular, argument as to proof was the appropriate form of speech and in the classical view of rhetoric: 'it is manifest that the artistic [technical] rhetoric is concerned with proofs. The rhetorical proof is a sort of demonstration, for we entertain the strongest persuasion of a thing when we conceive that it has been demonstrated. A rhetorical demonstration is an enthymeme[1] – this being, generally speaking, the most authoritative of proofs ...' (Aristotle, *Rhetoric*, I.I.1355a). For Aristotle indeed an ideal rhetoric would seek only the most simple of styles, such as would cause 'neither pleasure nor pain; our facts ought to be our sole weapons, making everything superfluous which is outside the proof'

(III.I.1404a). The real virtue of rhetorical style was originally that of clarity or of perspicuity and it was only several centuries later that literary rhetoric came to be much more and eventually wholly occupied with questions of style and of the verbal devices or tropes – the figures of speech.

Although it is often argued to the contrary, it was only in relation to the literary and poetic genres of rhetoric that style became a primary focus of study.[2] Within the religious and legal genres of rhetoric a concern with style, with speaking well or with eloquence, was really no more than a concern with presenting in the most favourable light possible the topics and probabilities of the case to be argued. Rhetoric in these instances was never consciously immoral; it was rather eloquent in support of arguments as to the truth of the case, a position most forcefully expressed by St Augustine, a Christian rhetorician of the fourth century AD: 'who would dare to say that truth should stand in the person of its defenders unarmed against lying, so that they who wish to urge falsehoods may know how to make their listeners benevolent, or attentive, or docile in their presentation, while the defenders of the truth are ignorant of that art? . . . the faculty of eloquence . . . is in itself indifferent, why should it not be obtained for the uses of the good in the service of truth . . .?' (St Augustine, 4.2.3). Eloquence or an appropriate and persuasive style can serve both good arguments and bad, both the probable and the improbable. Of itself, eloquence is simply a functional device. It aids the task of persuasion by making the speech relevant and accessible to the audience, it pleases and moves the hearer according to the beliefs and purposes of the speaker. The uses of eloquence are as numerous as the purposes of speech and it is consequently somewhat misleading to view rhetoric as being of itself untruthful or mystifying: a rhetoric which is systematically obscure, deceptive or ambiguous is strictly speaking bad rhetoric. It is speech that represents the closure of the public sphere and the further decline of democracy as participation in open debate as to the terms of the political life of the community.

Just as the rhetorical topics and probabilities seek to be appropriate to the audience to be addressed, so too the rhetorical tradition has tended to view style as a question of finding a mode of address or presentation which will appeal to, enliven and move or persuade the specific audience. The goal of style is that of persuading and eloquence is its means:

> Just as the listener is to be delighted if he is to be retained as a listener, so also he is to be persuaded if he is to be moved to act . . . he is persuaded if he likes what you promise, fears what you threaten, hates what you condemn, embraces what you commend, sorrows at what you maintain to be sorrowful; rejoices when you announce something delightful, takes pity on those whom you place before him in speaking as being pitiful . . . and is moved by whatever

else may be done through grand eloquence toward moving the minds of listeners not only that they may know what is to be done but that they may *do* what they already know should be done. (St Augustine, 4.12.27)

The good style is an effective one and it was increasingly to become the task of the rhetorical analysis to classify the linguistic devices, figures or tropes that would best create the effects specified as desirable in St Augustine's statement of rhetorical goals. We will examine first the earlier and more general rhetorical accounts of effective style and then briefly list some of the more specific classifications of rhetorical figures.

In general terms, style should be unobtrusive and should not interfere with the content of a speech, that is to say, the appropriate style will facilitate rather than obscure the arguments or proofs being put forward. Obviously enough, since each rhetorical genre or discipline has different topics and goals of argument, a different style will be required. For the legal audience it is best, for instance, to concentrate upon a logical style, upon a style which emphasizes proof and the balance of probabilities. The political speech, on the other hand, will be more appropriate if it adopts a dramatic style and presents its arguments in such a manner as to exhort the audience and induce the decisions or courses of action viewed as beneficial to the community. Only the ceremonial or panegyric speech, the speech originally concerned with praise and blame, honour and dishonour, would occasionally concentrate on an ornate style or see embellishment of the arguments as being an end or purpose in itself.

The three basic styles referred to above are clearly not wholly separate. Political and moral discourse will often make use of elements of a more self-conscious or ornate style, while on other occasions the political speech will be presented with a legalistic determination to appear to exclude all stylistic considerations save those of presenting proofs as cogently as possible. Similarly, the judicial speech may well, on occasion, exhort the audience and moralize or, when the case is a politically controversial one and has attracted wide media coverage, the court may well sense that the best style of justification for the decision would be the ceremonial or ritualistic – a style whose import is less argumentative than literary or persuasive. If the different styles of rhetorical address are frequently mixed together, it is also the case that study and advice on style can apply to all of the genres. The general rule is that style should reinforce argument; where the argument is or wishes to appear to be a logical one, then clarity is the chief stylistic virtue: each stage of the argument should be clearly proposed and easily distinguished from the other stages or premises of the proof. Clarity here is primarily a narrative clarity and it renders the progress of the argument – whether factual or logical (categorial) – easily visible. The style in such a case is, in classical rhetorical terms, predominantly *metonymic*[3] – a style based upon the figure of metonymy being one which concentrates upon figures of speech and argument which are based upon relations of contiguity or co-occurrence. Metonymy itself is a figure which designates a thing or phenomenon in terms of one of its elements. The designation is based upon a fairly clear form of connection between element and thing, as in cause for effect – Bacchus for wine, a Dickens for a work of Dickens; instrument for its uses – the second violin for the second player of the violin; place for the thing – Bordeaux for wine, Westminster for Parliament. The figure of metonymy enables the argument to develop by virtue of the connection or contiguity between its elements or topics. The connection in question is most usually a factual one – the narrative proceeds according to a perceived or proposed combination of real elements or events, it sets out what 'really happened' and its style should be correspondingly realistic. The rhetorical figures or tropes that accompany such a speech will tend to be most appropriate if they reinforce the realistic quality or factual character of the argument, the most usual instance of the metonymic figure being 'synechdoche', the replacement of the whole by a part – more for less or less for more: for example, crown for king, sail for ship, court for law and so on. One quality or aspect of the broader context is used to define it for argumentative purposes; to use a legal example, the convicted person is defined in terms of the evil deed although that deed is obviously of itself only representative of one of innumerable past actions. The metonymic style will constantly move the hearer or reader from the general context to material particulars, its logical value being that its narrative will either indicate or suggest the significance of the relation that exists between the whole and the material part; the relation between, for example, the accused person and the act (deed) in legal cases, or between the act and its means, or between the means and its product.

Metonymy as the form and style of logical and legal types of argument is viewed by the Aristotelian tradition of rhetoric as being the most effective style, the most eloquent and persuasive speech in particular kinds of situation or before certain audiences. Clarity of argument is not, of course, the only virtue of style nor need it be utilized only by itself or to the exclusion of other figures. Clarity and the various other metonymic figures which are associated with discourse as to real acts or events can be and often are joined to *metaphoric*[4] figures which will render the narrative more striking or more vivid to its hearers. Metaphor itself is a figure of substitution and according to Aristotle 'metaphor consists in giving the thing a name that belongs to something else . . .'; metaphor states a resemblance either explicitly (by way of an analogy/simile) such as 'the moon was like a bloodstain in the sky', or implicitly, as in direct reference to 'the bloodstained moon'. Metaphor and a style of presentation or argument which makes use of frequent metaphoric figures is primarily associated with literary genres of rhetoric which seek either to please or entertain or alternatively to argue and persuade not by proof of probability but rather by vivid or dramatic presentation of the case. While the metaphoric style has its logical element or constituents, the figure of *analogy* explicitly states (predicates) a likeness or relation of similarity between two acts, situations or things. The figure of analogy does not, however, of itself explain or prove the basis of the similarity predicated: if we accept that each situation before a court of law is in principle unique, analogies are always evaluative or interpretative. To say, as the higher courts often do, that case X is 'on all fours' with case Y is simply a vivid (metaphoric) way of asserting an interpretative choice as to the features of the two cases which render them similar. Any metaphoric figure suggests *comparability* and it does so most effectively when appropriate to its subject-matter and audience. For the legal audience, in the conventional view at least, the proportional metaphor is most likely to be effective because it retains the appearance of logic, whereas the political and literary genres are more frequently or explicitly concerned with vivid or dramatic metaphors that will increase the audience's sense of presence (hypotyposis, repetition, amplification) or of belonging (allusion, quotation) to the situation described.[5]

The metonymic and metaphoric poles of argument outlined above refer loosely to styles of presentation, the first being primarily realistic or factual, the second primarily abstract or symbolic. The study of style obviously includes numerous considerations other than those mentioned and rhetorical handbooks list innumerable other figures of speech which can be described broadly as linguistic devices that will strengthen, embellish or emphasize particular kinds of argument. The lists of figures vary between authors and between different periods of the discipline of rhetoric. Today, metaphor and metonymy are the most frequently utilized as a means of analysing discourses in terms of their structure and effects but there is no reason why more detailed techniques and lists of figures should not be used. All language usage is rhetorical and considerable insight into a discourse can be gained by examining the rhetorical figures and argumentative devices which it normally uses precisely because these characteristic figures will indicate the communicational features of the discourse; how is the discourse constructed, what effect does it intend, what audience does it imply, what status and authority does it claim? We have already on several occasions referred to and made use of the example of the legal genre of rhetoric, but it remains to look more closely at the principal features of the rhetoric of the law and to comment upon its style of argumentation.

6.3   LEGAL RHETORIC: DEVICES OF LEGAL ARGUMENT

The legal hermeneutics which we examined in the previous chapter offered
a reading of the law which was more or less internal to the legal community
and the legal values to which it adheres. Legal hermeneutics does not often
challenge the self-perception or lawyer's view of the law, rather it mirrors
the normal textbook claims as to the character and content of legal method.
In the previous chapter we therefore allowed ourselves no more than a brief
commentary upon the necessary interdeterminacy of legal rules and upon
the element of choice or judgment which accompanies every act of law
application. If we now turn to reassess the common-law tradition of precedent from a position within the discipline of rhetoric our task is both more
critical and more extensive than that of hermeneutics. It is that of re-
examining the legal institution in terms of the language that it uses and the
effects that such language-use produces: what image of a language does the
law require, to whom is it addressed, how does it communicate and by what
means (devices or figures of argument) does it achieve its effects? A
rhetorical reading of the common law, in other words, is a critical reading
which seeks to look at legal discourse or speech as active argument within a
social and political context.

The very oldest of the rhetorical enterprises was that of studying speech
in terms of its effects. The discipline attempted to classify the ways in which
a speaker (or institutional discourse) could best influence or persuade its
audience and bring that audience or community to share certain attitudes
and values, and where appropriate to act in a particular way. Legal speech
retains that active and political character. Any reading of the law which
seeks to understand more than the pale appearance of the law and aspires to
go beyond the deceptively abstract general rules of the legal textbook, needs
to look behind the vague formulations of *rationes decidendi* and examine the
audiences and effects of the decisions reached. While it is obviously not
possible to analyse directly the varied contexts or the material constraints
upon specific areas of legal decision-making in relation, for example, to
commercial practice, international trade or industrial relations, certain
general rules or guidelines for critical rhetorical readings can be set out. We
shall examine first the broad rhetorical form of legal argument and subsequently look at more detailed figures of the legal speech.

6.3.1   *Law as a unitary language*

The most common complaint against lawyers is probably that they hide the
law behind an obscure, convoluted and unnecessarily difficult language. We

have already observed at several stages of our account of legal techniques that the early history of the western legal tradition has been almost entirely that of foreign languages, and frequently that of foreign legal cultures as well, being grafted on to native customs. The civil-law tradition took the model and institutions of Roman law and of the Latin language as the basis for the European national legal systems, while in England the common law also borrowed heavily from Rome although its legal language was law French rather than Latin. By the mid-eighteenth century most legal systems in Europe had adopted the vernacular (national) language but the structure of legal language and the model for its usage was by then well established. The fact that the law was no longer couched in a foreign language did not greatly alter either the number of people who could understand and utilize that language or the image of the legal institution that the inaccessibility of its language served to maintain.

Interestingly enough, the point is well made by Jeremy Bentham, a legal reformer of the nineteenth century who observed and within limits welcomed the transition of the common law from law French to English. He comments that a large portion of the law had been 'by the bigotry or artifice of lawyers, locked up in an illegible character, and in a foreign tongue.' Now that lawyers were forced to give up 'their hieroglyphics and to restore the native language to its rights' a great advance had been made but 'fictions, tautology, circuity, irregularity, inconsistency remain' (Bentham, 1932, p. xvii). Elsewhere Bentham is even more graphic in describing the rhetorical way in which the common law develops; the work of judge-made law or precedent is that of 'wrapping up the real dispositions of the law in a covering of nonsense, the knowledge of it is rendered impossible to the bulk of the people – to the bulk of those whose fate depends upon it . . . every law book is an institute of vice; every court of judicature is a school of vice' (1932, p. 149). However paradoxical it may seem, one of the principal effects of legal discourse is that of limiting communication to a restricted and specialized audience. Simply by using a language and arguments that are incomprehensible to the majority of the population, the rhetorically correct forms of legal address or of formal legal discourse work to exclude participation in the law and act as barriers to communication – as systematic non-communication – in a far greater number of circumstances or contexts than those in which they will make sense or be directly understandable to those affected by them. In many respects the language of the law is historically much better fitted to expressing the power or authority of the law than it is to communicating the specific content of legal regulation in the material terms of who does what to whom and for what reason. The image conveyed by legal language is much more that of generalized authority requiring application and obedience if only because it is the legal experts alone who actually 'know' what the law is. Two aspects of this process or rhetoric can be singled out and briefly illustrated.

(i) *The devices of legal monologue.* A unitary language is a language and usage, or rhetoric, which rigorously endeavours to control both its own meaning (the way in which the law is to be read) and the meaning of other related languages or genres – those for instance of morality, religion and politics – where they come into contact with the discourse of the law. The unitary language actively attempts to control language-usage, to impose 'correct' meanings which are simply the assertion (though seldom the practice) of uniform meanings within the genre and to argue, in the name either of science or of professionalism, that legal language can be 'exact', 'objective', 'logical' and 'value free'. The unitary language attempts to centralize and standardize meanings and in the case of legal language in particular it denies that words have other meanings or connotations, rhetorical and symbolic usages which will frequently belie or at least challenge the correct or 'true' meaning as it is found by the law. The point is simply that any language-usage (meanings at the level both of words and of sentences) has a history and its terms have already been disputed and debated – by the courts, Parliament, academic legal commentators and from time to time the media more generally. Language carries with it the meanings and accents or connotations that previous usage and dialogue have created. Language is disorderly and dialogic, it is historical and stratified: 'no living word relates to its object in a singular way; between the word and its object, between the word and the speaking subject, there exists an elastic environment of other, alien words about the same object, the same theme. The object is always overlain with qualifications, charged with values . . .' (Bakhtin, 1981, p. 276) and the construction of meanings is consequently always an act of selection or choice between different possible meanings available in the particular context of the utterance.

In practice, language is dialogue – dialogue between different levels of the national language, between different discursive genres or formations (political, ethical, legal and so on) and between differently oriented contemporary usages. The professional language, and legal language in particular, however, strives to construct a unitary language which stands above the conflicting usages and differently oriented accents of social dialogue. The language of the legal decision strives for the appearance of objectivity and for the exclusion of dialogue in favour of monologue. Its principal aim and function is that of achieving an image of incontestable authority and of correct legal meanings. Such a task is essentially a rhetorical one: the monologue is the language-usage of authority, it precludes dialogue or any questioning of the meanings given, and it closes legal discourse by privileging the voice of the judicial author as the supreme arbiter of meanings. In rhetorical terms the legal use of language is characterized initially by its use of distancing devices or argumentative figures, particularly its use of the language of logic and its frequent recourse to figures of exclusion. The first function we shall term the construction of an 'elaborated' or closed code, the second oratorical definition.

Despite the highly argumentative and socially charged character of legal decision-making, the common-law text is predominantly expressed in the apparently strict language of legal logic. Although judges will often state that the life of the law is that of experience and not logic, the style and argument of the case report is most usually impersonal, objective and authoritative. The details and devices of such a style or 'image of a language' are mainly reasonably obvious. The elaborated code is a context-independent set of abstract meanings – meanings which are defined in dictionary terms and independently of their usage or contexts of usage. The first task of the legal utterance is to translate the facts of a case and the everyday perception of the facts into legal categories or normative propositions (rules) that are expressed in a language that is both obscure to the non-legal participants in the case and is far more general than the issue in the case itself. In traditional rhetorical terms the case (*causa*) is replaced or translated into the language of a problem of legal rules and rule-conflict or rule-application (*quaestio*). In positive terms this means that the legal pronouncement or judgment will have distanced itself from the particular case and will judge the case less upon its immediate merits than upon its legal significance. Our point is simply that the judgment will make use of a large number of distancing devices of which we list some of the more frequent.

The elaborated code or logical style requires first the distancing of the judge from the judgment, the orator from the speech. Of the many forms that this takes we shall concentrate on what has been aptly described as 'pseudo-objective' motivation (Bakhtin, 1981, p. 345). Rather than being an opinion or a particular individual's speech, the legal text is typically expressed in the shared language of objectivity. First, in terms of syntax, the most common form of linguistic connective is impersonal ('thus', 'because', 'for the reason that', 'in spite of') and in rhetorical terms indicates the voice of necessity, not of choice. The modality of the judgment and its terms of logical sequence, 'therefore', 'consequently' and so on, reinforce the impression that it is not a discussion or a dialogue that is being presented but rather the inexorable onward march of legal truth. Second, in much more general semantic terms we would note the correlative use of the rhetorical syllogism – the *enthymeme* or *apta conclusio* in the traditional rhetorics.

The enthymeme is the invention of Aristotle and is regarded by him as the most appropriate style of legal argument. It is a syllogism or logical proof used in matters that are indeterminate and contingent. It has at its basis a probability and not a necessity and in Aristotle's account it consequently lacks the status of objective proof. Later rhetoricians tended to forget that the enthymeme was based upon opinion or probability and, more importantly, if we look at how the enthymeme is used in legal texts, its form is virtually always indistinguishable from that of the syllogism. The text will not in general indicate that its outcome is based in the end upon a matter of opinion (the legal communities' *communis opinio*), at best upon an enthymeme, but will rather formulate its judgment as though it were, either explicitly or impliedly, a logical inference or deduction:

(a) There is a rule which applies to cases of the type before the court – for instance, carriers who transport manufactured products between different states in America must obtain a transport certificate from the Interstate Commerce Commission.

(b) On the facts of the case before the court it must be shown that the rule either applies or does not – for instance, a carrier transporting eviscerated chickens is transporting agricultural and not manufactured products.

(c) The rule is then applied to the facts of the case to infer or deduce a conclusion which follows necessarily from the first two stages (or premises) – eviscerated chickens may be carried in the USA without the transporter having to obtain an ICC certificate (*Interstate Commerce Commission* v *Kroblin*, 113 F. Supp. 599, 1953).[6]

There is, of course, nothing whatsoever inevitable in the argument presented above. It is only its form that is necessary; its style of argument suggests that it is an impersonal or logical decision, but nothing can dictate why the court should decide that eviscerated chickens, which are factory produced, are not manufactured products. In other examples further sources of ambiguity, of rule conflicts and of gaps in or obscurity of the law, may increase the indeterminacy or contingency of the decision – but decision there must be and, in terms of its style, it is more likely than not to be couched in the coercive rhetoric of the legal institutions' preferred style, that of the law as a specialized and peculiar logic. Thus in *Mandla* v *Dowell Lee* [1983] 1 AER 1062 at 1072, to take a recent example, the question raised was whether or not a member of the Sikh religion was a member of a 'racial group' for the purposes of the Race Relations Act 1976, s. 1. The Act defines 'racial group' in terms of 'ethnic origins' but provides no further relevant definition of what constitutes a racial group. Lord Templeman states that the meaning of ethnic origins is to be 'deduced' from the Act as a whole. The 'true construction' of the expression constitutes Sikhs as a racial group by virtue of their being a distinct and separate community. Why they are to be defined as such is argued by Lord Templeman with reference to the geographical, historical, physical and colour characteristics of Sikhs. He also refers to what Parliament 'envisaged' in drafting the Act, and by implication he further refers to a long list of additional relevant considerations: those of cultural tradition, religious observance, language, literature, memory and manners. Only in the most superficial or figurative of senses could Lord Templeman's judgment be said to be deducing the 'true' meaning of the words in question. The language of logic has an argumentative significance far in excess of its actual utility in providing a solution to the case. Nor, in the numerous other instances where judgments are expressed in terms of premises and conclusions, inferences, deductions, inductions and analogies, is any great light likely to be thrown on the real or material basis of the decision. The reason for selecting or 'inventing' a probability or topic as the starting-point of the argument is not clarified but more frequently is obscured by such language and by that further series of rhetorical figures that loosely support the image or rhetoric of legal logic.

The elaborated code or context-independent language of logical categories creates a language of inclusion or identification. A legal text which fell outside the legal institutions' requirement of logic and impersonality of expression would be discarded rapidly by the legal profession as lacking one of the major requisites of legality, the authority or distance that the language provides. Distance, however, is also produced negatively. Numerous figures or devices of *exclusion* support the general image of logical sequence. We refer here to the numerous devices or insignia that differentiate the legal text from other texts and legal argument from more mundane, non-professional, arguments. As one critic expresses it, 'we are clearly in the region of rhetoric when considering the identifications whereby a specialised activity makes one a participant in some social or economic class. "Belonging" in this sense is clearly rhetorical . . . the very stress upon the pure autonomy of such activities is a roundabout way of identification with a privileged class . . . serving as a kind of insignia promising preferment' (Burke, 1969, p. 28). In brief, legal argument is a specialized and privileged form of discourse which constantly makes the reader aware of the technical or 'artistic' character of the decisions being reported. Quite frequently this information is passed on explicitly in statements that argue that, for example, 'fortunately the court does not have to consider the political dimensions to this industrial dispute' or that it 'is the strictly legal and not the religious, moral or policy dimensions to the administrative decision that the court must decide upon.'

The most graphic or striking rhetorical figure used to exclude non-legal arguments is that of *oratorical definition* – the definition of the issue in the case or underlying the case is formulated in such a manner as to imply the legal solution or conclusion that will eventually be arrived at. The oratorical definition either identifies a true meaning which resolves the issue faced by the court by providing the basic premise of a later enthymeme, or dissociates and excludes undesired arguments and solutions. A good example of both aspects of the oratorical definition can be found in the judgment of Lord Diplock in the case of *Home Office* v *Harman* [1983] 1 AC 562. Very briefly, the case concerned whether or not a solicitor was entitled to show to an investigative journalist documents legitimately in her possession but belonging to the Home Office. The documents in question had been read out in open court and were available, at a price, from the court itself in the form of the transcript of an earlier case. The Home Office brought an action against the solicitor for contempt of court and on appeal the House of Lords upheld its action. Lord Diplock begins negatively by dissociating the legal from the non-legal: 'My Lords, in a case which has attracted a good deal of publicity, it may assist in clearing up misconceptions if I start by saying what this case is *not* about. It is not about freedom of speech, freedom of the press, openness of justice or documents coming into the public domain.' Somewhat later the legal issue in the case receives its definition as being 'an aspect of the law of discovery of documents in civil actions in the High Court'. Further, 'the case turns upon its own particular facts which are very special.' The definition itself prepares if it does not wholly determine the conclusion eventually reached, that the solicitor in question was in (civil) contempt of court and had acted both immorally and illegally.

Another example of oratorical definition can be drawn from the much-cited case of *Donoghue* v *Stevenson* [1932] AC 562, a case concerning the delictual liability of a manufacturer for defective products. Lord Atkin, in formulating the principle underlying liability in negligence, first dissociates the legal argument to be examined from moral sentiments of wrong-doing and then from religious rules of conduct concerning the account that should be taken of one's neighbour's interests:

> The liability for negligence, whether you style it such or treat it as in other systems as a species of 'culpa', is no doubt based upon a general public sentiment of moral wrongdoing for which the offender must pay. But acts or omissions which any moral code would censure cannot in a practical world be treated so as to give a right to every person injured by them to demand relief . . . The rule that you are to love your neighbour becomes in law, you must not injure your neighbour.

The dissociative strategies are followed by a statement of the legal principles of 'neighbourhood' in such a manner as resolves the case before the court by clearly stating that parties not in a contractual relation may nonetheless owe each other a general duty of care.

To the oratorical definition can be added a number of lesser figures of argument, all of which reinforce the authority of the legal judgment and are generally utilized in an axiomatic form, that is as definitions and not as arguments that are open to question or that are either persuasive or not. The traditional classifications of such figures are not of any great importance in that the argumentative function of figures such as *correctio* (dismissing alternative and opposed arguments as errors), *prolepsis* (anticipating and discounting possible objections), *meiosis* (mocking the opposed argument) or even the more common literary figures such as irony, paraphrase, collusion, hyperbole and so on can be understood in simpler terms as discursive functions in legal argument. Where they are used to support the assertion of an axiomatic argument we can accurately read a large number of rhetorical devices as covertly expressing the unitary power of legal language and the unquestionable authority of the judge in the form of a very repetitive assertion of the specialism of legal discourse: the legal text is distinguished again and again from possible political or economic or ethical alternatives to its judgment. Within its domain the law is sovereign and its most powerful argument for persuading its audience is precisely its refusal to acknowledge the terms or languages that its non-professional audiences would understand. The legal monologue is rhetorical and effective, its justificatory arguments work by and large by refuting the need to provide any justification at all outside the narrowly legal exercises in legal word-magic or the ritual incantation of legal norms. In more sober and critical terms we shall now move to reconstruct the elements of legal rhetoric as dialogue or, in the terms of the preceding account of the legal monologue, we shall endeavour to read the monologue as an act of communication.

(ii) *The devices of legal dialogue.* The most crucial point to be made in relation to the concept of law as a unitary language – as monologue and as authoritative speech – concerns the sense in which such an image of a language or ideological impetus is the construction of the legal institution. The legal monologue with its various claims – especially that the legal text is a logical, rule-governed discourse; that legal meanings are special or 'artistic' and essentially univocal meanings – is not given to the legal institution in advance but is made by it. Legal texts are historically and rhetorically organized so as to suppress the conflict of differently orientated social meanings. The monologue of the legal text is simply a dialogue aimed at controlling the hearer by means of authority rather than persuasion, coercively rather than dialectically, that is, by means of reasoned dialogue. Nonetheless, however distorted the character of legal communication and however socially restricted or exclusive its audience and codes, the specialized discipline does have its audiences, and its texts can be read in the rhetorical terms of their appropriateness to their audiences or hearers. What topics of argument, probabilities or stylistic figures are most effective within the legal community and further, what can such facets to the legal text tell us about the functions or the role of the law?

The style and content of legal speech clearly varies very greatly according to the different kinds of political institutions to which it is tied. In classical Greece, to take the most extreme example, the legal speech was simply a particular form of the political speech, having as its object past rather than future actions. It was conducted in front of the political assembly and drew upon a range of probabilities and topics that were to a large degree generic to both the forensic and the deliberative genres. The rhetorically appropriate speech in such a context was orientated directly towards the public sphere, at the citizen of the city-state, and it endeavoured, unashamedly, to persuade. According to contemporary descriptions of classical legal hearings, the very large juries of the Greek and Sicilian democracies were open to persuasion by means of the most convincing advocacy before the court and were little interested in any purely legal technicalities. The legal decision, in other words, was the product of open debate before a non-professional group of hearers and the most appropriate speech would communicate directly, clearly and on occasion vividly. The rhetoric of the early democracies was, however, exceptional. The subsequent history of the western legal tradition has been one of the constant restriction of the public sphere of legal dialogue.

There are, of course, important elements of dialogue and of rhetoric built into the adversary system of justice within the common-law tradition, but it is important not to overemphasize their actual effect upon legal communication. Historically, rhetoric as the art of speaking well in civil matters and more generally as the art of persuasive discourse had a role within the development of the common law but its role was systematically subordinated to the language of logic and of doctrinal assertion – the argumentation of textbook expositions and law teaching which fully came into their own only towards the late seventeenth and early eighteenth centuries (Simmonds, 1984). Although the subject has not been studied very thoroughly, it is probably accurate to observe that the role of rhetoric as a practical discipline in English law has always tended to be subsidiary and marginal to the primary impetus of the legal text as authoritative text requiring the responses of reverence and obedience. The audiences and purposes of the law were always somewhat concealed behind a technicality which rhetorical study and the rhetorical practice of the moot (*disputatio*) would reinforce rather than clarify. The medieval training in law certainly included a brief instruction in the rhetorical categories of public speaking but this exercise became increasingly replaced by the language and study of logic (or dialectic as it was then termed). Eloquence was recognized as a valuable asset in the lawyer's craft, pleadings in particular required expertise in verbal formulations, and students were commended, both by their teachers and by the judiciary, for their ability to argue but, in common with continental developments (Ong, 1981; Goodrich, 1984) the prevailing view was that argument should depend upon strict logic and not upon the rhetoric of probability. Writing in 1588, for example, Abraham Fraunce depicts the method of the common law as follows: 'I then perceived, the practise of Law to be the use of Logic, and the method of Logic to lighten the Law. So that after the application of Logic to Law, and examination of Law by Logic, I made plain the precepts of the one by the practise of the other, and called my book, the Lawyer's Logic.'

The audience of logical arguments is in principle universal. An argument which is necessary or strictly logical in its presentation and proof must be true and it will in potential at least be addressed to the entire audience of rational human beings, for the simple reason that anyone who can understand the arguments demonstrated will be convinced of their validity. However much it might benefit lawyers and judges to claim the status of rationality for the workings of precedent, we have already seen that legal rules and the requirement of their concrete application preclude the law becoming a logical demonstration. The law deals in probabilities and the claim to logic is therefore to be understood rhetorically, that is as a peculiarly persuasive form of argument or as a conscious attempt to produce a specific effect upon the audience. The logical argument is, in terms of its historical origins within the European legal tradition, a doctrinal one. It is primarily a form of classification and of teaching and as such it requires the subordination of the pupil to the teacher or of the hearer to the knower. The devices of legal argument which we shall now examine in terms of legal dialogue have their origin in this conception of the legal text as doctrine or 'doctrination' – as instruction in legal values and the legal order as a way of life.

6.3.2 *The figures of legal speech*

For rhetorical purposes the best or most persuasive legal speech is the one which appears the most authoritative. We have seen that such a requirement finds expression in the logical form in which most legal arguments are

presented. It is also to be found in the general educational character of the
legal judgment as a statement of legal teaching (doctrine), a statement of the
general attitudes, perspectives and moral beliefs of the legal institution. The
legal text inevitably expresses how society ought to live, how social arrange-
ments are best ordered and how individuals ought to behave, but it does so
somewhat covertly and always in relation to the individual case. The legal
text can always cover its tracks and it can always appear to be simply
restating previous law or doctrine. It is the responsibility of the rhetorical
reading to examine critically and evaluate which features of the judgment
indicate its most socially significant meanings. In the very loose list of
figures which follows we shall concentrate upon the more typical forms of
argument and justification to be found in common-law decisions.

(i) *Axioms and assumptions*. Axiomatic arguments are arguments which are
treated by the court as self-evident legal truths. There is no need to justify
an axiom; it merely has to be asserted for its persuasive power to be
recognized. Axiomatic argument is very common within the case-law systems of decision-making according to several recent studies[7] and is to be
aligned with the historically persistent 'formalistic' mode of judicial decision-making. Formalism as a decision-making technique or mode of
reasoning refers to the belief that there is an abstract solution available to
any legal problem and that such a solution should be preferred to others.
Formalism is broader than simple axiomatic answers to legal questions and
will not be analysed in detail here.

Axiomatic arguments are posed in numerous different forms. The figure
of oratorical definition discussed above is frequently an instance of axiomatic argument in so far as no justification is given for the way in which the
legal problem is stated. More broadly, an axiomatic argument may be
defined as any argument which is simply put forward as legally true ('this is
the law') without further discussion or argumentative support. Generally it
will be a broad principle of law that the court will accept as valid, as taken
for granted or too well settled to require further precedent: 'it is so clear
that no authority is needed to establish it', 'it is fundamental to our law', 'it
is obvious that' and so on, being regular forms of judicial invocation of the
axiom. Where the axiom is not explicitly asserted as axiomatic or incontestable it takes the form of an assumption or implication underpinning the
legal argument. Here it will be found that a maxim or category will explain
the legal usage in the instant case as 'natural', 'commonsensical' or self-
evidently 'reasonable'. In the case of *Photo Productions* v *Securicor* [1980] 1
AER 556, to take an isolated example, Lord Diplock hinges his judgment
on an axiomatic assertion followed by a lengthy elaboration of the implications of the principle asserted: 'every failure to perform a primary obligation

is a breach of contract. The secondary obligation on the part of the contract breaker *to which it gives rise by implication of the common law* is to pay monetary compensation to the other party for the loss sustained by him in consequence of the breach' (emphasis added, 566 g–h) and the passage continues to spell out the further implications of a somewhat obtuse and unnecessary terminology of primary, secondary and tertiary obligations. The axiomatic argument will tell us what the law is to be taken as being, it will tell us authoritatively how the law affects certain situations, but it will not tell us why it is taken to be what it is – why it is interpreted or constructed in a particular manner – nor why it implies the outcome arrived at. Elsewhere the axiom is used to state the absurdity of other possible interpretations or to ridicule opposing hypotheses: 'it could never be envisaged that', it would be 'absurd to suppose that', 'nobody could believe . . .' and so on.

(ii) *Repetitions and analogies.* Argument by axiom or assertion lays claim to an absolute authority and validity for the interpretative choice being made. Quite frequently the claim will need to be supported or justified as well as elaborated and explained. Where such justification is required, the figures of citation, quotation and analogy are amongst the more frequently used. The broadest figure is that of analogy and we shall concentrate upon it as one of the primary, non-axiomatic, modes of argument used simultaneously to distance and to persuade the audience.

In rhetorical terms the most important use of analogy is that of bringing the case before the court within the accepted sphere of legal values and languages. As we saw in examining the hermeneutic tradition, the tradition of legal precedent is largely contained within the notion of the repetition of traditional values, the belief that the present case can be decided according to previous patterns of resolution to similar cases. Rhetorically the analogy provides first the language to be used: the precedent cases referred to will present a vocabulary and categories to classify the problem before the court. Second, the precedent, the prior decision on similar (material) facts or on a similar point of law, will provide authority; it will bring the present utterance into the sphere of recognized legal utterance or speech-act by identifying the legal terms of the problem and the authoritative language for designating and resolving such problems. Finding the precedent is always a question of selection, a choice as to which case, which formulation of the rule and which judge to quote or transpose and finally and most importantly which similarities and which differences are significant to the particular situation. The analogy or reference to case-law authority of itself suggests that the present decision is legally justified, that the present utterance is a fully legal statement of law, that the text is a member of the genre and will speak directly to the qualified legal audience without needing to give any non-legal justification for itself. We would note that the logical value of the analogy as a figure of legal argument is always specific to or contingent upon the case being decided and will have to be evaluated on a case-by-case basis. The work of the legal analogy is always precarious – it is not itself a logical figure of argument and it is consequently always necessary to enquire precisely what work the precedent cited or quoted does within the instant text.

In very general terms we can also refer to a number of rhetorical functions that are either performed by the analogy or by associated figures. While we have dealt with the functions of authorization, it remains to point out that the analogical argument can have several strongly persuasive figures attached to it. As a variant form of metaphor, the legal analogy can persuade in several different ways. First, as a statement of factual similarities between past and present cases, it can act as a figure of presence and bring the issue faced to life. The figure of *hypotyposis*, for example, is defined as argument 'which sets things out in such a way that the matter seems to unfold, and the thing to happen, under our eyes' and such a figure can act as a general formulation of one of the more important of the uses of analogy (or proportional metaphor), that of stating resemblances between different factual situations, that of persuasion by making the instances of the rule or *ratio* come to life or 'acquire presence'. Second, the very notion of precedent as doing the same thing in similar circumstances (analogy itself is the rhetorical figure of *similitudo*) incorporates several of the figures of repetition as persuasion and as a means of 'presencing the argument'. Legal uses of repetition of course vary between different levels of argument. At the level of lexicon and syntax, repetition is common to the law in the use of synonyms (metabole) and paraphrases (periphrasis) to express the same idea by means of different words or in a different way. Common legal expressions such as 'null, void and without effect' or more lengthy para-phrases of simple ideas are both frequent, tedious and often persuasive – tedious because lengthy, persuasive because emphatic and noticeable. Of the other related figures of repetition, those relating to the logic of argu-ment are of the most interest and importance and include *dubitato* or dwelling upon a point in endeavouring to drive it home (also termed *commemoratio*), and amplification or *auxesis* in its various forms, whereby a point is stated, repeated and developed or built up by means of minor variations or extensions of the central theme. To give a non-legal example, the following brief passage drives home the wickedness of its subject by aggregation: 'your eyes are made for impudence, your face for effrontery, your tongue for false swearing, your hands for plunder, your belly for gluttony . . . your feet for flight: so you are all malignity.' The point is made forcefully, the evil or undesirability of the person described is stated most vividly and graphically, although the theme itself is simply repeated in different ways.

The more striking the figure of argument used, the more likely that the audience is somewhat broader than that of the legal profession or parts of the profession. The more numerous the figures of repetition, the greater the probability that the point being repeated is contentious or without any immediately obvious justification – the argument is in that case purely rhetorical. By such we mean merely that its sole function is to persuade its audience, to make the audience identify with or agree to the theme presented on the grounds of its verbal presentation rather than upon any explicit account of its content or effects.

(iii) *Policies and consequences.* It could well be supposed that the sphere of precedent in which most account is taken of the wider audience and effects of legal decisions, those beyond the legal audience and institution itself, would be in that area where the courts take account of what are termed policy considerations. Here at least legal argument would appear explicitly to recognize the need to examine closely the empirical effects of particular decisions and so seek to justify legal outcomes in terms of their consequences for the institution, groups and social relations generally that are implicated in the issues before the court. Policy considerations, which are traditionally defined as considerations of the effect of a decision upon the wider community, explicitly include economic, administrative, social, political, and indeed moral consequences of the legal outcome.

It should be noted first that the appeal to policy or consequence is selective, cautious and frequently ambiguous. Policy is not law – it is not even principle – and reference to it in the justification of a judgment is, in legal theory at least, never of greater status than *obiter dicta* or incidental remarks made by the way of background to a decision. Policy is described as an 'unruly horse' which, if mounted, is likely to carry its rider in directions which she or he might not wish. Policy in other words cannot be controlled and in consequence the courts tend to endeavour, usually rather successfully, to ignore it – lawyers, it is claimed, are neither sociologists nor politicians and should therefore not attempt to elaborate policy. In rhetorical terms, however, policy is of great consequence in the decision-making process and the rhetorically effective lawyer would be unwise to ignore policy considerations in making an argument or presenting justifications for a decision. What we would wish to argue here is that policy, the wider desirability of the decision, is always a significant factor in decisions but whether or not it is appropriate to refer to such factors in justification of the decision will depend upon the topic and audience of the case. If policy refers to the

effects of a decision then no judgment, however routine or however legalis-
tically framed, can avoid paying some attention to them. On the other hand,
it may often be the case that the rhetoric of policy is not the appropriate
rhetoric to invoke in presenting a particular interpretation of the law. It can
be briefly suggested that certain standard formulations of policy are frequently utilized as justificatory arguments or as rhetorical devices and we
shall list some of the more usual or frequent below. Before doing so we
would note two reservations. First, the policy factors invoked in a decision
need not be the only policy factors or effects which are actually taken into
account in determining the decision; other considerations, prejudices and
assumptions as to the consequences of the decision may be evident but
inadmissible in the text itself. Second, a critical reading of the policy factors
explicitly formulated in judgments tends to indicate that they are frequently
a poor guide to the actual effects that the decision is likely to have. The
courts work in terms of stereotypes of actors and consequences and equally
use a rhetoric of ritual policy considerations whose real effects are often
likely to be unknown in the particular case.

While it would be possible to provide very different classifications of
policy considerations we shall limit ourselves here to listing only a few of the
more obvious ones which can be readily found in most areas of law and can
be critically examined with relative ease.

1. *The interests of the State* form a blanket policy consideration bridging the
entire common law – civil and criminal, private and public. The most
rigorous version of the argument relating to the protection of the interests of
the State is to be found in relation to issues defined as matters of 'national
security'. In the case of *R* v *Secretary of State for the Home Department, ex parte
Hosenball* [1977] 1 WLR 766, for example, Lord Denning explicitly states
that where issues of national security are involved, then the rule of law ends;
the balance between the interests of national security and the freedom of
the individual is not to be adjudicated by a court of law, and it is for the
government of the day in the person of the Home Secretary, to decide. A
more recent example can be taken from the case *CCSU* v *Minister of State for
the Civil Service* [1984] 3 AER 935, where it was held that whether or not a
decision to ban trade unions from a government intelligence-gathering
centre was in fact necessitated by the requirements of national security was
'non-justiciable' since the executive was the sole judge of what national
security required. More generally, it should be observed that as a branch of
the administration, it would be surprising if the courts did not uphold the
general interests of the administration, the State, in which they serve. In all
other branches of law, categories can be found which will allow, more or
less directly, for the protection of the interests of the State. Thus, for

example, consideration of the State's interest in the conviction of criminals is a constant policy factor relevant to the definition of police powers (e.g. *Chic Fashions Ltd* v *Jones* [1968] 2 QB 299), the admissibility of illegally obtained evidence and so on. Again, the common law has traditionally recognized the illegality of contracts which threaten the interests of the State or are injurious to public safety in a manner comparable to that in which any action will be debarred or remedy refused if the court considers it to be *ex turpi causa*, or for whatever reason it offends the judicial conception of public policy as, for example, in *Ashton* v *Turner* [1981] QB 137. In *Ashton* v *Turner* the issue of public policy related to an action brought by A for injuries caused by T's negligence in driving a getaway car from the scene of a crime committed jointly by A and T. The broad head of public policy was sufficient grounds for dismissing the action.

2. The interests of the efficient *administration of justice* form a further broad set of policy arguments or topics which are generally available and applicable to legal justificatory procedures. Here the interests of the State are reduced to the interests of the legal institution in the efficient administration of the legal workload. The most obvious example of such a policy factor is to be found in the law of Torts where one of the most common of limitations to be placed upon actions for recovery of damages in negligence has traditionally been the straightforward public policy argument which claims to limit recovery to such a number of cases as can be reasonably dealt with by the courts. An interpretation of a rule which raises the possibility – however slight – of widespread recovery of damages, of opening the floodgates of litigation, is to be rejected for that reason alone. Traditionally, for example, 'pure economic loss' could not be recovered in a negligence action because, among other things, such loss was likely to be widespread (*Spartan Steel and Alloys Ltd* v *Martin and Co* [1973] QB 27, 38–9) and although such loss is now recoverable the so-called 'floodgates argument' – the requirement that the class of potential plaintiffs be limited in number – is still of considerable importance (see, e.g., *Ross* v *Caunters* [1980] Ch. D 297; *Yianni* v *Evans and Sons* [1981] 3 AER 597), and was considered most recently in *Leigh and Sillivan* v *Aliakmon* [1985] 2 WLR 289, where Goff LJ comments somewhat superficially on recent authorities that 'some of us prefer a controlled opening of the gates, permitting the flooding of a reasonably foreseeable area, rather than a wholesale inundation of unforeseeable and uncontrolled proportions.' In broader terms, the common law will always attempt to avoid what in one case was rather quaintly termed the 'fantastic possibility of an infinite realm of liability'. The administration of justice must not become overburdened, to which one could add that this self-interest on the part of the legal system has an even greater significance

as a practical consideration in relation to the day-to-day administration of the courts. The pressure to plead guilty in the courts of first instance, the identity of interest between enforcement agencies and the court officials all the way up the hierarchy, the weight given to the evidence of officials and so on are all important lower-level facets of one and the same policy expediency on the part of the court process as a whole (Carlen, 1976; McBarnet, 1982).

3. *Maintenance of moral standards* forms another interesting and generally applicable topic of legal argument and while we have looked at one facet to this argument already in terms of the 'community of legal values' (chapter 5, s. 5.3.2), that is, the values that the courts are likely to see as deserving protection, we would refer here to the rhetorical arguments available in terms of the effect of a decision upon the moral policy of the law. As as general rule moral or ethical considerations are not law but are rather treated as secondary justificatory arguments which support or go against the outcome of the particular case. The theory is that a sharp distinction is made between moral rules and legal rules: no matter how vicious or how exemplary the behaviour before the court, it should not affect either the outcome or the remedy available at law. In practice, however, the morality of the conduct is of considerable rhetorical importance at each stage of the legal process. Not only is an element of moral conscience built into the common law in the form of equity and arguments relating to particular justice (chapter 3, s. 3.2) but it would also be foolish to suppose that the courts, in interpreting or applying legal categories to individual cases, would be oblivious to what they consider to be normal patterns of moral conduct.

The influence or persuasiveness of arguments as to moral standards is difficult to evaluate within a system which claims to take little account of moral factors that are not also explicitly legal considerations. There is an element of 'ellipsis', of covert or undisclosed argumentation in the role of moral standards and it is consequently necessary to reconstruct the moral force behind specific arguments or forms of conduct in any given decision. To start with the most obvious example, arguments as to the morality of conduct are explicitly the issue in any common-law action seeking equitable relief. Where, for example, a bargain is thought to have been caused by undue influence or pressure being placed upon one or other of the parties to the agreement, the court has an equitable power to set the contract aside. In the recent case of *National Westminster Bank PLC v Morgan* [1985] 2 WLR 588, 602, Lord Scarman observes that here we are in the 'world of doctrine, not of neat and tidy rules ... The court in the exercise of this jurisdiction is a court of conscience ... Definition is a poor instrument when used to determine whether a transaction is or is not unconscionable;

this is a question which depends upon the particular facts of the case.' In other words, it is for the reader or audience to attempt to construct the pattern of decisions or the likely manner of exercise of this discretionary legal power.

Where the court is not explicitly sitting as a court of conscience, moral arguments have an even more indeterminate role which can only be hinted at in the present context. First, one can point to explicit terms of moral approval or disapproval as they appear in the judicial accounts of the factual circumstances and conduct of the parties to the case. The courts are certainly not slow to characterize their attitude to the morality of the conduct of the parties before them. In very general terms, certain kinds of activity and of motives are morally desirable and others are not so. An example of desirable conduct would be that of acting as a rescuer at the scene of an accident. However rash your behaviour, the court will try as hard as it decently can to exonerate that behaviour and, where the rescuer has been injured, to allow an action against the party that caused the accident. In the case of *Baker* v *Hopkins* [1958] 3 AER 147, for example, a qualified doctor arrived at the scene of an accident in a farmyard and was warned not to go down a well in which two workmen employed by the defendant company had been overcome by carbon-monoxide fumes. Despite the warning which explicitly indicated the general risk he was taking, the doctor went down the well and died. The company which was responsible for the original accident was held to be liable to the doctor's estate in negligence and it seemed to the court 'indeed ungracious' even to suggest that the doctor was in any way responsible for the harm he suffered. More contentiously, we shall take one example of morally undesirable conduct or, more accurately, undesirable character, the issue here being the topical one of the relevance of evidence as to the character of the complainant in a rape trial. Although it has frequently been recognized, both at common law (*R* v *Riley* [1887] 18 QBD 481) and in the 1976 Sexual Offences Act s. 2) that evidence that the complainant is of promiscuous character is of no legal relevance to the particular complaint being tried, in practice it is frequently still regarded as relevant.[8] In *R* v *Krausz* [1973] 57 Crim. App. Cases 460, Stephenson LJ remarks that 'in an age of changing standards of sexual morality it may be harder to say where promiscuity ends and prostitution begins, and it may be unnecessary to decide on which side of the dividing line the particular conduct falls . . . Evidence which proves that a woman is in the habit of submitting her body to different men without discrimination, whether for pay or not, would seem to be admissible.' The attitude of the judge towards the morality – and so also apparently the reliability – of sexually undiscriminating complainants is clearly one of disapproval in this instance, and such an attitude is clearly likely to affect the justificatory rhetoric and indeed the outcome of the trial. Recent studies do indeed suggest that arguments as to the moral history of the complainant in rape trials is not only extremely frequent but also highly effective (see, e.g., Edwards, 1981, 1984; Atkins and Hoggett, 1984).

In more general terms, any judgment is likely to indicate approval and disapproval of conduct or character at some stage of the trial or judgment. Any adequate reading of the legal text will need, consequently, to be aware of the role of arguments as to moral standards and to seek evidence of them in the language of the text. Of particular importance as indicators of moral argument or sentiment are the figures of the eulogistic (praise) and dys-logistic (blame), of the euphemism (understatement) and dysphemism (deprecation). In short, any judgment is an interpretation and entails a degree of choice. Reading the judgment critically will entail examining the way in which acts and actors in the case are characterized and events are categorized. Are the terms used favourable or unfavourable, are act and actor identified as members of the legal collectivity, of common sense or 'we', or are they rather excluded as other, extreme, unreasonable or 'they'? In any case there are likely to be many narratives within the one legal text and each plot or discourse should be pursued (Davis and Walton, 1984).

4. *Individualizing the case.* We would refer finally to a broader point concerning the structure of legal argument which develops from the last-mentioned concern with policy as the attribution of morality or immorality to actor and conduct in the case before the court. It is of the very essence of legal rhetoric that it individualizes the issues before the court. Legal meaning is always to be attached to individual acts and legal explanation is correspondingly biographical and moral rather than sociological or historical and contextualizing. Although the point is a very broad and complex one concerning the nature and functions of the legal subject and of legal responsibility, there are certain immediate and more practical considerations to be looked at.

The legal individual or legal subject is a very specialized and distinct rhetorical person. Rather than being a complicated and changing personality with a social and emotional background to be considered and understood, the legal person is a unity constructed upon the basis of its past actions. The legal subject cannot revoke or renounce its deeds, the legal subject is the straightforward cause of its deeds (acts) and it is morally and legally responsible for those deeds – utterances, actions and omissions. The legal subject is a static unity in the sense that it cannot avoid the legal imputation of a causal relation between past acts and present responsibility. There is no absolute reason for supposing that the individual 'now' still identifies with or is defined by past actions; it is only in the legal and rhetorical notion of the individual as a biographical unity based upon past acts that the past is irredeemable.

The legal form of individuality has its literary basis in the rhetorical form of biography and autobiography associated originally with the Greek funeral oration or 'encomium'. The speech would remember and lay bare the public life of the deceased. There would be nothing secret or private revealed by the funeral biography; the image of the person was already entirely public, external and formal, 'on the surface' and most importantly unitary, because there was nothing other than, or supplementary to, the public person and the responsibility that such a person bore for his or her life. All the details of that past life would be paraded before the funeral audience as coherent examples of the deceased's personality as a public figure, as politician, military leader, rhetorician or whatever other unitary calling the deceased may have had. In short, the encomium denied the possibility that the individual might change, that the particular act was an instance of 'becoming someone else' or simply of changing direction. Similarly, the encomium and more importantly the legal speech to which it gave rise, both insist on reducing rhetorical and legal events to individual causes and assigning praise and blame, innocence and guilt solely upon that basis of rhetorical and moral responsibility.

The final challenge which we would suggest for the rhetorical reading of legal texts is that of questioning the individualizing tendencies of the text. The individual, or indeed the various forms of corporate individual or personality, exists in a context and is the product of a wide variety of economic, social and environmental conditions as well as being a temporal or historical entity – the subject of change or becoming over time. The law, however, pins all legal meaning to individual acts without allowing – save in a few exceptional circumstances – any great weight to be given to factors external to individual responsibility. Thus to take a topical and quasi-judicial example, the *Scarman Report on the Brixton Disorders of 1981* (Cmnd. 8247) is of interest for a number of rhetorical reasons. Without entering into any great detail we may separate out, in fairly commonsense terms, two sets of actors – 'police' and 'blacks', and two corresponding conditions of action – the 'rational' and the 'irrational'. The police, for Lord Scarman, are very clearly characterized as rational actors; their behaviour is 'objective', their judgments are 'reasoned' and their actions are 'considered'. The vocabulary and syntax used by Lord Scarman to report the actions of the 'blacks' is almost the precise reverse of that used in relation to the police. Blacks are characterized in subjective and irrational terms – they 'believe in myths', they are 'driven by feelings', they are 'subject to rumours', they are 'insecure', they suffer a sense of rejection, are distrustful, suspicious and so on. The police are the 'we' or acceptable standard of judgment in the case to be considered by Lord Scarman, that of the causes of the riots. The blacks on the other hand are the figure or persona of 'they', of exclusion and irrationality. Not only are the blacks irrational, however, but we are also told that they are the victims of a context which they cannot control and of causes that exceed those of individual volition or will. Lord Scarman comments upon the social context and conditions that prompted the riots: unemployment, discrimination, poor housing, deprived environmental conditions and lack of adequate or relevant educational provision. Where 'deprivation and frustration exist on the scale to be found among the young black people of Brixton, the probability of disorder must be strong.' In a splendid example of the rhetorical legal conception of cause and responsibility, Lord Scarman moves from describing the social conditions of inequality and deprivation to assigning blame or responsibility for the riots. The conditions described do not 'provide an excuse for disorder. They cannot justify attacks upon the police' for the simple reason that it is always individuals who must accept responsibility at law: 'all those who in the course of the disorders ... engaged in violence ... were guilty of grave criminal offences, which society, if it is to survive, cannot condone.' Finally, on a note of explicitly moral exhortation, young black people 'share with the rest of *us*' (emphasis added) a responsibility for public order.[9] We would ourselves end rhetorically by asking exactly how the discussion of the social conditions of the riots is to be reconciled with the attribution of individual responsibility?

NOTES

1 The enthymeme is, for Aristotle, the rhetorical equivalent of the syllogism or deductive proof. Like the syllogism the enthymeme proceeds by means of three stages of proof – those of major premise, minor premise and conclusion – but it supposedly differs from the syllogism in being based upon a probable or likely major premise rather than upon a necessary premise leading to a necessary conclusion.

2 For an alternative view see, most notably, Plato, *Phaedrus* and *Gorgias* in *Collected Works* (Princeton, 1978); also T. Todorov, *Theories of the Symbol* (Oxford, 1982), ch. 2; T. Eagleton, *Walter Benjamin* (London, 1981), p. 101 ff. While an adequate history of the rhetorical disciplines still remains to be written, useful accounts which broadly support the interpretation given here can be found in E. R. Curtius, *European Literature and the Latin Middle Ages* (London, 1953); E. Grassi, *Rhetoric as Philosophy* (Pennsylvania, 1980); W. Ong, *Ramus, Method and the Decay of Dialogue* (Cambridge, Mass, 1981); J. J. Murphy, *Rhetoric in the Middle Ages* (Princeton, 1974).

3 The classic source of the distinction here used between metonymy and metaphor as separate powers or axes of the language-system is R. Jakobson and M. Halle, *Fundamentals of Language* (Amsterdam, 1956), Pt. II. For more sophisticated

discussions of linguistic features to the distinction, see G. Genette, *Figures of Literary Discourse* (Oxford, 1982), ch. 6; C. Metz, *Psychoanalysis and Cinema* (London, 1982), Pt. IV; U. Eco, *Semiotics and the Philosophy of Language* (London, 1984), p. 114 ff.

4 For more detailed discussions of metaphor, see particularly P. Ricoeur, *The Rule of Metaphor* (London, 1978); J. Derrida, *Margins of Philosophy* (Brighton, 1982), p. 207 ff; J. Culler, *In Pursuit of Signs* (London, 1981); U. Eco (London, 1984), ch. 3.

5 We shall return to these figures in the next section. The generic figure of *hypotyposis* is defined by Quintilian as the figure, 'which sets things out in such a way that the matter seems to unfold, and the thing to happen, under our eyes'.

6 For the legal meaning of 'chicken' in the USA, see also the illuminating case of *Frigaliment Importing Co v BNS International Sales Corp* (190 F. Supp. 116 SDNY, 1960) where an expert witness testified that 'chicken is everything except a goose, a duck and a turkey. Everything is a chicken but then you have to say, you have to specify which category you want or that you are talking about.'

7 See particularly R. B. Ferguson, 'The Horowitz thesis and common law discourse in England' (1983) 3 *Oxford J. of Legal Studies* 34; W. Murphy and R. Rawlings, 'After the Ancien Régime' (1981) 44 *Modern Law Review* 617, (1982) 45 *Modern Law Review* 34; F. Burton and P. Carlen, *Official Discourse* (1979).

8 Specifically on the workings of the 1976 Act, see Z. Adler, 'Rape – the intention of Parliament and the practice of the courts' (1982) 45 *Modern Law Review* 66. For another vivid illustration of judicial stereotypes of sexual mores see, *Thompson v R* [1918] AC 221 at 259.

9 For discussion of the *Report* and especially of its language see A. Norrie, 'Freewill, determinism and criminal justice' (1983) 3 *Legal Studies* 60; M. Barker and A. Beezer, 'The language of racism' (1983) *International Socialism* 108.

REFERENCES AND FURTHER READING

Aristotle, *Rhetoric* (trans. Welldon) 1925, London.
Atkins, S. and Hoggett, B. 1984: *Women and the Law*. Oxford.
Atkinson, M. 1984: *Our Master's Voices*. London.
Augustine, St *On Christian Doctrine*. (Robertson, ed.) 1958, Indianapolis.
Bakhtin, M. 1981: *The Dialogic Imagination*. Texas.
Bell, J. 1983: *Policy Arguments in Judicial Decisions*. Oxford.
Benson, R.W. 1985: 'The end of legalese'. xiii. 3. *Rev. of Law and Social Change* 519.
Bentham, J. 1932: *Theory of Fictions*. London.
Burke, K. 1969: *A Rhetoric of Motives*. California.
Carlen, P. 1976: *Magistrates' Justice*. Oxford.
Davis, H. and Walton, P. (eds) 1984: *Language, Image, Media*. Oxford.
Eagleton, T. 1982: *Literary Theory*. Oxford.
Edwards, S. 1981: *Female Sexuality and the Law*. Oxford.
Edwards, S. 1984: *Women on Trial*. Manchester.
Elshtain, J. 1981: *Public Man, Private Woman*. Oxford.
Goodrich, P. 1984: 'Rhetoric as jurisprudence'. 4 *Oxford J. of Legal Studies* 88.
Harrison, A.R. 1971: *The Law of Athens*. Oxford.

Humphreys, S. 1985: 'Social relations on stage: witnesses in classical Athens'. 1
   History and Anthropology 313.
Kennedy, G. 1979: *Classical Rhetoric*. London.
McBarnet, D. 1982: *Conviction*. London.
McDowell, D. 1978: *The Law of Classical Athens*. London.
Ong, W. 1981: *Ramus: Method and the Decay of Dialogue*. Cambridge, Mass.
Perelman, Ch. and Tyteca, O. 1958: *The New Rhetoric*. Indiana.
Simmonds, N. 1984: *The Decline of Juridical Reason*. Manchester.
Tacitus, *A Dialogue of Orators*. 1911, Loeb Classical Library edition. London.
Todorov, T. 1982: *Theories of the Symbol*. Oxford.

7

Conclusion: Law and Modernity

Error (belief in the ideal) is not blindness; error is cowardice . . . I do not refute ideals; all I do is draw on my gloves in their presence.

(Nietzsche, 1911a, p. 13)

The discipline of law constitutes one of the most prodigious and formidably Utopian of human social endeavours. It aims to rationalize sociality, that is to say, it claims to confine social interaction within the boundaries of reason or, in one relatively mild doctrinal formulation, law is 'the enterprise of subjecting human conduct to the governance of rules' (Fuller, 1975, p. 96). In this traditional representation the discipline of law is always, in the last instance, an enterprise in strict reason or logic, and human social behaviour is correspondingly, in its most basic principles at least, to be viewed legally as the consequence of reasoned intentions and explicitly formulated goals. In short, lawyers have always been indecently zealous to reduce behaviour to rules and, in constructing the abstract world of the doctrine and science of law, have tended to be forgetful both of the irrationality and chance embedded in social life as well as of the instability and change intrinsic to human purpose and human personality. In so far as the present work, in its broader implications, has challenged the doctrinal conception of legal regulation as a rigidly scientific and peculiarly rational enterprise in the exegesis of legal texts, it would seem fitting to discuss, by way of conclusion, the status of a (critical) legal studies centred upon the hermeneutic and rhetorical features of legal power. We will do so first by briefly examining the character and role of legal rules, and second by redefining the concept of the legal text in the light of theories of reading the law. The first issue relates most broadly to the problems of the source of law and the definition of the legal text as studied in Part I of this work; the second issue relates more closely to the question of the characteristic manner of interpreting legal texts which was raised most explicitly in Part II.

7.1 NIHILISM AND LEGAL STUDIES

The faith which the legal community places in the doctrinal ideal of the foundational rationality of law and in the correlative concept of the comprehensiveness of legal rules has always been a matter of degree. In terms of legal practice, the professional community has a powerful interest in sanctioning and protecting the varied rhetoric and symbols of justice as reason but it would be inaccurate in the extreme to ignore the generally instrumental and pragmatic character of practical legal reason in the self-consciousness of the law. Even at the level of legal doctrine and of education in the law, history indicates a degree of caution and clearly evidences that the community of legal science is far from immune to self-doubt and crises of faith in which the foundational value and objectivity of the law have been denied.

Interestingly enough the last major instance of such crisis within the common-law world dates back to the end of the nineteenth century and to a movement within legal education which came later to be known as (American) legal realism. In its origins legal realism may plausibly be traced back to the legal expression of a more general social pessimism, insecurity and radical doubt associated with the *fin de siècle* or twilight of the nineteenth century. Aligning themselves most closely with philosophies of pragmatism and scepticism, the legal realists expressed their loss of faith in the legal ideals or idols in terms of the 'hard-headed' educational claims that students of law ought to focus less upon the law in books or 'paper rules' and more upon official practice, informal processes and the empirical effects of the law more generally as an instrument of discipline and control. The law was defined as what happened to people in legal settings and the study of law was consequently to move from the library to the courts and from abstraction – brooding 'omnispresence in the sky' – to the concrete practices of everyday legal routines. While the more general and theoretical of the realist proposals were to be superficially accepted by the legal community and tentatively incorporated into the legal curriculum, the traditions of textbook and casebook jurisprudence survived the challenge of realism with relative easy and only minor reform (Tushnet, 1981).

The intellectual and cultural climate of the late nineteenth century was, in Europe at least, strongly imbued with the atmosphere of radical transition. The Industrial Revolution had, with unprecedented speed, begun to destroy the traditional agriculturally based communities and customary orders throughout Europe. The emerging modern nation-state had not yet begun to tackle effectively the social ill-effects of the unbridled pursuit of profit and the poverty, dislocation, industrial injury, pollution and ill-health that accompanied rapid and uncontrolled industrialization. Urbanization long remained largely unregulated by either administrative or legal agencies. The widespread cultural sense of dispossession, disinheritance and disorder received striking expression in the political philosophies of the period. The radical, rapid and uncontrolled economic and social change threw up the mildly apocalyptic sense that everything was possible, that the world would soon be either lost or gained, destroyed or saved, that the immediate future would, in the terms of Karl Marx, be one of either barbarism or socialism. The thought of the period correspondingly fluctuated between the polar opposites of radical pessimism and equally radical Utopianism, between the revolutionary programmes of ana rchism and socialism, and the more inward and individualistic predictions of philosophical pessimism and nihilism.

The cultural alternatives posed in such a fashion towards the end of the nineteenth century expressed strong sentiments of foreboding, of alienation, incomprehension and fear for the future. While these developments clearly had some degree of influence upon legal studies in helping to radicalize and politicize legal education, their effect was immediate, relatively anodyne and short-lived. It is a century later, towards the close of the twentieth century and in the context of a renewed pessimism most obviously associated with the various forms of nuclear power and pollution, with the renewed intensity of the technological revolution and with the perceived failure of reformist and revolutionary movements in the western industrialized economies, that the legal institution is most likely to be significantly affected by a general tide of cultural self-doubt. The cultural context of such contemporary *fin de siècle* ill-ease is to be found in terms of renewed sentiments of pessimism and nihilism, of loss of faith in ideals or absolute values, and in a fear for the future which finds varied expression in the philosophies of modernity and post-modernity and, in more academic terms, in theories of discourse and deconstruction, difference and decay (Anderson, 1984).

Obviously it is not our purpose here to provide any adequate account of the very extensive range of theories of modernity as applicable to literature, art and social science more generally. Our concern is simply to locate the intellectual context and condition within which legal studies have, as yet rather superficially, come to debate the foundational rationality and attendant value of law. Legal studies have been infected by modernity and the legal educational institutions have unwillingly begun to come to terms with the need to debate, if not yet to teach, the rhetorical status of law, the political character of legal discourse (Hutchinson and Monahan, 1984) and even the relation of nihilism (of the refusal to believe in absolute values) to the exegetical exposition of law as a system of rules (Rose, 1984; Singer, 1984). In such a context it is clearly relevant to examine briefly the key terms of the debate over modernity before examining their import for legal studies. In broad terms our argument will be to the effect that the various forms and expressions of modernism have been misunderstood by (critical) legal studies and misapplied to the analysis of law. On the one hand, metaphors, images and fashionable expressions of mood and lifestyle have been uncritically transposed on to legal studies and used as therapeutic consolation for a somewhat neurotic dissatisfaction with the state of the legal discipline. The catchphrases of a superficial eclecticism can all too easily stand in the place of historical consciousness and political argumentation. On the other hand, the fundamental conditions, concerns and concepts debated under the rubric of (post) modernity deserve careful examination and stand to contribute much to the renewal of legal studies.

At the risk of presenting far too selective an account of the principal themes of (post) modernism, we would maintain that the inter-related social experiences of powerlessness, irrationality and loss of faith (nihilism) are the three issues most closely connected to critical debates within legal studies. Each theme has an extensive history as well as specific usages within particular disciplines and the following remarks are intended solely in terms of introductory commentary. The first two themes may be dealt with together: the experience of modernization and of modernity as fundamentally irrational processes engenders a sense of powerlessness and of incomprehension which, while it dates back as far as the Industrial Revolution itself, appeals with particular force to the growing apocalyptic sense associated with the close of the century. The sense of irrationality is directed towards the political structures and institutions of modern State bureaucracies which seem largely irrelevant to the lives, needs and desires of modernist existence while at the same time appearing impervious to fundamental change. On the one hand, 'to be modern is to experience personal and social life as a maelstrom, to find one's world in perpetual disintegration and renewal, trouble and anguish, ambiguity and contradiction: to be part of a universe in which all that is solid melts into air' and all that is sacred is profaned (Berman, 1982, p. 15). The experience of this atmosphere of disorder is a fluctuating one and incorporates both exhilaration and disturbance, self-enlargement and self-derangement, the expansion of possibilities as well as the destruction of moral boundaries and personal bonds. Irrationality in its modernist cultural guise is never to be thought an unmitigated disadvantage and its essential insight is beautifully captured in a recent work on the *Critique of Cynical Reason*: 'what appears in reality as an objective state of affairs is . . . what we consider in logic a paradox and in literature a joke. This shapes a new consciousness of "objectivity"' (Sloterdijk, 1985).

The sense of powerlessness adverted to in terms of the experience of irrationality is also two-sided. It is both a potential motive for political change and for resistance to power and also, in other contexts, an incapacitating view of the world, a form of resignation to the 'power of things' and of cynicism as to the possibility of change. In its most negative sense the experienced condition of powerlessness is well expressed as the cynicism of incorporation and conformity, of loss of hope in the face of perceived necessity – the counter-enlightenment begins at £800 per month. Cynicism here means acquiescence to a power-structure experienced both politically and morally as unjustifiable. It is an unhappy consciousness of the absurdity and iniquity of officialdom and bureaucratic structure combined with a certain knowledge that 'the objective situation and the instinct for self-preservation speak the same language' and pose the stark alternatives of integration into a social world which one neither created nor desired, or self-sacrifice upon the altar of impossible revolutionary Utopias, the various dreams of totality and plenitude.

Underlying the experiences of both irrationality and powerlessness is the much broader and more pervasive experience of nihilism. Nihilism may be provisionally defined as a combination of elements; as a sense of the absurdity of existence and of the unwarranted pretension of social life; as a perception of the nothingness to which all things lead and as the consequent realization of the contingency of all values and the fragility of all claims to objectivity. Very briefly, the term nihilism in its modern artistic and cultural usages derives from the work of the classicist and philosopher Nietzsche and is to be understood as a specific stage in the history and especially modernization of European culture. Although Nietzsche does not provide any comprehensive analytical account of a concept of nihilism, it is reasonably apparent that certain ideas associated with nihilism were of particular significance and may be listed here. First 'What does nihilism mean? – That the highest values are losing their value' (Nietzsche, 1909, p. 8). Nihilism is thus defined initially in negative terms as the expression of a generalized loss of belief in the extant order and as a breakdown in the credibility of the prevailing religious and political ideologies, the dominant contemporary modes of social organization and belonging. The loss of purpose associated with nihilism is thus not absolute; it is rather the expression of incomprehension and disbelief in a specific order and specific values. Second, following on from the last comment, nihilism, which Nietzsche explicitly linked to modernity, is based in the rejection of the rationalist tradition of the nineteenth century and the Christian moral culture to which it belonged. Nihilism is born in the heart of Christian morality. It is the natural-law tradition of divine reason as the source of

morality and law which nihilists have wished to jettison and eschew. In this
sense, it is 'the belief in the categories of reason' which is the cause of
nihilism and nihilism, as the rejection of Christian doctrines of 'unity',
'purpose' and 'being', is a historical consciousness of the death of a
particular mode of organizing and belonging to society and the rejection of
the values and 'truths' upon which that moral culture was based. Third,
nihilism represents an 'intermediary condition' (1909, p. 15) and 'is an
expression of the uselessness only of the *modern* world, not of the world and
existence as such' (p. 29). Here we face one of the most paradoxical of the
features of nihilism, the possibility of viewing nihilism as a powerful positive
force and as an essentially affirmative and active will to create new values,
new modes of organization and of collective belonging. Nihilism is weari-
ness and despair in the face of a transcendental and life-destroying moral
culture, of a Church bound to archaic principles of hierarchy and value, in
short a decayed culture. Nihilism is also, however, the hedonistic possibility
of displacing that culture and those values and of creating new forms of
community and virtue.

Despite the prevalent tendency to caricature nihilism and to present it as
an absurd philosophy preaching absurdity and despair, we hope to have
outlined a fuller meaning of nihilism as an active historical and political
consciousness. Nihilism was and is a reading of and response to rationalist
Christian ideology which concludes that the orthodox and highly legalistic
definitions of truth and of lawful knowledge have outlived their purpose and
are indeed absurd when placed in the context of modernity. Nihilism as a
philosophy and mode of life denied the claims of religious metaphysics and
proposed, in the place of divinely given certainties, a rational dialogue as to
the choice of values and as to the terms of collective existence, 'happy,
unlike the metaphysicians, to possess in oneself not an immortal soul but
many *mortal* ones' (Nietzsche, 1911b, p. 134). Nietzsche's injunction was
not that we acquiesce in irrationality and purposeless absurdity but that we
become aware of and participants in the social conditions of value-choice,
or in Rose's terms, not that we cease reading our culture but that we read it
better, more competently and more thoroughly (Rose, 1984). In short, the
nihilist attack upon the objectivity and unity of a divinely given real world
was to clear the way for a movement beyond the old community and values,
the tradition and establishment, of the late nineteenth century. Interestingly, however, Nietzsche always claimed to be writing not for his contem-
poraries but for an audience which would come into being a century later.
He saw himself as writing not for the immediate future but for the
modernity and community which would develop by the close of the twentieth century. If we turn now to nihilism and legal studies we find, fittingly
enough, that Nietzsche's definitions of nihilism, of reason and value in the

history of a culture, are peculiarly relevant to contemporary experience, not least by virtue of having been in turn vilified, forgotten and misunderstood.

The concept of nihilism at work within what has come to be termed critical legal studies is on many occasions a peculiarly vacuous and ill-informed one. While the problems raised and debated by the reference to nihilism are important ones for an understanding of law, modernity and the future development of legal studies, the arguments against legal doctrine and the false ideals of textual objectivity and deductive rule-application are only likely to be effective if initially proposed in moderate and serious terms before moving to the equally valuable terrains of satire and polemic. To that end we shall here follow the account of modernity and nihilism outlined above and put forward first a brief outline of legal modernity in terms of the experiences of irrationality and powerlessness, and then we shall comment upon the basic characteristics of legal nihilism understood in its full historical and political context.

First, the related legal experiences of irrationalism and powerlessness, of absurdity and cynicism, as the expressions of a belated legal encounter with modernity. We have already noted in passing the close-of-the-century atmosphere within which legal realism challenged the orthodoxies of legal doctrine at the end of the nineteenth century. Rather than viewing law in terms of the guaranteed objectivity of textually established rules, realism had given expression to a confused sense that the rules of precedent were so vague and so numerous as to make any outcome legally possible. Within a jurisdiction in which reported cases often seemed quantitatively 'as grains of sand on the beach', the legal tradition's claim to the objectivity of rules and the rationality of their application sounded hollow to the realistic educators. Legal doctrine and the legal academy survived the challenge of realism and it is in that context, that is in the context of a continuing tradition of legal objectivism, of a doctrinal faith or orthodoxy which continues to assert the rationality of law as a 'system' of rules, as a 'grammar' of norms or even as the 'correct' expression of fundamental legal principles and rights, that the various expressions of the critical legal studies movement are to be understood. The sentiment of irrationalism is not new and it is indeed something of a commonplace to hear legal practitioners talk in terms of the *ad hoc* or fundamentally contingent and pragmatic character of legal decision-making. Cynicism, however, as to the actual role of rules in the process of law-application, should not be confused with a more fundamental and more serious debate at the level of legal tradition, especially at the level of doctrine and education in the law (Unger, 1983, pp. 567–76).

The refusal to continue to believe and promulgate an unreflective ideal of legal rationality has a dual significance. On the one hand it represents an endeavour to open the law to debate. The refusal to acquiesce in the shallow orthodoxy of a determinate system of legal rules is in effect a demand for dialogue within the law and a plea for systematizations of the law that will take into account more than the singular internal logic of legal texts themselves. The other feature of the sense of legal irrationality flows from the first. The demand for dialogue is not radical in itself but it is radical in the context of the prevailing orthodoxy and legal educational practice. It is a paradoxical feature of the development of the legal discipline during the past half century that while it has frequently been acknowledged, even by the highest ranks of the English and American judiciary, that decision-making involves discretion, or that experience governs legal development quite as much as logic, these acknowledgements in no whit alter the formalism and objectivism, the authoritarianism and orthodoxy, of legal textual practice. Even within the legal academy the situation is not one of debate but rather of cynicism. While most members of the legal community have certainly experienced the contingency, the elements of irrationality, choice and subjectivity, that enter into the application of law, the overwhelming response has been reactive, fearful and self-protective. Such are the elements of legal cynicism and of a thoroughgoing legal 'resistance to theory' which reduces the real message of the legal curriculum to teaching that 'a mixture of low level skills and high grade sophistic techniques of argumentative manipulation is all that there is – all there is and can be – to legal analysis and, by implication, to the many methods by which professional expertise influences the exercise of state power' (Unger, 1983, p. 669). Cynicism precludes active participation in the development of law being viewed as an intrinsically historical and political form of activity; cynicism refuses to address the question of what, at the level of everyday activity the law might strive for and the lawyer might strive to do; 'the attitude of professionalism thus ends up recommending submission to the status quo because it cannot imagine alternatives and does not think it should. This is the real cynicism of the legal profession: that there is not much that anyone can do about the way things are, that we must accept "reality" as a soldier accepts his orders' (Gordon, 1985, p. 5). In short, the sense of the irrationality of legal development, the experience of a textual tradition which is arbitrary in its authorities and narcissistic in its elaboration of meanings, engenders a sense of powerlessness within the profession and academy alike. The law is perceived to be subject to forces that it cannot control as well as being the object of powers external to it; the only feasible response to the uncontrolled and irrational development of the law is consequently resignation or simple cynicism, the recourse of the profession being to a model of the lawyer as a 'technician of practical knowledge' for whom issues of value, belief, aspiration and political hope are essentially only aspects of private life and private desire.

In the context of professional cynicism, legal nihilism arrives as an essentially optimistic force bent upon rejoining the humanity of private aspirations with the language and roles of public life. Nihilism in the context of legal studies simply means loss of faith in the community of legal doctrine and refusal to succumb, acquiesce or otherwise believe in the foundational myths of legal doctrine and legal regulation. Legal nihilism speaks to the possibility of a public language of legal modernism and of open debate as to the values contained in and resulting from the practice of the law. The point is a crucial one in the light of frequent and possibly wilful misinterpretations of the meaning of nihilism within legal studies. The prevalent reaction to the term has indeed been one of exclusion and caricature, of 'defining out' those who would admit to even passing acquaintance with the siren of nihilism. Nihilism is here taken to mean no more than purposelessness and despair engendered by the impossibility of arriving at objective, or singular and 'correct' interpretations of legal texts. In a somewhat extravagant defence of the American Constitution, a professor of law at Yale University suggests that: 'nihilism would drain the great public text of modern America, the Constitution, of all meaning . . . it [nihilism] calls into question the very point of Constitutional adjudication; it threatens our social existence and the nature of public life as we know it in America; and it demeans our lives' (Fiss, 1982, pp. 762–3). Such a statement, of course, says nothing much more than that the old order feels threatened and sees a need to lash out to protect itself. In turning now to the more specific issues of rule, interpretation and value, we hope to rectify briefly the profound conservatism underlying this rejection of nihilism.

7.2 LEGAL VALUES, LEGAL INTERPRETATIONS AND LEGAL TEXTS

If one is incapable of imagining any alternative to the established values and order of social life then loss of faith in those values and that order is bound to appear as a loss of purpose and, more profoundly, as despair. In such circumstances the unwilling nihilist would be left denuded of hope, most likely becoming an agnostic with little else left to do save tend to the garden (Voltaire) or revert to nature (Rousseau). It is precisely such lack of imagination and lack of political will which underpins the refusal seriously to debate the political values, choices and future possibilities contained within legal texts and available to a critical reading of those texts. The legal institution is everywhere concerned to inculcate values, to teach modes of living and .belonging, to authorize texts and interpretations as the written embodiment of the reason underlying the law. As a totality of discourses and practices the legal institution continuously strives to present the legal code as the symbolic representation of an ideal sociality, as a way of life and as the fundamental morality of belonging to the social whole. To challenge the values specifically established in legal texts and legal practices, to question the morality of the written symbols of justice, to refuse to accept passively the legal communities' doctrinal equation of law with reason – these positions are quite the opposite of the insignia of despair, they are the last vestiges of hope, the final flailing of historical consciousness and of political sensibility in the face of a pathological cynicism. The nihilist, to paraphrase Nietzsche, is fearful that 'in so far as we believe in law, we condemn existence' and consequently seeks to displace the world of legally established transcendental values with an account of the everyday world of the law, with an account of a very fragile, very finite, very mortal world in which human beings and human institutions are constantly in the process of becoming, for 'from this standpoint, the reality of becoming is the only reality that is admitted' (Nietzsche, 1909, p. 14). To be human, in short, is to become, to become other and to cease.

Legal doctrine, as constituted by and expressed in legal science or the jurisprudence of legal rules, endeavours to avoid the transiency of positive law and the contingency of legal values by establishing and authorizing a tradition of written texts. In the face of purely polemical and usually rhetorical claims to the effect that 'all interpretations are possible', that legal texts hide a limitless plurality of meanings, the legal institution responds by asserting the written form of law – the conjunction of *logos* and *graphos* – as representing the immortality of the law and the transcendental objectivity of legal meaning. The law comes from books and it is the books of the law that guarantee it permanence, its survival beyond the momentary legal order constituted in each act of law application. The conjunction of writing and law is intrinsic to the foundational value of western legal order: writing places the law beyond the spatial and temporal limitations of oral tradition and unwritten power. The written texts of the law, legal doctrine implies where it does not explicitly so state, provide the legal order with an objectified existence independent of any specific historical institutions sustaining that tradition. In short, it is because it is written, because of the ideational unity which the written law claims to represent, that the textual tradition of the law manages to maintain its status of incontestable professionalism guaranteed by a priesthood of interpreters empowered to gloss but never to create the law (Derrida, 1979).

The concepts of text and of textual meanings as rules presented by legal doctrine are the explicit object of a varied group of critical polemics. While we have thus far outlined motives for ceasing to believe in that doctrine it remains briefly to outline a position which would displace that faith and those idols while posing the question: would it be easy to be a modernist in law? The answer presented here by way of provisional definition and conclusion is necessarily partial and non-dogmatic and it should also be clear that the modernity we allude to as the contemporary context of legal studies is stratified and complex in its attack upon the exegetical concept of legal text.

The first point to be made is one of ample common sense. To deny the claims of legal doctrine as to the monumental or documentary status of legal texts is *not* the same thing as denying the existence of the historical community of legal doctrine and the textual teachings and disciplinary rules in which it places its faith. It is simple obfuscation to propose that the claim that texts are inherently ambiguous or polysemous is the equivalent of saying that 'anything goes' or that 'all meanings are equally possible' (Fiss, 1982, p. 763). The explicit political and interpretative task of the historical legal community as a profession has been precisely that of restricting and constraining the scope of possible interpretations, that of defining the dictionary of legal language and of establishing the paradigm of normal legal knowledge: one cannot drain texts of meaning simply because they were never repositories of settled meanings to begin with (Fish, 1984, p. 46). Similarly, what meanings may be established at any given time and in any given context is always a complex negotiation between reader and text, between the hermeneutic or interpretative community and the audience that such a community speaks to: 'readers will have a range of plausible meanings set by the conventions of the historically and socially situated communities of interpretation to which they belong' (Gordon, 1984, p. 13).

Legal doctrine represents the manner in which lawyers read legal texts and those readings are by and large predictable once the history and contemporary constituents of that interpretative community have been studied. What is at issue, however, in the debate as to law and criticism is not so much the reality of the meanings and values wearily peddled by the legal doctrinal community but rather whether or not it is desirable to allow the profession to continue to transmit those values and doctrines, that ideology and those myths, without being made explicitly accountable for the political choices underlying the development of the law. Although that issue is much broader, it can be usefully posed in relation to legal education and the more general pedagogy of the legal text. The second point we would raise is thus one which may be broadly termed that of deconstructing the written law, that of opening law to the dialogues and disciplines which legal doctrine has traditionally endeavoured to exclude from legal studies.

Initially it is necessary to expand somewhat the concept of legal doctrine to include not simply the concepts and values transmitted within the legal tradition but also to recognize legal doctrine as the instantiation of hierarchy. A body of doctrine is an organized set of 'truths' but it is also a mode of transmitting those 'truths'; 'their authority is incorporated into the transmission of the doctrine. To be more accurate, it is inherent in the relationship linking a plurality of receivers with a single sender who stands above them' (Debray, 1983, pp. 246–7). Doctrine is a way of administering and teaching discourse which consistently presents the doctrinal teaching in the form of a monologue, as the elaboration of a scientifically established and so incontestable authority, as the exegesis of a primary text. Doctrine as teaching demands obedience on the part of its students or pupils and it is consequently less than surprising that the doctrinal community should treat those who do not believe the teachings or who wish to engage in dialogue with the primary texts as schismatics, heretics or other counsellors of despair: the critics of legal doctrine, we are told, have 'an ethical duty to depart the law school', in precisely the same fashion that 'a professor of divinity for whom atheism is the primary message to profess ought to recognise that he has a conflict of interests' (Carrington, 1984, p. 227; 1985, p. 10).

It is, of course, the function of doctrine to provide an authoritative and closed discourse for its disciples and the doctrinal community guards the boundaries of that discourse by administering the criteria of inclusion and exclusion, of orthodoxy and heterodoxy. The desire to deconstruct the primary texts of legal doctrine, however, also has strong historical support: power creates resistance and, in more specific literary and linguistic terms, texts necessarily engender the 'conflict of interpretations'. For a modernist, or let us say deconstructive, reading of the legal tradition it is not the unified textual teachings of the law that are to be studied and obeyed but rather it is the conditions under which those teachings are possible that should be opened to dialogue. The shift of emphasis is a crucial one: the issue raised by the conflict of interpretations is that of the text as an intersection of competing discourses, the text as a point of fracture in which different systems of signs are transposed, translated and articulated to form the contemporary utterance. The text is here to be understood as productivity, as the active 'absorption and transformation of a multiplicity of other texts' (Kristeva, 1969; 1984), together constituting the space of 'intertextuality' in which the text is conceived and read as a tissue built from and leading to other texts and other discourses.

The principle of intertextuality may be loosely summarized in the view that the logic of modernity refuses to recognize any singular or unitary and unifying textuality. The text inevitably refers to and incorporates other texts. More than that, however, the principle of intertextuality opens the way to an analysis of the text as discourse: an analysis of the manner in which the intrinsic dialogue of the text, the polysemy, plurality, polyphony and play of the textual discourse is controlled by the imposition of meaning, by the

power of the political and doctrinal communities to define the discourse and
to silence dissent. Thus we may move to examine the nature of a deconstructive reading of legal texts by comparing legal intertextuality with what
may be termed legal interdiscourse, the latter term referring to the manner
in which the legal text may be read as an active gesture, as a speech-act or
intervention into the texts and discourses of a heteroglot and frequently
irrational sociality. First, we would note the sense in which legal method is
almost entirely contained within the process of defining and controlling
legal intertextuality. From the work of the glossators to that of contemporary textbook jurisprudence, legal method has, for practical purposes, limited
itself to the study of the means of textual restriction and recollection
(*procedere ad similia*). The legal text and legal judgment are to be presented
within the literary canon of jurisprudence as complex (philological) recon-
structions of the figures, metaphors and meanings elaborated in earlier
texts. Citation and quotation dominate legal writing. Concentration upon
the explicit elaboration of intertextual meanings should not, however,
detract attention from the indicative silences of the legal text as to its role as
discourse, as intervention into the order of discourse and the hierarchy of
social meanings.

Whereas legal exegesis searched behind the legal text, as behind a ready-
made veil, for a more or less hidden meaning (truth), the deconstructive
reading is more open and more hedonistic: the nihilist has no confidence in
the text as a transcendental value and meaning, the doctrinal unity of the
text, far from hiding the voice or speech of its source, rather veils the
historical and political conditions of its existence as meaning. The text is
here to be constituted as a generative and creative act of meaning. The
signs, symbols and figures of which the text is composed are consequently
to be read historically and politically as indicators of semantic choice: the
text is semantically structured according to the manner in which it supplements given meanings and discourses (Derrida, 1981, p. 37 ff), according
to the mode in which it administers the insignia of inclusion and exclusion
at the linguistic level of assembling the legal surface text. There is, in short,
no text – legal or other – which cannot be read as an exercise in organizing
the signs of belonging. The text is only ever an apparent unity and to
understand that appearance requires a reading of the margins of the text, a
reading of its figures of incorporation, of translation and inclusion, but also
and more radically a reading of its demarcation of self and other, of the
points of diffraction of discourse wherein the discourse of the text becomes
incompatible with the discourses external to it (Foucault, 1972, pp. 64–71).

Finally and by way of conclusion, a third point concerning the interplay of
modernity, temporality and the unity of the legal text. As befits a conclusion
we must here alter the level and context of discussion. From the doctrine of

the unity of the text we need to move to doctrines of the unity of life, from linguistics to metaphysics and more crudely from questions of how we live to questions of what we live. The natural-law tradition is in essence based upon the unity of life as perceived through the eyes of God. In terms of temporality, Christian theology has always refused to accept the finality of death, a position whose consequence is that of a linear conception of deferred (incomplete) time: each moment is a step in the direction of a metaphysical plenitude. At the level of biography the temporality of individual life is to be measured against the conditions and unities of an 'after-life', while in terms of human history social life moves from ignorance and disbelief towards the inevitable 'second coming', the much-vaunted and much-delayed millennium. In relation both to biography and to history the temporal rationality or indeed unity of human existence is situated at a point external to it and only beyond living does life have a meaning. The temporality of the individual life is fulfilled (unified) in death – live each day as your last – while the temporality of historical sociality is only to be fulfilled once Christ has returned and the human political order has given way to the rule of God on earth.

The Christian conception of time as preparation for judgment and as prelude to a future unity is hardly the temporality of modernity nor is it easily recognizable as a description of the lived time of contemporary secular communities. The abstract religious metaphysic, however, still guards and guides the terms and categories of the legal text. In the crudest of terms we need merely observe that the community of legal doctrine still clings to the metaphysical certainties of time, tradition and text: the law remains the same and certain over time and as a consequence the temporality of human biography can be rendered linear by reference to the unifying rules and goals represented in the legal text. A life lived in the gaze of the law is a life rendered rational over time by the arbitrary metaphysical plenitude of legality. The legal biography, like the Christian biography, is rendered unitary and rational for the purposes of judgment by reference to a point beyond temporality and external to the contingent and merely human biography of becoming. For the law, a biography is a museum cluttered with relics – past deeds – each or any of which deeds may be isolated and excised to be linked in a linear and causal fashion to the contemporary legal subject. For the law there is only one biography, the legal record of a life, and that biography is a unity which transcends both time and context to lead its second life within the abstract contours of the legal text. In the harsh reality of linear time the individual life is always already past: like linear temporality itself, the legal life is built up of moments succeeding one another, each moment being potentially definitive in itself of the individual legal subject to which it is attached. In the rhetoric of modernity, individual and collectivity, subjectivity and history, cannot be so separated. Not only does the individual necessarily possess numerous interrelated and conflicting biographies but the plural temporality of historical existences means that all actions are to be correlated to the contingent terms of collective life. Rather than creating the singular causal narrative of individual biography by removing the legal subject from both time and history, the logic of modernity points in the direction of individual biography as a constantly changing production within a history which constantly needs to be changed. Legal nihilism as we defined it earlier at least allows for that possibility of change.

REFERENCES AND FURTHER READING

Anderson, P. 1984: 'Modernity and revolution'. 144 *New Left Review* 96.
Berman, M. 1982: *All that is Solid Melts into Air*. London.
Carrington, P. 1984: 'Of law and the river'. 34 *J. of Legal Education* 222.
Carrington, P. 1985: Correspondence. 35 *J. of Legal Education* 10.
Cotterrell, R. 1983: 'The sociological concept of law', 10 *J. of Law and Soc.* 241.
Debray, R. 1983: *Critique of Political Reason*. London.
Derrida, J. 1979: 'Scribble (writing-power)'. 58 *Yale French Studies* 24.
Finman, T. 'Critical legal studies, professionalism and academic freedom'. 35 *J. of Legal Education* 180.
Fish, S. 1984: 'Fish v Fiss'. 36 *Stanford Law Review* 1325.
Fiss, M. 1982: 'Objectivity and interpretation'. 34 *Stanford Law Review* 739.
Foster, H. (ed.) 1985: *Postmodern Culture*. London.
Foucault, M. 1972: *The Archaeology of Knowledge*. London.
Fuller, Lon. 1975: *The Morality of Law*. Yale.
Goodrich, P. 1984: 'Review'. 12 *Journal of Law and Society* 241.
Gordon, R. *et al.* 1985: 'Nihilism and academic freedom'. 35 *J. of Legal Education* 1.
Hutchinson, A. and Monahan, P. 1984: 'Law, politics and the critical legal scholars'. 36 *Stanford Law Review* 199.
Kairys, D. 1983: *The Politics of Law*. New York.
Kristeva, J. 1969: *Semeiotike*. Paris.
Kristeva, J. 1984: *Revolution of Poetic Language*. New York.
Lyotard, J. 1984: *The Post-Modern Condition*. Manchester.
Mitchell, W. (ed.), 1982: *The Politics of Interpretation*. Chicago.
Nietzsche, F. 1909: *The Will to Power*, 2 vols. Edinburgh.
Nietzsche, F. 1911a: *Ecce Homo*. Edinburgh.
Nietzsche, F. 1911b: *Human All Too Human*, 2 vols. Edinburgh.
Rose, G. 1984: *Dialectic of Nihilism*. Oxford.
Singer, J. 1984: 'The player and the cards: nihilism and legal theory'. 94, *Yale Law Journal* 1.
Sloterdijk, P. 1985: *Critique of Cynical Reason*. Minnesota.
Tushnet, M. 1981: 'Legal scholarship: its cause and cure'. 90 *Yale Law Journal* 1205.
Unger, R. 1983: 'Critical legal studies'. 96 *Harvard Law Review* 563.

Index